Spirit

Communication

Spirit Communication

The Soul's Path

Kevin Ryerson
and
Stephanie Harolde

BANTAM BOOKS
NEW YORK · TORONTO · LONDON · SYDNEY · AUCKLAND

SPIRIT COMMUNICATION
A Bantam Book / September 1989

Library of Congress Cataloging-in-Publication Data

Ryerson, Kevin.
    Spirit communication : the soul's path / Kevin Ryerson and
Stephanie Harolde.
        p. cm.
    ISBN 0-553-05388-4
    1. Spiritualism.   2. Channeling (Spiritualism).   I. Harolde,
Stephanie.   II. Title.
BF1261.2.R94   1989
133.9′1—dc20   89-6915
                                                                CIP

Published simultaneously in the United States and Canada

Bantam Books are published by Bantam Books, a division of Bantam Doubleday
Dell Publishing Group, Inc. Its trademark, consisting of the words "Bantam
Books" and the portrayal of a rooster, is Registered in U.S. Patent and Trademark
Office and in other countries. Marca Registrada. Bantam Books, 666 Fifth Avenue,
New York, New York 10103.

PRINTED IN THE UNITED STATES OF AMERICA

BG   0 9 8 7 6 5 4 3 2 1

This book is dedicated to all members of the human family, both incarnate and discarnate, who move, live, and have their being in God, who is love.

Acknowledgments

The authors would like to thank the following people:

Kevin's family—especially his wife, the lady Kwan Lynn Tate Ryerson; his sister, Bonnie, her husband, Lou, and their children; his "other" sister, Lisa Tate; his mother and father-in-law; his father, Walt, and his family number two, Sandy, Pammy, and Michael S.; and his Sandusky and Oklahoma families.

Stephanie's family—her parents, Ira and Miriam, sisters Alison and Lori, brother, Richard, nephew David, and Tara.

The spirit entities John, Tom MacPherson, Atun-Re, Obadiah, Japu, and the many others who have spoken through Kevin's trance state.

Shirley MacLaine, Dr. Anne Marie Bennstrom, Alan Brickman, Gabriel and Nora Cousens, Joyce DeWitt, Christian and Victoria Eddleman, Tara Harolde, Allen and Gudrun Hicks, B.J. Jefferson and Beva, Dr. William Kautz, Terri Kram, Danaan Lahey, Lin and Stacey Martin, Penney Peirce, Elaine Rock, and Jason Serinus for their friendship and support; all the others, too numerous to name, who have contributed to Kevin's work over the years.

Kevin would also like to thank: the Edgar Cayce family, the poet Maya Angelou, Katerina Hedwig ("the Cat"), Aumakua (Elizabeth), Terrell, Danny Boy and bro, Peter, Diana, Jeff, Santa Barbara, Connie, Angelique, Rainbow, Barbara, Terry Church, "the Goldman," Aura and Marta, Takanori and Reiko, and Alexander's "Sumo."

A special thank you from Stephanie: to Kevin, for his friendship and trust; to my friends at Nolo Press and, in particular, Jake Warner, Nolo publisher, for his support and encouragement; to Antonio Costa e Silva for being there; to all my friends for their love and patience through the years. Also, my very deep gratitude to the Twelfth Tai Situpa and the family of the Golden Rosary.

Lastly, both authors would like to express our sincere appreciation to Barbara Alpert, our editor at Bantam, and Berkeley attorney Brad Bunnin; and to Betty Bower, Alan Brickman, Fran Fisher, and Elizabeth Hodson for their invaluable editorial assistance and feedback.

Contents

Perhaps at times your burden will seem heavy and you will feel as though you have passed the same way many times; yet, in reality, you are on an ascendant path which spirals gracefully upward and onward.

—John

The meaning of life—like the meaning of a journey—lies not in the arrival at a certain place, but in the progress toward it; in the movement itself and in the gradual unfoldment of events, conditions, and experiences.

—Anagarika Govinda

Introduction

Spirit once said, "That which is worth learning comes directly from the experience of individuals, and all that isn't worth learning is stored in books." Books are simply two-dimensional images, sequences of thousands of words printed upon flat surfaces called pages. The value of any book isn't in the tangible object itself, but in the ability of those organized words to inspire thought. This then becomes the activator of human experience. Therefore in making these materials available, my primary intention is to inspire thought. Like any other book, ours will be of value only to the degree that it stimulates an active thinking process within the reader.

In the following pages, we will examine the dimensions of the human mind. We will explore how our thought processes can facilitate our growth and transformation in relation to our inner spirit, as well as help us to fulfill our practical everyday needs. We will explore the answers to such questions as: Are we here for a universal purpose? Do we each have an individual life purpose that is uniquely our own? How do we discover what that purpose is?

Once we have knowledge of who we are, how do we best apply that knowledge in our lives?

The principles and methods I introduce here come from many sources, including Judeo-Christian values, Buddhist psychology, and Egyptian texts, as well as from the works of Andrew Jackson Davis, Edgar Cayce, Manly P. Hall, Carl Jung, the Bhagavad Gita, and many shamanic traditions. These sources have all, to varying degrees, contributed to my inner growth. It isn't an easy task to objectify one's private knowledge and communicate it to others, but I have tried my best to be both emotionally and intellectually honest in the process.

The title, *Spirit Communication: The Soul's Path,* reflects a journey in examining our inner spirit, our inner values. The soul does indeed have a sojourn, and we, as souls, are collectively examining and exploring who we are in the human community. This is the soul's path. And since the soul's path leads us ultimately to the divine, it is an ascendant path as well.

We are currently amid a spiritual renaissance. People are once again asking the classical metaphysical questions about the meaning of life. Over the last twenty years, vast amounts of information on esoteric and metaphysical subjects have become available. I refer to this as New Thought, or New Age Thought.

Many are questioning the purpose of this renaissance. How can it serve us individually, as a society, and as a world community? I believe that, as a society, we are in the process of re-embracing one another. We are beginning to break down the barriers of communication and rediscover things about ourselves, both politically and psychologically, that we have long since forgotten. This is having far-reaching effects, even on what is called the mainstream of our society, or the human community as a whole. Indeed, we are the mainstream. We are reclaiming those inner spiritual values.

There are many techniques and methods available to us if we wish to increase our awareness of our spirituality and spiritual values. Trance channeling is only one of these techniques, but it is one that has been receiving a great deal of attention over this past decade. Many people are familiar with trance channeling through the work of Jane Roberts, who, in the 1960s, published the teachings of a channeled entity known as Seth. Others had exposure to the vast library of materials based on the channelings of Edgar Cayce, in the early part of this century. There has also been a resurgence of interest in the Swedish channel Emanuel Swedenborg, who lived in the eighteenth century. Trance channeling is certainly not a new phenomenon. It is simply that our society is engaged in the process of refamiliarizing ourselves with the various spiritual abilities inherent in all of us. Having channeled professionally for fifteen years, I devote the first two chapters to discussing the dynamics of the trance channeling phenomenon, as well as the implications of spirit communication for all of us as beings of mind, body, and spirit.

Although most of us are aware of the vast differences that exist between the various cultures on our planet, in fact there are as many common spiritual values as there are differences revealed by the bodies of knowledge of these seemingly divergent cultures, which have been preserved over the centuries. One of my favorite stories illustrating the universal nature of truth comes from Paul Reps, *Zen Flesh, Zen Bones* (Charles E. Tuttle Company, 1958):

A university student was visiting a Zen master and asked the master if he'd ever read the Christian Bible. The master said that he hadn't, and asked the student to read to him from it.

The student read first from St. Matthew: "And why take ye thought for raiment? Consider the lilies of the field, how they grow. They toil not, neither do they spin, and yet I say unto you that even Solomon in all his glory was not arrayed like one of these. . . . Take therefore no thought for the morrow, for the morrow shall take thought for the things of itself."

The master said: "Whoever uttered those words, I consider an enlightened man."

The student continued reading: "Ask and it shall be given you, seek and ye shall find, knock and it shall be opened to you. For everyone that asketh receiveth, and he that seeketh findeth, and to him that knoweth, it shall be opened."

The master remarked: "That is excellent. Whoever said that isn't far from Buddhahood."

Truth recognizes truth. This universality has been expressed in contemporary psychology by both Freud and Jung. The use of myth, archetype, and other devices conveys and expresses our common humanity. Psychology and spirituality are tools that we can use to help us rediscover who we truly are. The intention of this book, then, is to assist with, and inspire, that rediscovery.

If we take the spiritual dimension literally, when we exhaust all of our past lives and all of our future potentials, the only thing lying outside the limited dimension of time and space is the being we call God. Everything comes from God and everything returns to God. This renaissance in spirituality is returning us to the root of discovering who we are. We are co-creators with a greater spirit that is God.

Some time ago I read a wonderful article in *Discover* magazine, which is part of the Time-Life series. It was written by an intellectually honest physicist who had concluded that physics was actually a search for truth, for understanding our relationship to the cosmos. An axiom in science is that in order for something to exist, it has to be observable and measurable. This scientist speculated that perhaps the universe created stars so that stars could cool and create carbon molecules, so that carbon molecules could create life forms and evolve to create physicists, so that physicists could observe the universe, so the universe could exist. No matter how we phrase it, our purpose for being here is to rediscover and reclaim who we are. Everything else merely witnesses or testifies to that.

That many of us are able to identify past lives suggests that we are immortal beings, that we do not, in fact, die when our bodies die. Trance channeling has particular implications for the study of the afterlife. Literally, we are unlimited beings. Research bears out that, in some cases, we can access vast bodies of knowledge through extrasensory perception, bypassing our five physical senses. Knowledge just arises within us, spontaneously. According to the rules of inductive logic, all answers lie where the questions originate, and those questions originate inside us. We can express our questions in an endless variety of ways, and search the far corners of the globe, but the answers reside in us. Together we will examine ourselves, and ask many of the same questions, but in the light of a new spirituality—a spirituality based on identifying clear, universal, and at the same time individually relevant human needs. We'll explore a new spirituality that is based on meeting those needs for ourselves, which then empowers us to help meet the needs of others.

The material is arranged in a manner that was particularly relevant to me in developing my own thought processes. There are three distinct parts. Parts 1 and 2 consist of materials adapted from my lectures and seminars over the last ten years, and are written in an informal essay style. Part 3 contains a body of inspirational materials from Spirit.

In Part 1, "The Medium and the Message," I share my own growth and developmental processes and some of the basic principles of spirit communication and trance channeling that characterize my work ethics and life philosophy.

Part 2, "Human: Being of Light," is a more theoretical presentation of the wisdom I've synthesized from the many sources I acknowledge above. It will enable the reader to explore both the mystical and logical dimensions of the material.

Part 3, "Spirit Communication: The Ascendant Path," consists of teachings from the spirit entities John, Tom MacPherson, and Atun-Re, the predominant teachers who speak through my trance state. This part allows for Spirit's own voice(s) to communicate to the reader a unique and diverse body of information, inspiration, and insight. These spirit entities were a major source of knowledge and inspiration for me as well as for many others, most notably Shirley MacLaine, who has written many books based on her metaphysical explorations with these teachers.

In the appendix ("The Storytellers/Other Voices"), we've included communications from some of the other teachers, such as Obadiah and Japu, who speak through less frequently, in order to show the richness and diversity of their cultural backgrounds.

★   ★   ★

A major tenet of reincarnation is that the relationships that have great value to us in this lifetime usually evolve over many lifetimes. I have no doubt that this applies to myself and Stephanie Harolde, my friend and co-author. Stephanie and I have been working on various projects together for many years. This relationship has been invaluable to me, because we learned from, and were inspired by, many of the same sources, and have together drawn knowledge and inspiration from the spirit entities over the course of our friendship. I would like to take this opportunity to thank Stephanie, who, through her many years of study, support, and dedication, has brought together a cohesive body of information that will be part of the reader's journey.

Finally, we are living in a period where a great human adventure is beginning. All of our lifetimes—past, present, and future—are happening simultaneously, and creating, in this moment, the multidimensional personality. I hope the material presented here will further the reader's spiritual journey. As the saying goes, "Any journey of value begins with the first step."

Kevin Ryerson
San Francisco, 1989

Part I

The Medium and the Message

Chapter 1

The Medium

People have come up with the most peculiar ideas about trance mediums, or trance channels. About eight or ten years ago, I was channeling at a retreat facility in the middle of the Arizona desert. Because I'm occasionally subject to heat exhaustion, I wear a hat most of the time to keep the sun off my head. Before I channel, I always take off my hat and set it aside. A rumor began to circulate that if I took my hat off, I would instantly fall into a trance state. The speculation was that my hat was made out of a special material that covered my crown chakra and that it prevented me from going into trance whenever I wore it. During a program break, two women from this particular group approached me. Gentleman that I am, as the women drew near, I removed my hat. They practically passed out in unison because they were convinced I was going to go into trance on the spot. So, before we proceed, let me reassure you that the ability to trance channel has nothing to do with one's choice of crown (hat)—it has much more to do with the development of one's crown chakra.

So, to eliminate any confusion from the start, I would like to talk about what a "medium," or in my own case a "trance channel," does, and how he or she does it. I'd also like to share some of my experience with the phenomenon of channeling and discuss some of its implications for us as individuals as well as for society as a whole.

Actually, the term *trance medium* has been around for a long time. It came into popular usage in the United States in the mid-1800s, with Andrew Jackson Davis, Daniel Douglas Home, and Lenore Piper, who were all recognized mediums in those days. Subsequent investigations into spirit communication by academicians such as F. W. H. Myers, Edmund Gurney, and the noted American psychologist William James further popularized this phenomenon, which in those days was more commonly known as *spiritualism*. Such investigations into spirit communication were essentially an attempt to design a model by which the rationalists of that day could view and interpret the phenomenon of the afterlife and other evidences of the spiritual nature of man.

The word *medium* is applied to individuals who bridge the physical and nonphysical worlds. A medium, or mediator, is one who negotiates between parties. A trance medium is someone who enters into what is alternately called an altered state, a trance state, or an ecstatic state to accomplish that form of communication. Toward the middle of this century, both Eileen Garrett and Arthur Ford practiced this classic form of mediumship, which attempted to prove the survival of the human personality after death.

Traditionally, a trance medium brings through a discarnate entity, or discarnate intelligence, who gives philosophical commentary. Trance "channels" such as Andrew Jackson Davis and Edgar Cayce gave knowledgeable discourse and answered complex questions on a broad range of subjects, functioning more as information resources or data bases than as demonstrators of communication with the dead. They appeared to have an intuitive faculty that enabled them to discourse on a much broader range of topics than survival into the afterlife.

Edgar Cayce, probably the best-documented trance channel of the twentieth century, had only an eighth-grade education and yet was able to accurately diagnose illnesses and outline complex medical treatments for a wide variety of physical diseases while he was in a trance state. He also gave intelligent discourse on many academic subjects, including physics, ancient history, and archaeology, although he'd never studied or even read about them.

Edgar Cayce's contact was with his superconscious mind instead of with an independent entity, which clearly distinguishes him as a trance channel, rather than a medium. In fact, the term *trance channel* was introduced in order to distinguish between the latter form of channeling and the more traditional mediumship, which was intended primarily to demonstrate evidence of the afterlife.

A trance channel is simply a person who has developed the ability to set aside one level of consciousness and allow another level of consciousness to come through. I consider myself both a medium and a channel. Like a medium, my sources are discarnate intelligences, which are independent of my own thought processes, but they give broad commentary on topics commonly associated with channeling. In other words, in outward form my channeling parallels classical mediumship because the contact is with discarnate intelligence; but in content and subject matter, it is more like channeling.

The consciousness that I set aside when I go into trance is the personality named Kevin Ryerson. The other levels of consciousness that come through are spirit beings such as the entities John and Tom MacPherson, who have had numerous incarnations on the earth plane but are currently in the discarnate state. So, my trance channeling is directly related to the survival of the personality after death, and demonstrates that discarnate entities who lived in the past can, and do, communicate with us and convey information that relates to our present society, particularly on the philosophical levels. At the same time, the range of information that is channeled through shows a clear accessing of the superconscious realms, reminiscent of Edgar Cayce.

There are also individuals who are known as psychics. *Psychic* merely means "of the mind" or "of the soul." A psychic accesses information in much the same way that a trance medium does, but rather than having the information "channeled through" by an independent entity, the psychic him/herself becomes the "medium" for the message. Jean Dixon was a classic example of a psychic. She derived most of her information through clairvoyance rather than spirit channeling.

The Mechanics of Trance Channeling

Having provided some basic definitions, I'd like now to explore the actual mechanics of trance channeling. The best way to do this is to compare trance channeling to a radio broadcast. If two stations are competing for the same frequency on the radio, by slightly adjusting the dial we can tune down one vibration or channel and the other will come in more clearly. The personality named Kevin Ryerson is one vibration, channel, or frequency. By tuning down this particular frequency, other frequencies, such as Tom MacPherson and John, can speak through me.

Spirit is able to access information telepathically, through a process of thought transference. All of us broadcast thoughts or energy through our human energy fields. These fields are generally referred to as the human aura. Just as we can turn on the TV and receive information broadcast from Los Angeles, New York, or even by satellite from Japan or the Soviet Union, these entities are able telepathically to "view" the energy or thoughts that we broadcast and then reflect them back to us in the form of constructive insights.

If we believe that the human spirit can survive independently of the physical form, as the growing body of parapsychological evidence of telepathy and remote viewing suggests, all I really do is open myself up, or—not to mix metaphors—turn myself on, like a radio, for this consciousness to broadcast through me. This ability is, in itself, further evidence that the personality can survive the passing of the physical body.

We broadcast and receive information all the time, although we are generally more open to receiving it during sleep, or in a hypnotic or trancelike state. The human personality is able to survive death because we consist of energy, and energy can't be destroyed. Thought patterns are simply energy that maintains the "frequency" of the human personality even after the physical body passes away.

The communication with spirit entities, or discarnate intelligence, is not really any different from that of two ham radio operators who live on opposite sides of the globe. They can talk for years and years and never physically meet. They know each other by personality, by voice inflection, by what they've shared with each other over the "airwaves," and are just as much a "disembodied voice" to each other as anything you'll ever receive through a trance channel.

These frequencies or vibrations, which we call Spirit, are available to me anytime I go into trance, because they "broadcast" twenty-four hours a day. For example, even when we are not listening to the radio, it is still broadcasting. By turning a knob or pushing a button, we can tune in to music, news, or a weather or traffic report anytime of day or night. Spirit is available in this same way.

Spirit has said that we aren't incarnate in the physical body, we're incarnate in a human personality. This is a good principle to bear in mind. There's nothing esoteric in our having the ability to hold on to our personalities after leaving our physical bodies. Our personalities dissolve and reemerge all the time, particularly when we sleep, daydream, and meditate. We have all had experiences with daydreaming, where we enter into a greater state of relaxation, clarity, and creativity. People with highly developed intuition, whether artists, scientists, or businesspersons, are familiar with these mild altered states of consciousness. The insights that come in such moments are our perceptions of ourselves. Our personalities start to reform themselves. We often seem more mature, more "centered," and think and behave differently from before. Just as we are no longer the child we once were, even our adult personalities and perspectives continue to change. We embark on this path of evolution or transformation when we meditate or work with any other information that causes us to grow.

Accessing Altered States of Consciousness

There are several means of accessing the various altered states of consciousness, the most common being sleep, hypnosis, and meditation. Edgar Cayce channeled through a sleeplike state. In fact, he was known by many as "the sleeping prophet." Sleep is a natural channeling state. We tune in to our subconscious and superconscious dimensions when we sleep. Our subconscious minds communicate with us in sleep through the symbolic language of dreams. People who are skilled in dream interpretation can read these symbols and gain information about themselves that they were not conscious of before.

Trance channeling is much like meditation or sleep. It is an ability to turn inward and tap information that already exists in our collective unconscious, or the universal mind, but of which we aren't yet consciously aware. Like Edgar Cayce, I go into an altered state of consciousness not unlike sleep. It is more of a telepathic phenomenon. I do not have out-of-body experiences, nor do I travel to different dimensions—I'm one of the very few people who literally gets paid for sleeping on the job.

Many people associate the trance state with hypnosis. Portraying someone in a hypnotic trance has traditionally been a favorite theme of grade-B movies. Off the silver screen, a trained psychologist or hypnotherapist can, indeed, access information from an individual's subconscious mind. The technique has been used successfully by psychiatrists and psychotherapists since the days of Mesmer and Freud. Many trance channels consciously use self-hypnotic techniques to induce, or deepen, their trance state.

Classical hypnosis has routinely been used as an intellectual tool by Western psychologists primarily to access the subconscious levels. In contrast to this, meditation and trance channeling attempt to contact more spiritual resources, such as the superconscious and the collective unconscious. Since most Western psychology, with the exception of Jung, has not been open to exploring those realms, which are considered metaphysical, or "beyond the physical," meditation and trance channeling have not made the same inroads in Western thought.

Meditation and trance channeling are essentially spiritual tools. They are attempts to contact an even deeper expression of the self, rather than just the events of this lifetime. I consider my own channeling a spiritual process because it emphasizes the spiritual rather than the intellectual. Remember, classical hypnosis is an attempt to harness the subconscious, whereas trance channeling attempts to tap our spiritual resources, or the superconscious mind.

In the chapter "The Human Condition," I will explore the different levels of consciousness—conscious mind, subconscious mind, and superconscious mind—in greater depth. For now, let us simply say that the subconscious mind is the repository of the events of this lifetime as we understand it, and as classically defined by Freud. However, according to Carl Jung and Edgar Cayce, the events of this lifetime actually have deeper roots in the superconscious, in past lives. They have asserted that each of us possesses a collective unconscious as well as a superconscious dimension that consists of the sum total of all of our past lives and future potentials. In trance channeling, both the conscious and subconscious resources are set aside to access this broader range of superconscious information. But since the superconscious mind functions through the subconscious, past-life memories do at times come up using the technique of hypnosis. A skilled hypnotherapist with spiritual intention can, using guided meditation, tap in to superconscious resources.

Sir Isaac Newton and Albert Einstein possibly accessed these superconscious and intuitive resources. Edgar Cayce and Andrew Jackson Davis certainly did. "Intuition" simply means direct knowing, no matter what the source of, or mechanism for acquiring, information. Any information that comes to us through a process of direct knowing, which bypasses our empirical or logical faculties, is intuitive in nature. This doesn't mean that all intuitive information is psychically derived. Information may lay dormant in our subconscious until stimulated by a question or a critical thought process, at which point it will come up to conscious awareness through an intuitive channel. But it is not physically derived because we took the information in through our five physical senses in the first place. Maybe we read it, smelled it, or touched it. Only information that we gain through our extrasensory faculties—say through thought transference, or prognostication—is psychic in nature. But psychically derived information would definitely be considered intuitive, because it comes in through a process of direct knowing.

Discarnate Intelligence or "Spirit Entities"

The spirit entities who channel through me are just like you and me, except they have a broader world view and can more easily harness their intuition within the vast ocean of consciousness that is available to us all, and in which they exist and have their being. In other words, spirit entities can access superconscious information because they swim in the cosmic ocean of cosmic consciousness.

Although they access information through the mechanism of telepathy, once we are speaking with them, it is human need, as expressed through our questions, that triggers their responses. If the spirit entities have the information, they will channel it through. If they do not have it, they will say so.

From their state of "knowingness," these entities offer evolved bodies of information that I haven't consciously accessed in this lifetime. This is all channeling is—a source of information. It is not an omnipotent source of information, but it can offer us fresh insights into how we function as human beings of mind, body, and spirit.

Tom MacPherson will, on occasion, teach people object lessons. A client once asked him when a certain person was going to die. Tom said, "Just a moment. We'll see what we can find for you." Tom paused and then said, "We find that the person you're inquiring about is going to pass to our side in approximately six to eight months. Does that answer your question?" The client acknowledged that it did and thanked Tom. Tom then interjected, "We also discovered something else of interest to you. We find that the person you're inquiring about is going to be delivering the eulogy at your funeral."

As the client gasped for breath, Tom quickly said, "No, no, no. We're just pulling your leg. We discovered that you stand to inherit money when this person leaves the body, and we find that waiting for this inheritance is holding you back from accomplishing your goals in life. You have talents you should be exercising as the source of your livelihood. We also feel it is important for you to understand the impact the question would have on the other party. You wouldn't want them to feel the way you just did when you thought that your passing was imminent."

This is an example of how spirit entities can interact with us to nudge us along on the path of our own development. Indeed, we shouldn't think of spirit entities as being any different from ourselves, even though they are in the discarnate state. Using our own extrasensory faculties and intuition, we can access the same bodies of information as they can, both from our past lives and present circumstances. The only difference between ourselves and discarnate intelligences, as mentioned earlier, is that these discarnate souls occupy a greater gestalt, or a greater state of knowingness. Existing outside the three-dimensional perimeters of time and space, they have easier access to the collective unconscious, or universal mind. They are only objectively feeding back to us information that we, ourselves, hold as a potential, but of which we aren't necessarily conscious.

To say this another way, whenever we ask a question, the answer is already contained within us. If we were to probe our own creative resources through an intuitive process, we would inevitably arrive at answers to our questions. Spirit simply objectifies the inquiry we are making and then goes that extra nine yards by telepathically accessing the energy (or the "answer") that we are already "broadcasting" and then reflects it back to us. It is not that spirit entities know everything about us, but they more fully apply their knowingness or intuition to isolate information that can help us accomplish our goals.

The Childhood of a Trance Channel

People are usually curious about how and why I became interested in trance channeling. I'm not sure I can answer that, precisely, but I recall that when most of my classmates were busy putting together model airplanes and trading off Mickey Mantle baseball cards, I was reading books on parapsychology and psychic phenomena.

Some of my early interest in these areas was stirred by the conflicting versions of creation and of man's essential nature I was exposed to as a child. At Sunday school, I was taught the biblical story of the creation, and about angels and archangels, "the hereafter," and souls. In public school, my science teachers called these "superstitions" and taught, instead, the more mechanistic "big bang" theory of the origin of our universe. Considerations of higher purpose or moral principle were relegated to the domain of "religion," or, at best, philosophical speculation. In any case, neither of these versions of reality matched my childhood experiences of déjà vu, out-of-body experiences, and prognostic dreams. So, at the tender age of eleven, I set out to resolve for myself these apparent contradictions.

In junior high school, after countless hours at the library, I came across a book on dreams by Carl Jung. His experiences with the dream state paralleled many of my own. From Jung I was guided to the parapsychology section, where I discovered that paranormal phenomena had been tested and documented over the last two decades, and that data in support of telepathy had already been introduced into scientific literature. I recognized parapsychology as the bridge between theology and science I was looking for. From that point on, I read every book I could find on telepathy, extrasensory perception, astral projection, reincarnation, and other evidences of man's spiritual nature.

In high school I discovered the works of Edgar Cayce, whose parapsychological models of the human psyche closely paralleled my ideas. The more I read, the harder it was for me to understand why this vast body of parapsychological research had not been entertained as worthy of even a footnote all through high school. If it had been, who knows how many minds might have been stimulated to pursue these studies.

I continued to research these areas quite seriously on my own, then started to consciously develop my ESP abilities through psychometry, divining, and inspired writing. By the time I graduated from high school, in 1969, I'm sure I had the equivalent of a self-taught bachelor's degree in parapsychology. When, after graduation, my family moved from Sandusky, Ohio, to Phoenix, Arizona, I temporarily shelved my interest in parapsychology and went into partnership with my father in graphic arts.

After several years in business, I began to feel that I had dried up artistically. Desiring to stimulate my creativity, I joined a meditation study group that was using Edgar Cayce techniques. After about six months, the meditations seemed to trigger a trance channeling state.

My first trance was spontaneous. I was meditating and seemed to drop off to sleep. When I awakened thirty minutes later, the group was very animated. They played back a tape of the channeling that had taken place while I was "sleeping." This was the first time I heard the entity "John." In his soft voice, John explained his reason for speaking through and then answered questions from the group. Most of the people present had a degree of familiarity with trance states through their exposure to the Edgar Cayce teachings.

Even though I hadn't intended to go into trance, what transpired was by no means against my will. I had consciously given permission for contact with the superconscious levels all my life. The form it took surprised me because I was partial to Edgar Cayce's method of directly accessing superconscious mind resources. It had never occurred to me that I would be channeling discarnate entities. But after continuously working with trance for about six months, I could go in and out of the altered state quite easily, and John was able to speak through almost as he does today. The other entities, such as Tom MacPherson, Japu, and Obadiah, came through several years later.

Most of the people I worked with in my early trance channeling sessions were familiar with mediumship and metaphysics. Their questions were primarily philosophical and metaphysical and drew responses from Spirit that were clearly above and beyond information I had read. But there was nothing to suggest that there was any extrasensory functioning, or that the trance state was communicating anything that wasn't already contained in my subjective experience or conscious resources. Then, one day a physician came to consult with John about some patients he was having a hard time in diagnosing. He also sought John's insights on some personal health concerns. Afterward, the doctor told me that John's responses had been extremely helpful, and that his summation of the doctor's own health had been precise and accurate.

This was the first demonstration that John had clearly tapped sources of information with which I had no conscious-mind familiarity. This gave me the confidence to apply the trance state to other topics, such as reincarnation, dream states, appropriate models of physics and medicine, and earth changes. I was fast beginning to see how the phenomenon of trance channeling could be harnessed to benefit individuals and society, both on the practical and spiritual levels. Desiring accreditation, I enrolled in a two-year program at the University of Life in Phoenix, a theological institution founded in 1962, and received my credentials as a teacher of metaphysics and a trance channel.

The Spirit Teachers

In the beginning, and for the first few years, John was the only teacher to speak through my trance. A soft-spoken personality, John identifies himself as an Essene scholar of Hebrew ancestry and a disciple of the man Jesus. On occasion, he has identified himself as

John, son of Zebedee, and has talked about his experiences as one of the twelve apostles. His manner of expression is what we would think of as "biblical," both in his language, such as the use of the biblical pronouns *ye* and *thee,* and in his many references from that time period. But John's knowledge is not limited to biblical times. He is able to give discourse on the spiritual and philosophical knowledge of all ages and cultures and seems to have spontaneous access to such fields as modern physics, medicine, and advanced technology. He is certainly the most universal of the entities to speak through me.

In contrast to John is Tom MacPherson, who was the second personality to channel through me. Tom identifies himself as an Irish pickpocket who lived about four hundred years ago, in Shakespeare's England. He applies his Irish charm and wit to helping individuals overcome emotional blockages and make career and other practical life decisions. Some people are troubled by the idea of speaking with a pickpocket, but Tom points out that his earthy and pragmatic personality contributes a certain humanity to the channeling process. Tom provides a common man's approach to the information John brings through. He also says he's no longer into picking pockets and doesn't advocate that trade to anyone. These days, he's more into picking brains.

Atun-Re, who started coming through me in 1981, is of Nubian descent. He lived in Lower Egypt around the middle 1300s B.C. and was a student of the teachings of Imhotep, the great Egyptian architect, and an adviser to the pharaoh Akhnaton. Like MacPherson, Atun-Re teaches with humor, but like John, he accesses a wide range of both spiritual and technical information. Atun-Re has channeled extensively on meditation, the chakras, the ancient mysteries, and intuition and dreams.

John, Tom MacPherson, and Atun-Re are the entities who speak through me most consistently. John usually opens and closes each session. In a group situation, he often gives an inspirational discourse on the subject of the evening's channeling and then steps aside for one of the other teachers to speak through. In personal consultations, either John or Tom, or sometimes both, will speak, depending on the nature of the inquiry. People most frequently consult spirit entities on personal relationships, health problems, career direction, creative blocks, or work-related problems. I find that it helps, especially with first-time clients, to spend the first hour just talking casually. Sometimes I can help people clarify their questions and phrase them in such a way as to elicit the most comprehensive answers from the entities. The channeling itself usually lasts for about an hour.

Two other teachers who often speak through in groups are Obadiah and Japu. Obadiah is a Haitian who lived about 150 years ago. He was an herbalist and storyteller. Drawing on his narrative skills, he entertains groups with anecdotes from his culture and time period. Japu is also a storyteller. An oriental teacher, he lived about 5,000 years ago, and used to bless the traders who traveled along the silk routes between India and China. Japu channels on reincarnation and past lives.

Although the backgrounds of these spirit personalities are diverse, their values are quite similar, and they appear to be knowledgeable about one another's cultures and beliefs. John often draws on Buddhist philosophy and parable, while Japu and Obadiah have, at times, clarified subtle points of Judeo-Christian values. To some extent, their similarities can be traced to their shared perspective as discarnate entities. But also, every society has teachings that embrace the idea of spirit survival, and these teachings in themselves are strikingly similar. The spirit entities who speak through me seem also to know one another from past lives at various points in history, although not necessarily in the lifetimes in which they are speaking through. This probably contributes to the similarity in beliefs.

Many people wonder why these entities all speak English, since it is clearly not their native language—with the exception of Tom MacPherson. The simple answer is that they speak through in English because that is the language spoken by the audiences I address. John, Atun-Re, Japu, and Obadiah all say they studied English while in the discarnate state. Although Tom MacPherson spoke a derivative of English in his lifetime, his brogue was so thick when he first came through that his message was often discounted. People couldn't understand him. So, he had to work on updating his dialect, which he did in a matter of months. Tom continues to use archaic terms from his own time period, but has also picked up some of our modern slang.

In addition to the teachers I've just mentioned, many other entities have spontaneously spoken through my trance state over the last fifteen years. Although some of them are teachers of mine from past lives, the majority were guides and teachers of individuals who consulted me for channelings.

Why These Spirit Entities Speak Through Me

Several conditions converged to shape my development as a trance channel and to attract these particular entities to me. I'm quite certain that I've known all the discarnate personalities who speak through me in past lives. For example, John has spoken of at least two lifetimes we shared among the ancient Essenes. And according to Tom MacPherson, I was an English magistrate in his time period, and some of his mischievous behavior occasionally brought him up before my bar.

The bond that exists between ourselves and Spirit is a human one. Bonds of familiarity and friendship survive not only over the course of a lifetime, but over the course of many lives. Because I knew these discarnate personalities in past lives, there is tacit permission given for our association, even if I was initially unaware of them. It is like an adoptive child who gives permission to his unknown parent to locate him, or to be in communication, because the connection already exists. Our relationships do not cease just because some of us have a physical body and some of us do not.

Another reason why these spirit entities teach through me is that I've always been interested in this phenomenon and see it as perfectly natural. As an artist, I kept my intuitive flows open throughout adolescence, so it was easier for these human bonds to reestablish themselves and for the entities to speak through. And since I've chosen to be a teacher of spiritual and metaphysical principles, there is high motivation for them to maintain an alliance with me.

But again, keep in mind that we are all psychic, and we all channel to one degree or another. How far we develop our channeling ability depends on our interest and our willingness to apply ourselves. Most of us can play baseball, but few of us care to pursue it professionally. People assume that because I have chosen this profession, I'm exceptionally gifted in it. The truth is that I've met channels with superior abilities to mine who have simply chosen to keep a lower profile with their work. So, I would not say that I was chosen to do this work, particularly, but only that I possess a talent or an ability for it and have the desire to work with it professionally. I may or may not be a "gifted" channel, but anyone can develop the skill. Trance channeling is a talent, not a "power." It is a natural human ability.

Spirit's Motivation for Speaking Through

Spirit's primary motivation for speaking with us is to help us explore the spiritual dimensions of ourselves and our universe. John has information he believes is relevant to the present time period. When appropriate, he gives illuminating discourse on the Bible, but more often he talks on alternative or holistic healing, world peace, futuristic technology, earth changes, and other topics of vital concern to us.

Tom MacPherson gets visibly upset when people refer to these communications as "talking with the dead." He is quick to say, "I am not dead, I am very much alive. I consider myself as much a human being as you are, because I have personality, I have feelings, and I have ambitions." Tom has an additional motivation to communicate with us at this time—he plans another incarnation in fifty or sixty years. The more he can contribute to our awareness of various spiritual principles, the better the world will be when he reincarnates. As he has often said, "We are counting on you to keep things together until we can get down there ourselves."

The Relationship Between the Channel and Spirit

Of great interest to many people is the nature of the relationship between a medium, or channel, and the spirit entity, or entities, who speak through. In my case, the entities I channel must, to some extent, align themselves with my personal ethics. When I first began to channel, I experimented with some of the classic spiritualist activities, such as trying to track down a certain client's recently departed uncle Charlie to find out where he hid his will, or bringing messages through from deceased relatives. It didn't take me long to realize that people who used trance channeling in this way seemed not to be developing mentally, emotionally, or spiritually in their exchanges with Spirit. On the other hand, those who were exposed to the philosophical concepts became inspired and started to explore their own spirituality. So, I consciously moved my trance work in this direction and Spirit aligned with my decision.

The entities who work with me have always had a positive philosophical orientation; however, on occasion I've had to put an entity "on notice." For example, in an early guides-and-teachers workshop, when Tom MacPherson had just started channeling through, our values came into conflict. Tom was introducing the various guides and teachers aligned with individuals in the group. At one point, an elegant Native American Indian guide by the name of Red Fox (not to be confused with the comedian Redd Foxx!) showed up. In the manner of any good Irishman of his day, Tom introduced Red Fox as "a savage with practically no clothing on." Tom's transmission was terminated instantly. It was as if a large invisible hook had come out and jerked him offstage. Several minutes later he returned and said, "Excuse me. I've just been dutifully informed that you now address these individuals as 'noble Native Americans.' " It sounded like he'd been dusted down on the other side.

When I learned of Tom's crudeness in introducing Red Fox, I put him on probation. In the meditative state, I put up a screen that wouldn't allow Tom through unless he aligned himself with my ethics and values. After some time passed with no repeat performances, I removed the screen.

On another occasion, a client of mine asked Tom if he could locate his wife, who was recently deceased. Even though my trance tends to be weak in this area, Tom told the man he would give it a try. After a few moments of silence, Tom said quite angrily, "You bloody liar. Not only do I find that your wife isn't over here, but she's in perfectly sound health!" The client, who was probably just trying to test MacPherson, was quite startled. Once again the big hook came out and jerked Tom offstage.

The hook that jerked Tom offstage both times was my own system of ethics. Our guides and teachers must align with our levels of consciousness, our ethics, and our manner of expression. It is practically impossible for them to express themselves above and beyond these perimeters. They are "guests" within our area of influence and are permitted to contribute only what is appropriate. My consciousness has an automatic screen that filters out behavior that goes against my values. In other words, spirit entities can make independent statements, but unless these statements serve the full intention of the channel, they will not be permitted expression.

Although the entities have on occasion spoken spontaneously in their own language, they do not often do so because it tends to leave residues in my subconscious mind. For instance, I was giving a public talk some years ago, and just as I was coming to a dramatic point and was about to say "and God goes to bat for you," instead I said, "God will take a shillelagh for you." (A shillelagh is a shepherd's crook. It is the old Irish word for *staff*.) So, even though Tom MacPherson's linguistics are close to our own, his archaic phraseology occasionally pops up in my vocabulary when I'm not in trance. Sometimes when I'm speaking, a word comes out that is alien to me on a conscious level but has the right feel at the moment. Often it turns out to be a foreign word known to Japu or another of the entities. The retention of such words is a side effect of the clairvoyant state.

Anyone Can Become a Channel

I've always believed that a good trance channel should be trying to put himself or herself out of business by teaching others to access their own higher resources. The best way to access these resources is through meditation. This is the key to any psychic or channeling ability. When we meditate, we go to our own inner resources. And that is all channeling really is—a form of meditation.

As I've said before, everyone has some degree of extrasensory perception. In the United States, recent polls show that 65 to 68 percent of the people surveyed have had some personal experience with extrasensory phenomena. A poll published in *New Scientist* on January 25, 1973, indicated that 25 percent of the scientists surveyed considered paranormal phenomena an established fact. Another 42 percent of them thought it was a likely possibility. Today's statistics show even higher percentages.

The only special ability one needs to be a good trance channel is an open heart and an open mind. It is also a good idea to get some academic underpinnings in the field of intuition and parapsychology. This helps to remove fear and superstition about trance and places it more in the realm of "normal" rather than "supernormal" behavior. Being creative or intuitive in our everyday thought processes is the only prerequisite for easily entering into these various psychic states.

We are all channeling on one level or another. Our personality, which is conditioned by our past circumstances, is being channeled from our subconscious mind and our superconscious states. We gain insights subliminally from guides and teachers, as well as from our environment, all the time. The sound of horns honking on the freeway tells us that commuter traffic is under way. The smell of warm bread tells us that dinner is ready. A disturbing dream affects our mood all day. It is merely the degree to which we apply these insights, or increase our awareness of them, that we call them "psychic" or "intuitive" or "trance channeling," but it is all the same phenomenon.

There are many forms of channeling, including trance channeling, psychometry, aura reading, clairvoyance, and clairaudience. Since high levels of information can be accessed by any of these techniques, I encourage people not to focus on any one form. Ultimately, the value of any insight is relative to the person who receives it. It is a mistake to consider trance channeling a superior method. It is just a little more dramatic than the other methods, so people get fixated on it. In truth, our own intuitive insights are equal to any information we get from any other source.

Trying to "Prove" Channeling
Is Like Nailing a Custard Pie to the Wall

I decided long ago that trying to prove to skeptics or disbelievers that the human spirit can exist outside of a physical form is a poor use of the channeling state. I prefer to channel information that helps promote well-being and enhance our own spiritual decision-making processes, so that is where I concentrate my work. Ultimately, you can't prove something to someone whose mind is closed. No matter what evidences are offered, they'll discount them. Some people say, "I'll believe it when I see it." A friend of mine gave me a unique way of rearranging that—"When you believe it, you'll see it."

Evidence for the kinds of phenomena we have been talking about has already been painstakingly documented in parapsychology journals, so anyone who is truly sincere about investigating this topic has many reliable resources to explore. The fact that most surveys taken over the last ten years show that the majority of Americans already believe in some form of afterlife is further reason not to invest energy in those who do not believe.

I personally believe that the entities John, Tom, Atun-Re, and all the others are separate and distinct personalities from my own, rather than a projection of my past lives, or an "alter ego." But I leave this open to each person's interpretation. Some people think of the entities as creative aspects of my subconscious, and others have no trouble at all relating to them as entirely separate beings.

A psychologist who'd been coming to see me for years once said, "Kevin, we are friends, and my trust level with you is very high. Your entities come through for me every time, and I've received a great deal of value from the channelings. I personally believe that they are who they present themselves to be. However, if my colleagues ever backed me into a corner, and I had to make a diagnosis of what I observed, from a psychologist's perspective, I would have to say you've developed a benign form of schizophrenia that you've learned to apply in a socially constructive manner."

Well, if that's what it takes for someone to be able to comfortably participate in this process, I'm open to it. We know that artists can be a little eccentric, but no one would deny that they make a positive contribution to the social order. Channeling, regardless of how you explain it, does make a valuable, though novel, contribution as a source of inspiration and insight.

How to Assess the Accuracy of Channeled Information

Suppose you're an archaeologist. A psychic you've consulted tells you, "Go into the Egyptian desert at such-and-such location and dig down two hundred feet. There you'll find a temple." Let's say you go to Egypt, to that precise location. If after digging two hundred feet you do not find the temple, I would say the information isn't proved accurate. If you find the temple, the information is verified.

This was a simple example, but the factors that affect the accuracy of a trance medium are sometimes quite complex. Many predictions made by mediums do not come to pass—such as Jean Dixon's prediction that Nixon, Haldeman, and Erlichman would not resign from office. The conscious mind, which is the controlling factor, can sometimes interfere with the information being channeled. For this reason, the medium needs to be totally detached from the information. Jean Dixon's strong attachment to Nixon's not resigning from office seemed to interfere with her predictions, which are usually from 70 to 80 percent accurate.

If a channel has fears, he or she may bring through a discourse on those fears. This can be as much a clearing process for the channel as a legitimate response to another person's inquiry. It is important to remember that we are all in different stages of our spiritual development. Some channels are in the beginning stages, and others have been working with metaphysical principles for many years. We need to be as discerning in dealing with channeled information as we would be with any other information. If the information feels right, we can work with it. If it doesn't, we just put it on the shelf. We have to trust our intuition about these things. If something we hear doesn't resonate with our inner knowingness, there's no need to overreact to it, because it is only information.

If we are trying to assess the accuracy of our own channeling, say of inspired writing, we need only to look at our past writings and see where we've had success, or brought through information that proved valuable to ourselves and/or to others. This builds our confidence. Some writing will be inspired and some may be just a cleansing process, to empty out the subconscious. Either way, it has value. We may want to evaluate our progress by making a series of predictions and seeing if we get synchronistic feedback from the environment. It could be anything from predicting earthquakes, to anticipating treatments for cancer, to foretelling the outcome of a particular governmental election. The ultimate criterion in weighing any information is whether it has human value—whether it is relevant to you or to others.

In assessing the accuracy of any trance channel, remember that although the spirit entities are usually in a greater state of objectivity than we are, which allows them to more easily access information, Spirit doesn't know everything. Only God knows everything. When we hear our own truth spoken, it will resonate in our hearts and we will recognize it. This is how we weigh the value of the information we receive from any source. And we shouldn't become so attached to this information that we run to an outside source for validation every time something comes up. I say this because many people do become attached to receiving information from spirit entities. They think Spirit knows everything because the entities are "up there" and we are "down here." The entities who speak through me are qualified teachers and are worth listening to as a source of information, but ultimately we have to heed our own source, our own inner guidance.

The Value of Trance Channeling

People consult with trance channels for reasons that are as varied as the people themselves. Often the reasons are pragmatic—individuals wish to explore their relationships, career potentials, or health problems. At other times, the need is quite specialized, such as an individual's desire to trace a particular karmic pattern back through many past lives to find its origin. Trance channeling can be particularly helpful when a person is in spiritual crisis. Many sociologists and psychologists acknowledge a spiritual dimension to the human psyche, which traditional therapy doesn't address. Some call it a "sickness of the soul."

In addition to its value in providing insights to help us define and achieve our life goals, channeling can be used as a research tool. It has already been successfully applied in the area of psychic archaeology. The Mobius Society, in Los Angeles, has submitted many reports on the value and use of psychic archaeology to scientific journals and to _Omni_ magazine.

Throughout world history, politicians have sought channeled information. Much to his regret, Julius Caesar ignored the advice of his seers to "beware the Ides of March." Abraham Lincoln was well known for his interest in the spiritualist movement. It is said that he consulted with a trance medium over the signing of the Emancipation Proclamation. He was encouraged at that time, by an entity who identified himself as the spirit of Daniel Webster, to sign the Emancipation Proclamation because it would establish, once and for all, the true principle of what the United States stood for—freedom for all people.

Trance channeling has provided tremendously valuable information for individuals involved with healing and medicine, particularly those researching and applying holistic principles of healing. Spirit has shared many "natural therapies" for preventing disease and enhancing general states of health. I'm not a medical doctor and I do not prescribe medicine or diagnose disease, but many physicians and chiropractors do research with trance channels such as myself. Edgar Cayce provides probably the most well-known example of how channeled information can be accessed to outline treatments for specific disease states, with very positive results. In 1983–84 I met with a group that gathered monthly to develop medical models for working with the AIDS virus. The research generated by this program is published in the book *Psychoimmunity and the Healing Process* (Celestial Arts, 1986), by Jason Serinus.

Because of my early interest in closing the gap between science and spirituality, some of my most gratifying work has been with Dr. William Kautz, founder and director of the Center for Applied Intuition, in San Francisco. Dr. Kautz has designed what he calls the "intuitive consensus" method, wherein he consults various individuals, whom he calls "expert intuitives," on such topics as sudden infant death syndrome and earthquake-triggering mechanisms. When he receives a consensus from these intuitive sources, it is written up and submitted for testing under the rigors of our traditional scientific methods. Intuition tells us where to look, and the left-brain rational process allows us to verify our findings and communicate them to other people. The intuitive state is now being acknowledged as a normal and necessary part of our thought process. In his book with Melanie Branon, *Channeling: The Intuitive Connection* (Harper & Row, 1987), Dr. Kautz discusses his work with expert intuitives.

A major aspect of my work is to educate individuals in their own channeling abilities. I often work with creative visualization and meditation techniques to assist people to access their deeper channeling states.

My own channeling has two major areas of impact. First, it has implications for the field of thanatology, or the study of death and dying. If the discarnate personalities who channel through my trance state are the beings they present themselves to be—and it is my belief and my experience that they are—they are certainly in a unique position to provide insights into the afterlife.

For example, we are beginning to document more and more cases of near-death experience (NDE), in which people who were declared clinically dead and then were revived reported strikingly similar descriptions of out-of-body states. Since these descriptions come from individuals of widely divergent cultural backgrounds, we can conclude that whatever near-death experience is, it is a common psychological human condition. And if there is an afterlife, as the documentation implies, and we survive into that dimension, it has tremendous implications for how we should conduct ourselves in our everyday affairs.

Trance channeling provides another valuable service as a source of information and inspiration. I see my channeling as an information base that can assist individuals to expand their sense of themselves as multidimensional beings and meet their human needs in constructive and creative ways.

Why Are So Many Channels Appearing in These Times?

Many people assume that our society's growing interest in spirituality is a new trend. The truth is that there have always been "spiritual revivals" in which people began to seek deeper insights into the human condition. Some societies reinforce this more than others. The United States has often had such revivals—most notably the transcendentalist movement of the last century, and the periodic resurgence of interest in spirit communication prevalent in our own century, beginning with Edgar Cayce, then later with Arthur Ford and Eileen Garrett, and finally with Jane Roberts and younger channels such as myself.

The consciousness revolution of the 1960s was a profound demonstration of interest in the spiritual dimension. I recall a cover of *Time* magazine from the mid-1970s that read: BOOM TIMES ON THE PSYCHIC FRONTIER, referring to the human potential movement of that decade. All of this, including the widespread exploration of psychic abilities in the 1980s, has contributed to a more open environment. Interest in these phenomena does run in cycles, but it is all part of the growth of human consciousness.

There have always been channels and mediums among us. Trance channeling was around before biblical times and both the Old and New Testaments are rife with references to mediums. This is true of the oral and written literature of most ancient cultures. Perhaps the most familiar to Westerners is the Delphic Oracle. But mediums were also prevalent among the Aztec and Incan cultures, and in Africa and Brazil. Two of America's best-loved presidents, Abraham Lincoln and Franklin Delano Roosevelt, consulted with trance channels. Roosevelt consulted with Edgar Cayce on a number of occasions.

Trance channeling continues to be widely practiced and accepted in Brazil and Nigeria. In those cultures, individuals who were trained in orthodox Western colleges and universities freely consult local "shaman"—practitioners of paranormal phenomenon—to come up with new insights and medical diagnoses. These shaman are the carriers of the oral traditions of their respective cultures and are thoroughly integrated into the framework of their social order.

So, spirituality has always been current in our society and many others. It is just that we are experiencing a revival of people's awareness of these phenomena.

Parapsychology and Social Change

I describe my work as "parapsychological." Parapsychology is the study of paranormal phenomena and how to apply them appropriately within our current social structure. It includes everything from precognition and astral projection to the more clearly defined near-death experience and death and dying. It also includes the metaphysical inquiries made by Shirley MacLaine into soul mates, reincarnation, and past lives.

There are more than just a handful of people exploring these various phenomena. Applied intuition and the psychic sciences are carving deep inroads into the direction in which we, as a society, are moving. One major social impact of these new forces is the extent to which meditation and self-hypnosis techniques have been acknowledged as valuable in restoring mental and physical well-being. These techniques are widely applied in the areas of medicine, business, and education, to name just a few.

These same forces have had profound impact in the area of nutritional foods. A little more than a decade ago, if we walked into our neighborhood Lucky or Safeway grocery store and asked for a loaf of sprouted wheat bread, some nice man in a green apron would point us in the direction of the nearest health food store. Now, most of the major food chains have at least a small section of organic and unprocessed foods.

There has been significant impact on orthodox medicine as well, particularly in the application of biofeedback and visualization techniques in the treatment of a wide range of diseases, including hypertension, heart disease, and cancer. More and more we are seeing empirical, scientific evidence of how the mind, or consciousness, and the body influence each other.

Many industries have sprung up as a result of the consciousness movement. Celestial Seasonings, an herbal tea and spice company, has garnered tremendous economic clout over the years. The growth of the organic cosmetic industry in the last decade is another direct outcome of the consciousness movement. There are numerous other examples.

The most encouraging trend we have seen recently, in my opinion, is the attention being given to the role of intuition in our lives. *Intuition* is the polite term for "psychic insight." It is a safe term to use whether we are talking with a conservative businessperson or a parapsychologist. Renewed interest in the intuitive process has had a tremendous effect particularly in the area of labor and management relations. One manifestation of this is our interest in Japanese models, in some cases more effective than our own, which seem to incorporate a form of thought transference, or telepathy.

The intuitive consensus method of Dr. Kautz, whom I mentioned earlier, has been applied, with positive results, to researching AIDS, calcium deterioration in the physical body in zero-gravity states, crib death, and earthquake-triggering mechanisms, to name just a few.

Jeffrey Mishlove's *The Roots of Consciousness* (Random House,

1975) provides an excellent overview of where parapsychology is today, as well as its historical antecedents. Any of the works of Carl Jung, whom many people consider the father of modern parapsychology, are excellent resources. William James, the American psychologist, wrote about psychic phenomena; actually it was James himself who coined the term *parapsychology*. I also recommend the publications of the Theosophical Society and any books by Elisabeth Kübler-Ross on death and dying.

In any study of the paranormal, keep in mind that the highest application of any paranormal or parapsychological ability is to discover ourselves in our relationship with God. That is the true goal of working with these energies. I work with a parapsychological model because I want to see the phenomena observed under controlled laboratory conditions, where they can be measured and repeated. At the same time, I also apply the model to my spiritual growth. Again, the highest application of any theory or model is in teaching us more about ourselves as beings of energy, and empowering us to achieve our fullest potential.

Closing Words

I would like to close this chapter with some words about my personal beliefs and how they influence the way I live my life. I consider myself a practicing Judeo-Christian metaphysician, both religiously and philosophically, and hold a strong belief that we are all part of God. I think that if we were to acknowledge the portion of us that is spirit, or soul, we'd have a deeper appreciation for the human condition, rather than continually dehumanizing it. I do not believe God is an impersonal or abstract concept; rather, I think God can be highly personal because we, as human beings, are personal.

My spiritual development, and the shaping of my attitudes and emotions, has been strongly influenced by a belief in reincarnation and the laws of karma. I believe that everything that happens to me in life has a meaning from which I can learn and grow. I attempt to practice the discipline of "Judge not, lest ye be judged."

I also subscribe to "the law of grace." I think it is essential that we learn to forgive ourselves and others, but at the same time we shouldn't forget, or take lightly, the lessons that come to us in life.

What happens to us is the result not of happenstance but of revelation. It is not that we are born, we live, and we die, and maybe contribute something to society on the way. Rather, life is a continuous cycle of birth, death, and rebirth, or incarnation and reincarnation, and our soul, our consciousness, and even our personality survives in these various states.

Being a trance channel has expanded my understanding and appreciation of who we are as human beings and has given me greater opportunity and freedom to grow and experience life in its fullness. Above all else, I feel a deeper bond with all individuals, and an absence of barriers, whether ethnic, social, or religious. In short, being a trance channel has expanded my sense of humanity.

When I decided to pursue parapsychology and trance channeling as a full-time profession, I set aside my career in graphic arts, which had been a source of deep personal satisfaction. I did this because I felt that parapsychology contained information that was both personally and socially transformative. Through my studies, I've come to respect the profound influence that mind, or consciousness, exerts over events, over matter. We see this all the time, especially in relation to health. It is commonly acknowledged that a good attitude has a miraculous effect on the body's ability to heal. And if one person's mind has the potential to affect matter, it is even more awesome to consider what "group mind" can do.

The growing recognition of the power of group consciousness motivated the flurry of Live Aid, Farm Aid, and Band Aid concerts in the 1980s. Such events managed to raise the international consciousness of our ability to bring an end to human suffering.

It is through our communications that we transform one another. There's also an esoteric principle at work here, which is that we are not in this alone. We are part of a universal mind, or universal intelligence. Spirit has said, rather poetically, "Even as ye have many thoughts and yet only one mind, so in turn there are many souls and yet there is only one God. Therefore, each of ye are as a thought within the mind of God." When we all think as one, we become that mind, that force, which transforms. So, our meditations, our prayers, and our dialogues—however we care to look at them—do indeed have an incredible historical and social impact.

If we think about it, we have witnessed an extraordinary leap in consciousness in the span of one generation. We have by no means eliminated racism, but when we consider the unbroken chain of thousands of years of racial discrimination in the world, we see that we have made a tremendous leap forward. Our consciousness was profoundly affected by the visions and efforts of both Mohandas Gandhi and Martin Luther King, Jr. And later, when our country seemed to have turned a deaf ear to the hungry in Africa, Mother Teresa came along and said, "Feed the hungry," and we were able to give billions of dollars. We need to become more conscious and more sensitive to one another. That is the real issue—consciousness and sensitivity.

I do not see us as separate from that perfect Spirit that we know as God, even at this point in time. I believe we are aligned with that perfection at all times, and it is only the degree to which we choose to realize it, and take responsibility for it, that we are expanded or limited. It is only when we judge something as lesser or greater that we feel we have dropped out of that process. If we can think of a moment in our lives when we felt totally inspired, and at one with all people, that is an example of how that perfection is with us at all times. The only challenge we have is to maintain the state of perfection we are already in. We have never left it.

Chapter 2

❦ *The Message*

Trance channeling is just one of many expressions of spirit communication, which is a vast subject in itself. Spirit communication is any dialogue between any of the dimensions of human consciousness that results in a more expanded awareness of ourselves as spiritual beings. This is the key to the value of trance channeling or any other form of spirit communication—that it results in the expansion of our awareness of ourselves as beings of mind, body, and spirit. This is the essence of what I've been teaching for the past fifteen years and is the single most important message that the spirit entities have attempted to convey. Our nature is three-dimensional. We live in a society that has been very thorough in uncovering the dimensions of ourselves as mind and body but less diligent in exploring our spiritual roots. With this in mind, I would like to explore this threefold dimension of ourselves in greater depth.

A Spiritual Paradigm for Human Potential

According to orthodox models of Western science and medicine, we consist of mind and body only—that is to say, our nature is strictly physiological. These models hold that matter somehow randomly evolved in a very complex physiological process that became conscious of itself. The model or paradigm that I work with acknowledges the spiritual dimension and the ability of consciousness to exist independent of the physical framework that we call the body. In other words, my model supports the supposition that consciousness, or mind, exists independent of matter, and that we are therefore more than just physiological beings.

A growing body of documentation strongly suggests that we are indeed more than just our physical minds and bodies. For example, when the phenomenon of near-death experience occurs, the people involved relate strikingly similar accounts. Most recall having traveled along a tunnel of light and passed through what they experienced as various planes of existence. The majority also report having met people they sensed to be highly evolved souls, and having found themselves reviewing the actions of their entire lives.

Carl Jung had an experience of this nature after suffering a heart attack at the age of sixty-nine. He was in a coma for three weeks, hovering between life and death. In his autobiographical work *Memories, Dreams and Reflections* (Vintage Books, 1961) Jung recounted this experience:

> I found myself in an utterly transformed state, in an ecstasy. I was floating in space a thousand miles above the earth, which I could clearly see below me. I felt safe in the womb of the universe, with a happiness that cannot be described. Soon I saw a gigantic stone, a huge asteroid, also floating in space. Inside it was a splendid, illuminated temple, and there—I felt with a great certainty—I was about to meet those people to whom I really belonged.
>
> Then a messenger arrived. I was ordered back to earth to finish the work that was expected of me. I was profoundly disappointed. Earth life seemed to me a prison. I had been glad to shed it all, and felt a violent resistance to returning.

Jung's report is typical of thousands of instances of near-death experiences that have been reported over the years. In the 1960s, Dr. Karlis Osis, the director of research at the Parapsychology Foundation in New York, investigated thirty-five thousand cases and found amazing consistencies. Raymond Moody, in his book *Life After Life,* and Robert Monroe, in his *Journeys Out of the Body,* researched this phenomenon more recently and had similar findings. These kinds of studies strongly suggest, or bear witness to, the spiritual dimensions that lie within us.

Telepathy is the clearest scientific evidence of this. If you lock two telepaths, or "sensitives," in separate rooms, under rigorously controlled laboratory conditions, eliminating any possibility of communication, they can still broadcast and receive intelligent thought between them. This phenomenon has been tested and observed so many times, under rigidly controlled conditions, that it's quite impossible for the scientific community, or for any of us, to ignore. The obvious implication is that human thought *can* survive independent of the physical body. And if a single thought, or a complex group of thoughts, can be communicated telepathically, why can't mind itself exist independent of the physical body, or the physical plane? And if mind *can* exist independent of the physical plane, independent of matter itself, we then have the principle called the human spirit, or the soul.

This mechanism of telepathy, this simple graceful exchange of energy between one level of consciousness and another, ·is the basis for most, if not all, spirit communication. Ultimately, it is exchanges of thoughts, ideas, and values that help us actualize as spiritual beings. While out-of-body and near-death experiences enhance our understanding of the phenomena, telepathy is the *cornerstone* or the mechanism behind spirit communication.

So, spirit communication is not some esoteric or supernormal occurrence that is independent of ourselves and outside the laws of nature. Quite the opposite. Spirit communication literally *flows from* our nature. It is a manifestation *of* our nature, and it can inspire us to fully align with ourselves and one another as beings of mind, body, and spirit.

The Nature of Spirit and Spirit Communication

Many people think of spirit communication, particularly trance channeling, as a person falling into a comatose state, or performing séances and tipping tables. Although these are legitimate expressions of what we would call classical spiritualism, which draw on natural psychokinetic activity, they represent only one aspect of spirit communication. The dialogue between ourselves and discarnate intelligence that takes place through a trance channel is another aspect of spirit communication. Talking to one another, going into meditation, and entering dream states to contact our own superconscious levels are also aspects of spirit communication, because we are all spirit. Spirit communication, then, is a way of accessing all the levels of expression of the human spirit that help promote our knowledge of who we are as human beings.

Our human nature is not defined by our physical bodies. Body simply means "perimeter" or "dimension." Even when we move beyond the physical body, our spiritual bodies survive. In other words, we continue to be "embodied" whether we have a physical body or not. We remain human beings whether we're incarnate in a physical form or not. As John often says, "We're not incarnate in the physical body, we're incarnate in the human condition."

The terms *entity, spirit, energy,* and *light* are all interchangeable in this model of the human condition. Spirit entities are beings of energy, or beings of light, and so are we. They are "discarnate spirit" and we are "incarnate spirit." We are just in different dimensions or states of energy. Our physical bodies are simply the mechanisms that enable our human souls to have focus in time and space, and to have experiences in the here and now.

Just as telepathic communication between two human beings is an aspect or expression of spirit communication, so are our conversations with spirit guides and teachers. But who are these energies, and where do they come from? Each of us is surrounded by a band of energy—like a radio band. This energy can be observed in a Kirlian photograph or can be viewed directly by individuals who can see or sense auras. This band of energy can also be seen as a spectrum of entities who gather in fellowship about us. We are in constant communication with these entities through our meditations, dream states, and direct dialogues with them.

The purpose of communication with spirit guides and teachers is human evolution. It is to keep us continually progressing with the general flow of the collective consciousness (some people call it planetary consciousness). John has suggested that the consciousness of our planet is reflected through us, and that in many ways we *are* the planetary consciousness, we *are* the evolutionary force on this plane. Spirit has also suggested that there's no progression in the earth plane without the physical body. In other words, we human beings have chosen to focus or anchor ourselves in the earth plane so that we can progress spiritually. Our spirit guides and teachers evolve through their association with us and the experiences we undergo. Thus, these entities communicate with us for the same reason we communicate with one another—to learn and to grow.

These discarnate entities are human personalities. According to Spirit, we don't occupy a physical body, we occupy a human personality. John once said, "The personality is the language through which the soul communicates in the earth plane." Spirit beings utilize their personalities as teaching tools to communicate and establish rapport with us, and to reinforce our understanding that the human personality survives the physical transformation we call death.

In the East, the personality is equated with the human ego. Eastern schools of wisdom have traditionally considered the ego the source of all suffering and teach that if we want to put an end to our suffering and return to our original nature, our Buddha nature, or God-like nature, we must eliminate the ego. In the West, it is quite the opposite. We are conditioned from childhood that to survive in our competitive society, we must build a "healthy" ego, a strong ego. We're taught that our suffering comes not from *having* an ego but from having *too weak* an ego. There is much emphasis put on whether we have a "good personality."

The truth probably lies somewhere in the middle. To the degree that we're physically incarnate, we are conditioned by our physical environment, so we certainly have to contend with that aspect of our nature. At the same time, it is essential that we get in touch with that deeper aspect of ourselves, which is our spirit. This means accepting ourselves fully in all three dimensions of ourselves—as mind, body, and spirit. Denying any aspect of this trinity interferes with our ability to be fully self-actualized, to live up to the potential of ourselves as spiritual beings. If we become too exclusively focused on the spirit, we lose sight of the practical. If we become too exclusively focused on the body, we can lapse into materialism. It is also possible to go too deep into the mind and lose ourselves in the intellect at the expense of both the body and the spirit. We have to balance these aspects of our threefold nature.

Because our personality, or our ego, is our vehicle for progressing in society, or as John says, "the language through which the soul communicates in the earth plane," it is very important that it be balanced. At the practical level, if we have an unpleasant personality, it will be harder for us to advance professionally. A salesman who is rude to his customers isn't going to make many sales; a professor who can't get along with his fellow faculty members might not achieve tenure; an overly temperamental aspiring actor is going to have a hard time finding work.

Our personality can also be a vehicle for our spiritual growth. In acknowledging our spiritual nature, and conceiving of ourselves as more than just mind and body, we expand our personality so that it can begin to serve our higher purpose. This is what our guides and teachers encourage through their communication with us. Rather than encouraging us to eradicate our ego, they inspire us to expand our perception of ourselves to include spiritual principles, as well as love and respect for ourselves and others. With this overview in mind, I'd like to briefly describe the individual dimensions of spirit communication.

The Seven Dimensions of Spirit Communication

According to Spirit, there are seven dimensions of spirit communication predominant in the band of entities who work with us. These are:

- spirit guides
- teachers
- master teachers

- saints
- ascended masters
- angels
- archangels

Spirit Guides

Spirit guides are beings whom we have known in past lives. They assist us with conditions that are karmic in nature, issues that we still need to work out in the context of this lifetime. If we argue with someone, the best person to work it out with is the person with whom we argued. Similarly, when karma is incurred, it's best to receive insight from a being with comparable karmic needs or experiences. Assistance from our spirit guides and teachers, or communication with discarnate intelligence in general, is an interactive process. Our spirit guides learn from us and we learn from them.

Spirit guides usually assist us with our attitudes and emotions, or our habit patterns. By the way, I make a distinction between "feelings" and "emotions." Feelings are those aspects of ourselves that we are beginning to consciously define, that we're willing to speculate upon and bring up into conscious awareness, although they remain in a more intuitive state. Emotions are those elements of ourselves that are suppressed into the subconscious mind. They are primarily those parts of ourselves that are unrealized, those issues we suppress and don't want to confront on a conscious level because they cause us some degree of discomfort. An emotional response is a classical conditioned response—something occurred to us in childhood that we react to on an unconscious level as adults. Simply put, emotions are issues that we are uncomfortable in confronting, while feelings are similar subliminal issues that we are at least willing to entertain on an intuitive level. Emotions are reactive, whereas feelings are a more sophisticated intuitive response. They may be subliminal, but they are not locked in the subconscious. Our spirit guides help us with those areas that we have emotionally suppressed from childhood or past lives and that we need to confront on a conscious level. John has said, "Even as our childhood actions shape our adult personality, so in turn, actions from past lives can shape entire lifetimes."

Our spirit guides are sensitive to our needs and issues even when we aren't aware of their presence around us. Because the human body is like a radio, we're continually broadcasting information. This information, or "message," is received by our guides and teachers, as well as by people with whom we have a strong connection. We're also receiving information that's being broadcast to us, at times over great distances, by our guides and teachers, and by individuals with whom we have rapport. It's no coincidence, for instance, that certain people always seem to contact us when we're going through some sort of crisis. They somehow "sense" that we are in need. Our spirit guides and teachers sense when we are in need in that same way.

As an example of how our spirit guides and teachers inspire and guide us, imagine you've had an argument with a close friend. You're feeling quite depressed about it and decide to take a walk along the beach. As you're ambling along, kicking at the waves, you have a "flash." The image of your friend comes into your mind and you're overwhelmed with a feeling of love for him. You realize that your argument was trivial. Maybe you can't even remember how it started. As soon as you get home, you call your friend and patch things up.

This flash, or sudden realization, could very well have been inspired by a spirit guide or teacher, since this is one way that Spirit frequently assists us. The entities plant seeds of actions or motivations that can help us resolve our day-to-day problems and transcend the various obstacles to our spiritual growth. But, of course, it's always up to us whether to act on the inspiration.

Or suppose you're struggling with an addiction. Perhaps an eating disorder is compromising your physical and mental health and keeping you from moving on with your spiritual development. Your spirit guides can help you understand the nature of your addiction and suggest ways to break it. Perhaps your obsession with food is a karmic condition stemming from an abuse of fasting in past lives. Or perhaps you starved to death in a past life and are still carrying the scars from that in your present life. Spirit guides frequently provide insights and inspirations through our dreams, reveries, and meditations that help us to move past such obstacles.

Spirit guides are transitory and are generally with us for cycles of three, seven, or nine years. These are not mystical numbers, nor are they an esoteric bonding process—they are psychospiritual cycles. Most psychologists agree that the foundations of the human personality are laid in the first seven years of life. In the second seven-year cycle, we leave behind physiological childhood and enter that magical time we call puberty. Seven years down the road, when we're twenty-one, we're at "the age of consent." This is often the body's last growth period. Seven years later, when we are twenty-eight, the body is fully matured physically. We have no more growth cycles after that.

These three-, seven-, and nine-year cycles are the natural cycles for reaching insights about ourselves on an attitudinal or emotional level—first bringing them up to a feeling level, then to a conscious level, and then to a level of resolution. Most studies bear out, for example, that it takes three, seven, or nine years to get rid of the smoking habit. If you can go three years without smoking, you're usually considered cured of that addiction.

I doubt that there are any hard and fast rules governing our relationships with our spirit guides, however. These are general guidelines for our various interactions, but the dynamic is always individual.

Teachers

Our spirit teachers help us evolve our life philosophy and conscious ethics—how we relate to ourselves and others. For example, if we impose our preconceived notions and prejudices onto others, we aren't dealing with them, or with ourselves, ethically. We aren't acting with integrity. It means we're not yet conscious of our own true nature as spiritual beings, as part of the divine, and we need to further evolve our life philosophy. Teachers help us develop higher qualities such as integrity and ethics.

There's really very little difference between spirit guides and teachers. It depends on a person's stage of growth. Both dimensions of energy assist us to elevate our attitudes and emotions to a more conscious and ethical level, so that we respond to people not out of prejudice and negative emotion but out of compassion, philosophy, ethics, values, and consciousness. That's the overriding step-by-step growth process that guides and teachers represent. Our guides help us resolve some of our more negative emotional issues so that our teachers can help us raise our consciousness, but actually the two work hand-in-hand most of the time.

Teachers are generally with us for seven-, nine-, and twenty-one-year cycles, because those are the cycles within which most of us develop our personal ethics in life. Psychological studies attest to the importance of these different cycles of growth.

Master Teachers

The next dimension is what is often referred to as a master teacher. He or she is with us from cradle to grave and has one simple function—to inspire us. Inspiration is the ultimate form of teaching. I can share information with you all day, but if it doesn't *inspire* you, then I haven't succeeded in teaching you anything. Without that inspirational component, the information will go in one ear and out the other. On the other hand, if you are inspired, you will more than likely retain the information, and apply it, and I will have succeeded in my role as a teacher. As an example, when Martin Luther King, Jr., gave his famous "I have a dream" speech, people were inspired to transcend their prejudices and limitations and went on to develop a higher life philosophy.

Master teachers represent the highest level of spiritual achievement we feel we could personally attain in this lifetime. Remember the *Kung Fu* series, where Master Po would come out and say, "Well, Grasshopper . . ."? There was something in Master Po's persona that inspired many people, and all master teachers have that quality.

I, personally, am somewhat uncomfortable with the word *master,* since it implies that some people are higher than others. The word *master* actually means "teacher," and the aim of these beings is to communicate information that's spiritually alive for us, that helps us recognize and actualize ourselves as beings of mind, body, and spirit. The word is also used for one who has "mastered" certain knowledge or skill. It doesn't entitle such entities to any particular degree of power, judgment, or influence over us; it simply certifies them to teach and inspire us in their particular area of expertise.

John has often said that there's no such thing as a hierarchy in Spirit. We don't have to complete certain assignments before moving on to the next level of progression. It doesn't work that way. Although we can receive different levels of teaching from various individuals, both incarnate or discarnate, that same understanding can come to us in many ways—while we're washing dishes, at the supermarket, driving along the freeway, or trekking in the Himalayas—because God is in all sectors of time and space. The key thing is that we have to be true to our own *inner master,* and that inner master is "love." We have to have unconditional, uncompromising love for all persons, including ourselves. This has to be our principle.

Saints

Saints are common to all cultures, whether we call them "avatars," "arhats," "bodhisattvas," "spiritual beings," or "messengers of God." They are primarily beings who dedicated their lives in service to God. Our guides and teachers may be quite knowledgeable about metaphysical principles, but no one is likely to mistake Tom MacPherson for Saint Francis.

In the West, we traditionally think of saints as historical or heroic personalities who possessed wonderful virtues. By contemplating on either the name or the life of a particular saint, those virtues become transferable to us, so that we can effectively practice them in our own lives. Mother Teresa may be an example of such a living saint.

Ascended Masters

This level of evolution is a little more controversial. Ascended masters are historical beings, such as Moses, Krishna, Buddha, Jesus, and Quetzalcoatl. In their lifetimes, they placed no barriers between themselves and their oneness with the divine. They knew that God was within them, that they were one with God. And they were willing to take the social and spiritual consequences of adhering to their belief. Buddha and Jesus clearly acted on their knowledge of their true nature and reshaped their lives in the light of that knowledge. And they took total responsibility for sharing the truth with others.

Ascended masters came here to teach us that we are of the same essence as the divine. They sometimes work with us on a personal basis, but because of their tremendous energy and resources, they more often work with a broader collective, or planetary consciousness.

Certain individuals and groups like to say that a particular ascended master can be contacted only through them. This is *never* the case. Each of us has a direct "hotline" to any of these masters, through the vehicle of meditation and our own ability to go to that inner divine.

In contrast to saints, who dedicated their lives in service to God, ascended masters fulfilled the knowingness that they were one with God. In other words, saints had a tendency to think of God as separate from themselves, and ascended masters affirmed that the essence of God was within. The ultimate goal, of course, is to acknowledge that the divine is in each of us, that we all are expressions of the divine.

Angels and Archangels

These last two dimensions, angels and archangels, are God-realized souls who've never been physically incarnate in the earth plane and are without human prejudice. They remain as messengers of the divine, which is what the term *angel* or *archangel* means. Angels can choose to incarnate, and when they do, we refer to them as "new souls." Archangels are souls that were here at the time of the first incarnation, and have neither the need nor the ability to incarnate in the earth plane. Angels inspire us to recall our own angelic nature.

Jacob's Ladder

All seven of these dimensions of energy attempt to inspire us to the realization of our true nature as divine beings. Their methods of working with us are appropriate to their state of evolution as well as to our own. The reason we communicate with any of these energies is to expand our awareness of ourselves as beings of mind, body, and spirit. The true aim of spirit communication is always to increase our awareness of ourselves as spiritual beings and draw us into that inner light, usually through meditation or the dream state.

If we view these seven dimensions of spirit communication as a ladder, most of us would place ourselves at the bottom (if we could see ourselves on the ladder at all). In other words, we might be able to acknowledge ourselves as evolving along the lines of spirit guides. And, if we stretch it a little, maybe we can even imagine ourselves as a teacher someday, someone who can inspire individuals. But a master teacher? A saint? An ascended master? Absolutely not. So, inevitably, there's a "Jacob's Ladder" effect, with God at the top and the rest of us at the bottom. We're certain we could never achieve what these higher dimensions of evolution represent.

But this is a mistake. The ladder isn't a vertical phenomenon at all. If anything, it should be tipped on its side, because these seven states of human evolution are transpiring simultaneously within us at all points in time. We've all been sinners and we've all been saints. These various dimensions are all part of the human condition; they're a blueprint of the human personality. As Jesus said, "Anything I have done, you can do and greater."

So, these dimensions of energy represent the progression of the human personality. The states of human evolution are continuous, because we are unlimited beings. God is in each of us because we already possess that spiritual dimension. This is what makes us completely human. The only thing that gets between us and this divine expression is our lack of awareness.

The Bond Between Ourselves and Spirit

Spirit guides and teachers are present with us at all times. They contribute information and insight that helps us to develop the highest degree of spiritual awareness. Since we've usually known these personalities in past lives, we often share similar karmic experiences. By helping us work through our karmic circumstances, they progress and gain understanding about their own. And eventually they, too, will reincarnate and experience the karma they incurred in their own past lives.

Spirit guides help us to establish a higher spiritual order by increasing our awareness of the spiritual lessons we need to learn at this critical point in our history. One of the greatest spiritual lessons of this age is learning to master our technology. Einstein once commented that, in spite of the fact that we've split the atom, we haven't yet succeeded in changing how we think. When we lose track of the common human spirit in each of us, we lose sight of our humanity, and the result of this is always human suffering.

Spirit casts an objective eye over our potentials, our emotions, and our talents. At times we might be too close to an issue to see it clearly. From their more objective state, spirit entities can reflect back to us what is already obvious, or is just below the surface of our awareness. Because they are discarnate, they can more easily access extrasensory dimensions, or tune in to other sources of information. Then we can work at our own pace and in our own way with the information they convey. It's important to understand, however, that Spirit can work with us only to the degree that we give our permission, on both the conscious and subconscious levels. Our guides and teachers are continually sending us inspiring messages, but unless we acknowledge and work with this inspiration, nothing happens.

The reason guides and teachers come through in the personality of one of their previous lives is to more easily establish rapport with us. After all, for most of us, the more similar someone is to us, the more relaxed we feel in his or her presence, and the more we feel we can trust that person. Remember, the human personality is the vocabulary through which the soul has chosen to express itself in the earth plane. All human personalities are points of relativity, points of understanding. They're actually a vocabulary through which we can speak to others.

We've all been guides and teachers to our own guides and teachers when they were physically incarnate. It's a constant process of give-and-take. Everyone has the capacity to teach, express, and learn at all times. Guidance is the sharing of information that contributes insight to circumstances and experiences. As long as we're occupying some dimension of human personality, we will probably be interacting with other beings who occupy human personalities. I recall a particular class where someone in the room told Tom MacPherson, "I have the uncanny feeling that I know you from somewhere." Tom replied, "You should. You were a guide of mine when I was physically incarnate as Tom MacPherson. Now I'm just returning the favor."

We also act as guides and teachers to one another. That's one of the mysteries about this whole process. We don't have to go outside of ourselves. Fellowship with inner guides and teachers, and with living guides and teachers, is just as legitimate a source of spiritual inspiration as fellowship with discarnate intelligence. It is all "human spirit."

People frequently ask how close these bonds of friendship between ourselves and Spirit can get. I have a story that illustrates this. Some years ago, my wife, Lynn, was conversing with Tom MacPherson while I was in trance. They agreed that I was working too hard and needed a break. Tom told Lynn that on my upcoming birthday he would treat me to a night on the town as he knew it in his day. He gave her an address in San Diego, where I was working that day, and suggested I show up at a certain time.

When I got there, I was astonished to find a restaurant that was a complete replica of a pub from Tom MacPherson's day. I believe it was called the Red Fox Room. It was a typical Irish pub, paneled in dark wood, with a large oak mantelpiece. Shortly after I'd finished my dinner of beef and ale, a client of mine, whom I hadn't seen in years, approached my table. I had previously extended him credit for a channeling, and he insisted on making restitution by picking up my tab for the evening.

On another occasion, Tom once again expressed his desire to treat me to a night on the town as he knew it. Following his directions, I found myself at a coffeehouse that had been converted to a publike atmosphere for the evening. A band called Spring Wind was playing authentic English and Irish folk ballads dating back to Tom MacPherson's day. My friends and I danced for hours to the tunes of lute, drum, and penny whistle.

But my favorite story involves a more spontaneous touch-in from Spirit. While I was still working as a graphic artist, I needed an idea for an album cover with a 1920s motif. My friend B.J. Jefferson and I went to a local antique store that had a good selection of postcards from that decade. After we had agreed on a few promising images, we found ourselves wondering which of them Tom MacPherson might have chosen. We decided to slowly go through the cards we had selected and see if Tom would indicate his preference. Just as we turned to one particular card, we heard a hardy Irish voice with a thick brogue saying, "Ay, lads, that's the one you want, it's the one, indeed." Next we heard an entire chorus of Irish voices chanting in unison, "It's the one you want, it's the one you need, it's the best there is. . . ."

B.J. and I were stunned. We thought we were having an extraordinary psychic experience. Moments later we realized we had been listening to an Irish Spring soap commercial broadcasting from a radio in the back of the shop. There was no doubt that the synchronous event was a touch-in from Tom, which he later confirmed in a channeling.

So, these are some of the ways that Spirit interacts with us in our everyday lives. As Tom MacPherson often says, "When you're feeling down and out and thinking you don't have a friend in the world, and at that moment you look up and see one of your Shamrock dairy trucks pass by, you'll know that ol' Tom is working with you on the problem."

Negative Entities, Spirit Possession, and Things That Go Bump in the Night

Many people are afraid that if they go into a meditative or trance state, they'll contact "negative entities" or "evil spirits." In fact, one of the questions I'm most frequently asked is how I protect myself from evil or negative spirits taking over my body when I'm in trance. I have to say that, to the best of my knowledge and experience, this type of spirit possession doesn't occur. I personally believe there's a psychic lock on the frequency or vibration of each person's physical body that only we, ourselves, can match. It would be impossible for someone else to "inhabit" our vibration.

On the other hand, obsession is a very powerful psychological state that, in the extreme, resembles what we think of as possession. For example, an individual can be dominated by a parent even to the point of taking on the personality traits of that parent. Until the individual learns to detach himself from that parent and is able to restore his own individuality, he will not be "exorcised" of that parent's influence. But we can't really say that the parent has literally "taken over" the child, only that he or she has dominated the child's psychology to such an extent that it appears the child has been taken over.

A psychological bond exists between the obsessed person and the so-called possessing entity that ritual exorcisms, magic, and displays of supernatural power cannot break. The only one who can release the issues that are causing the so-called spirit possession is the person who is allegedly possessed. And this can be done only through understanding. Without understanding the cause of the bond or attraction, the person will continually draw similar experiences to himself. Dramatic expressions such as obsession are rooted in the consciousness, in the mind, so only by expanding our conscious awareness can we free ourselves from these disturbing influences. I see it more as a condition of human reform for both individuals than as an issue of possession by evil spirits, since the so-called possessing entities themselves, whether incarnate or discarnate, also need to be educated to their higher potentials.

There are people who disagree with my thinking and strongly assert the existence of "demons," but as far as I'm concerned, we are all human personalities, whether in the physical body or the discarnate state. Spirits, even the so-called possessing entities or "mischievous spirits," are just personalities in different states of human development. To me, rather than being displays of power or magic, exorcisms are the equivalent of a religious education for these entities, informing them that they have a higher potential that they can aspire to, whether in the name of Jesus or Buddha. In fact, during such ritual purifications, spirit entities often make great leaps in their development. I would say, then, that to the degree that an exorcism is an educational experience, it can be beneficial.

Many people use terms such as *spirit possession* to instill fear in others. The movies we see about spirit possession, such as *Psycho* and *The Exorcist*, play on people's ignorance, fears, and superstitions, because that's what attracts most of us to the box office. The simple truth is that the occult, like anything else, can serve constructive or destructive purposes. The highest use of any occult phenomenon is as a source of insight or information for pursuing both individual and societal well-being. For example, we can use metallurgy to make swords or to make plowshares. Human consciousness determines the application.

I prefer to work within a parapsychological framework, where attempts are being made to scientifically document phenomena typically thought of as paranormal or supernatural. This places such phenomena within the context of human psychology but at the same time acknowledges our inherently spiritual nature. I believe that all of these so-called supernatural phenomena fall within the range of normal human behavior.

My experience has borne out that we attract those events and persons that we've set up as lessons for ourselves. For example, if we walk down a dark alley in certain sections of San Francisco with fifty-dollar bills hanging out of our pockets, we're almost certain to be mugged or robbed. We're attracting that experience to ourselves. Or, if we're obsessed with the need for parental approval, we'll continue to attract to ourselves people who remind us of our parents, until we work through our issues.

Another point I wish to make is that, just as there is a level of trust between human beings that overrides suspicion and fear, I have that same trust level with Spirit. Just as I would not worry about a friend robbing me of my possessions, I don't worry about Spirit robbing me of my body. As I said earlier, spirit entities never really inhabit my physical body in any case. They are simply energy; they broadcast or speak *through* me, using me as the instrument.

There are lesser-evolved discarnate spirits around us, of course, just as there are lesser-evolved incarnate spirits, but in the same way that I can have a rapport with you and trust your humanity despite the lack of ethics among certain others in our society, I have a rapport and trust with the spirit entities. Instead of putting up force fields and trying not to get zapped by lower entities, I simply trust that when lesser-evolved entities come into a clear presence, they'll become aware of their own higher nature and will therefore not interfere when I'm in trance. If anything, they'll just go on to a higher level of consciousness.

So, rather than working with protections and charms, I trust the transformative process of the inner divine. In other words, I believe that God acts as our personal bodyguard. And remember, our own psychology attracts these different dimensions of Spirit to us. Ultimately, our own free will determines the quality of any guidance that's brought through. Our inner insight and wisdom allow us to recognize truth when any source, whether incarnate or discarnate, speaks to us. These principles hold true whether we're referring to bonds with incarnate or discarnate energies.

Prayer and meditation are the best tools I know of to uplift our consciousness and expand our philosophical point of view. Prayer and meditation deepen our knowledge of ourselves as spiritual beings and enhance our understanding of how these various dimensions of communication work. As we uplift our consciousness, we begin to attract to ourselves entities of a more benign quality. If entities of a negative nature do show up, their purpose will be to learn of their greater human potential. In other words, in the same way that a person who is suffering from a psychological illness will go to a psychiatrist or psychologist for help, a discarnate entity who is suffering from a lack in his or her own development will seek out an individual with a higher level of philosophical and spiritual development. Traditionally, these have been persons with mediumistic sensitivities or members of the priesthood. Whether incarnate or discarnate, all human beings need opportunities to grow and to become active, healthy members of the human family.

Summing Up

Elisabeth Kübler-Ross has said that the only healing we can bring to bear on the human condition is to work with uncompromising love, and the only life that we can rightfully give or take is our own. I believe that taking personal responsibility for the way we conduct our lives is what spirit communication is all about. It's a communication of the human spirit. As it is written in the Tibetan Buddhist texts, all of our various demons and hell worlds are the products of our own minds.

We become fearful of one another when our loving nature is blocked. Ignorance is at the root of all bigotry and injustice. We are free of ignorance to the extent that we accept the uncompromising spirit of love, which is in each of us.

Ultimately, there is only one spirit—the being we know as God. All the great religions state that God is within us. The ultimate form of spirit communication is when we go into that internal process, when we have that personal relationship with God.

There are no barriers between ourselves and God. People ask me, "If you really believe that, why do you talk to the spirit entities Tom MacPherson and John?" I relate to John and Tom as fellow human beings and I carry on dialogues with them, but I never pray to them or elevate them above my own human nature. In the case of prayer, we eliminate the middleman and go right to the big cheese, which is God, and God then sends an appropriate messenger. The messenger may be a discarnate spirit or an incarnate spirit, but he or she will try to help us get in touch with the inner wisdom, the inner teacher, the God within. And what is God? All the great religions agree on this central principle—*God is love.*

It's so simple. We are all here to manifest a loving and altruistic nature—our God-like nature. We're here to serve ourselves and one another in appropriate fellowship so that we can bring this realization into our lives. When we meditate and go within, that is spirit communication. When we speak with our guides and teachers, that is spirit communication. Our communications and dialogues with one another are also spirit communication. That inner spirit exists in each of us. We self-actualize and become one spirit through our experiences with one another. God is in the human heart and is the vehicle by which we can communicate directly with one another.

Part II

Human:

Being of Light

Chapter 1

§ *The Human Condition*

The ancient holistic model of the human condition that we are about to explore is based on information I've synthesized from the wisdom of many cultures and civilizations, including Mayan, Egyptian, Hindu, Buddhist, and Judeo-Christian. All of these cultures agree that we are multidimensional beings consisting of mind, body, and spirit.

This is also a parapsychological model. Parapsychology is the application of observation and deduction to paranormal phenomena that lie just outside traditional bodies of knowledge. The word *parapsychology* was coined by the American psychologist William James to include shamanistic and spiritualistic models of human nature that addressed the elements of the soul, or the spirit of man, which science and even orthodox religion refused to examine. These models, which existed prior to our modern psychology, are still widely held in many cultures.

Such concerns are reflected in a number of contemporary psychological theories. Indeed, Carl Jung is considered by many to be the father of modern parapsychology. Also, much of what we consider "humanistic psychology" addresses the so-called intangible needs of

53

humankind, such as art, beauty, and culture, as well as the transcendental aspects of ourselves as human beings.

The first aspect of this trinity of mind, body, and spirit is mind. Here we mean "conscious mind." Our conscious mind is our life philosophy, our feelings, our reactions, and our knowingness, and the ethics by which we consciously interact with other people. The conscious mind is a realm or dimension of consciousness, but its seat isn't limited by the physical body. The conscious mind is the seat of our free will. It has the ability to discern the difference between right and wrong and to choose between them. It can decide whether or not to examine what's happening within us on the level of our subconscious. When the conscious mind chooses not to examine the contents of the subconscious, it is always at the expense of our conscious beliefs about ourselves, and it compromises the fullness of our potential.

The second part of our trinity is body. In our model, the body is synonymous with the "subconscious mind." It is that function of consciousness we think of as the classical Freudian subconscious, the repository of all our suppressed thoughts. The subconscious mind is the seat of our emotions and all the things that are unrealized about ourselves. It is the storehouse of all the issues we aren't willing to acknowledge from this life and past lives. The subconscious mind has no will or realization of its own. It is also referred to as the "unconscious."

The statement that the physical body is the subconscious mind has been corroborated by the body-mind theories underlying Reichian therapy. For many years, Reichian therapists have been documenting conscious memory patterns in specific muscle groups in the body. They have found that they can alleviate specific psychological conditions by manipulating particular pressure points on the body. The principle is that consciousness is stored in every cell in the human body, and that the physical body itself is the seat of all that is unrealized about us in this lifetime.

The physical body is an elegant and sophisticated system of energy. In the East, "energy," "time," "space," and "consciousness" are synonymous. Chi, which is the Chinese word for "energy," is an expression of consciousness. And that is what the physical body is—our densest aspect of consciousness.

Hindu and Buddhist texts refer to internal seats of consciousness called chakras. These correspond to what we in the West know as the endocrine system. The ancient Chinese believed that these gland tissues contain specific bodies of knowledge and emotion. The bladder, for example, is usually associated with anger, the abdomen with the feminine aspect, and the heart with the masculine. According to these theories, someone who has difficulties with his mother is more likely to develop stomach ulcers and other digestive disorders, while someone whose major difficulty is with his father is more apt to develop heart problems. Such correlations between specific emotions and particular muscles and organs have been demonstrated throughout the whole of our anatomical structure. More and more, these theories are becoming known in the West. Asian techniques such as acupuncture and acupressure, which are based on similar principles, have gained degrees of acceptance even within orthodox medicine.

We interact with our subconscious minds through the principle of suppression. This principle is even built into our language. We say, "I must hold down my feelings," or, "I'm not going to deal with this today because I need time to work through my feelings." We suppress our feelings and thoughts because we don't want to change who we perceive ourselves to be on a conscious level. Whether our perception of ourselves is positive or negative, it is the one that is familiar to us, and most of us would rather deal with the devil we know than the devil we don't know.

In simple psychological terms, if we had a painful childhood experience that was difficult for us handle on an emotional level, we would suppress the memory of that experience until we have the confidence to cope with the emotions it would bring up. Through suppression, the painful memory doesn't enter into consciousness. It remains unrealized, or "subconscious." If that memory continues to be suppressed, often it will manifest as a psychosomatic illness. Edgar Cayce said that karma, which is our actions from the past, is the source of all disease in the physical body.

The final dimension of this mind, body, and spirit trinity is spirit. In our model, spirit is the "superconsciousness," or the superconscious mind, which is comparable to Carl Jung's collective unconscious. The superconscious mind is the sum total of all of our past lives and future potentials. That is why it is designated as the *super*conscious. The superconscious mind is a pure life force, or a pure state of energy. The superconscious mind is also the ability of mind to function independent of the physical body. Telepathic communication is the best demonstration of this ability. Spirit has referred to telepathy as "the cornerstone of universal mind upon this plane of existence."

We interact with our superconscious levels through the principle of ascendance, or transcendence. This is our ability to gain a greater gestalt, or a greater overview, so that we no longer feel limited to our immediate circumstances, experiences, or knowledge. But for the same reason that we suppress painful memories in our subconscious minds, we often refuse to work with transcendence—we don't want to change who we perceive ourselves to be on a conscious level. In other words, we'd rather deal with the devil we know than the angel we don't know. This is why at times we close our eyes to opportunities that could help us transcend our limited circumstances.

For example, I'm certain you've all had the experience of reading a book or seeing a movie that inspired you spiritually, but you were afraid to pursue those feelings because you sensed they might create a wedge between you and your friends and loved ones. Such denial of our superconscious resources is the "refusal to transcend." A good example of this is cynicism. Our culture tends to romanticize cynics as "realists." But people confuse cynicism with discernment. Cynicism is the refusal to work with our higher principles and higher ideals. It's a refusal to ascend.

Consciousness, Time, and Transformation

The three functions of consciousness—subconscious mind, conscious mind, and superconscious mind—interact with time in very specific ways. For example, because the subconscious mind, which is the physical body, is focused and centered in the present moment, it occupies very little time. It keeps us anchored in the here and now. As I mentioned earlier, the physical body is our ability to have a focus in time and space. Curiously enough, it is the physical body, rather than the conscious mind, that gives us our focus. The physical body stays right here. It says, "I'm tired and I want to sleep *right now*," or, "I'm hungry and I want to eat *right now*." Whenever we deal with the physical body, there's always an urgency or impulsiveness to it. This is why the Buddhists say the body *is* the here and now.

Conscious mind, by contrast, can wander all over the place. It drifts into the past and projects into the future. If you are depressed or feeling bad about yourself, you can consciously examine the events leading up to the present to uncover the source of your malaise. For example, while you are meditating, you might remember the fight you had with your parents last year that led to your breaking off relations, and you suddenly realize that your depression set in not long after that event. Or you might recall a past life in which you drowned during an ocean voyage, and you suddenly understand why you refused to take that South Seas cruise your family had its heart set on. The conscious mind can also look into the future and draw on our dreams and hopes to enhance our self-esteem in the present. Perhaps your vision of yourself as a successful artist in the future gets you through your nine-to-five job at the bank, or your vision of yourself on the beach in that brand-new bikini keeps you from going off your diet. Since the conscious mind can access both the past and the future, it occupies more time.

The reason why this ability to access past and future time is important is that our ability to transform ourselves depends on our being able to consciously perceive of ourselves in a positive manner and to transcend the limitations of our present circumstances. For example, let us say that we had a fair distribution of positive and negative experiences in childhood. If as adults we've emphasized our positive experiences, we'll have positive self-images. If we've emphasized our negative experiences, we'll have negative self-images. When we begin to consciously acknowledge the positive, and integrate this into our self-image, we are working with the transformative principle. We are *choosing* how we perceive ourselves in the here and now.

To further illustrate the importance of being able to consciously access past and future time, I recall an interesting experiment where people were hypnotized so that they couldn't conceive of a past. As a result, they saw their future potential as unlimited. Without the weight of their personal history, they became more joyful, optimistic, and creative. But when these same people were hypnotized so that they couldn't conceive of a future, they became very depressed. Unable to see beyond their immediate circumstances, they had no dreams or hopes by which to lift themselves above the mundaneness of the present moment.

This illustrates quite succinctly how our present self-concepts draw on the total resources of both past actions and future potentials. In other words, how we feel about ourselves right now is based both on who we were in the past and who we conceive ourselves to be in the future.

When we work with the superconscious dimension, we're dealing with the absolute past and the absolute future. This is because the superconsciousness, or the spiritual dimension, is the sum total of all our past lives and future potentials. In traditional Western psychology, if we can get to the root of something that happened to us in childhood, we can take better conscious command of who we are as adults. Thus we can move more fully and confidently into the future. This is true of parapsychology as well, except that parapsychologists believe that we look back not only to our childhood, but even further back, to our past lives. Spirit has referred to our past lives as "the childhood of the soul."

Many researchers have documented cases in which people have struggled in vain for years to work through emotional issues using traditional psychotherapeutic approaches. Yet after a single past-life-therapy session, the same people experience a heightened sense of clarity and creativity in relation to their problems. Often just the clear recall of a past-life trauma is healing in that moment. The deeper insight itself becomes the goal of the therapy, because that deeper insight can transform the person. With extra insight, or a greater overview, we solve the problem by literally transcending it. Spirit has said, "When you're bigger than the problem, that's the solution to the problem."

To demonstrate how this principle of transcendence operates in everyday life, suppose you live in a small village and you're up to your neck in debt. You owe the butcher, the baker, and the candlestick maker, and there seems no way out of your predicament. One morning, feeling quite depressed, you climb to the top of a nearby mountain. Looking down from the mountaintop, the village suddenly appears very small. From such a height, even your indebtedness to the butcher, the baker, and the candlestick maker doesn't bear the same weight as before. After a while you descend the mountain and return to your village. On the surface, nothing has changed. You still need to settle your debts. But because of your recent change in perspective, you're feeling confident. You negotiate a new method of payment that works out better for everyone concerned, and you no longer feel helpless and oppressed by your indebtedness. That's how the principle of transcendence works.

Accounts of transformational experiences by individuals who have undergone near-death or other out-of-body experiences are well documented by Raymond Moody, Robert Monroe, and, of course, by Elisabeth Kübler-Ross. After these kinds of experiences, people seem to lose their fear of death. They no longer feel limited by previously perceived circumstances and can be more altruistic with themselves and others. Often they have psychic perceptions they didn't have before, and there's been a positive alteration in their thinking processes and their world views.

In his book *Deathbed Observations by Physicians and Nurses* (Parapsychology Foundation, Division of Research, 1961) Karlis Osis reports:

> The doctors and nurses in our sample reported that fear is not the dominant emotion in dying patients. On the contrary, a large number of patients are said to be elated at the hour of death. This strengthens the evidence of previous findings. . . .
> A general practitioner commented that such observations had changed his philosophy: "A peaceful, happy expression comes over the patient," he said. "It leaves me with a feeling that I would not be afraid to die."
> One doctor reported a near-death experience of his own: his near-drowning brought him to such a beautiful state of consciousness that he was unhappy at being rescued. This was true also of patients who had been close to death but were brought back . . . the predominant emotions at death's door were calmness, peace, and exaltation. . . .

This is what I mean by transformation. The fact is that when people get in touch with the purpose of their lives, they often undergo this form of transformation. They cease functioning from a limited perspective and begin to function from a greater gestalt, which is the superconscious dimension.

Memory as a Principle of Transformation

The principle of transformation is based on one primary function of consciousness—memory. When we remember an event from childhood, it becomes a transformative tool. This is basic psychology. Transformation has nothing to do with suppressing or denying ourselves. It is a process of becoming conscious of who we are, *remembering* who we are, and accepting responsibility for our actions and beliefs.

Memory is the mechanism by which we access all levels of consciousness. What we're conscious of is what we recall with ease of memory. Memory and consciousness are synonymous. Remember, the conscious mind is all the ethics of which we're consciously aware and can easily remember. This is the same memory process by which we find lost objects or recall experiences from the past.

When we consider it deeply, it is not so much our experiences from childhood that shape and contribute to our adult personalities as it is our *memories* of those experiences, whether conscious or subconscious. This is why psychologists and psychiatrists try to stimulate our childhood memories. By stimulating memory, emotions that we had suppressed into the subconscious can come into our conscious awareness and we can gain a clearer understanding of our present behavior. The goal of any psychotherapy is to consciously understand the roots of our behavior patterns so that we can alter them. If we're unable to retrieve these memories, we'll be limited in our ability to transform ourselves, because it's through these memories that we create the substance of who we become in the future.

Social scientists and psychologists call this the "self-fulfilling prophecy." For example, if as adults we continue to react negatively to authority figures because of issues with parents or teachers in childhood, we'll only progress so far socio-economically in our lives until we resolve these issues. Conversely, if on the basis of positive memories from childhood we move into adulthood with optimism and a sense of trust, we're much more likely to succeed in whatever goals we set for ourselves.

We can use this same memory process as a bridge to our past lives. This is what happens in past-life regression. Using this memory process, a good hypnotist or hypnotherapist can help us retrieve memories of past lives, which can have a liberating influence on us within our present circumstances. Jess Stearn wrote a fascinating book based on a series of past-life regressions, entitled *The Search for a Soul: Taylor Caldwell's Psychic Lives* (Bantam Books, 1981).

Conditioned Memory, a Process of Repetition

People have asked me, "Kevin, if it's really all the same memory process, why is it so much easier to remember our childhood experiences than our past lives?" The reason for this is that *memory is a process of repetition.* We can recall events from this lifetime more easily than those from past lives because our present memories are frequently reinforced. We get reinforcement from the modes of transportation in this lifetime, the language we speak in this lifetime, and the popular fashions and trends of this lifetime. We don't easily recall past lives because those memories aren't reinforced. They remain dormant. Memories that aren't reinforced atrophy—like muscles that aren't flexed. If we don't exercise our memories of childhood, they fade away—until we flip open the old family album and they come flooding up. Whether the memories are positive or negative, they come back to us as soon as we stimulate the memory process through repetition or reinforcement.

This is one explanation of our experience of déjà vu—the sense that we've been someplace before. Visiting the Acropolis in Greece or the pyramids in Egypt or the King Tut exhibit when it comes to town becomes the equivalent of opening up our past-life family journal. Suddenly we're receiving reinforcement for the memories of another culture, another lifetime, another childhood—the childhood of our soul—and all those memories come up.

Techniques for Exercising Memory

The more we work with our memories, whether through hypnosis, meditation, contemplation, or daydreaming, the clearer they become. Sometimes the memories are revived in such startling detail that we can even recall languages spoken in past lives that we didn't study in our present life.

Hypnosis and meditation are very effective ways of accessing memories, whether from childhood or past lives. They are both memory-enhancing techniques, not obscure esoteric practices. In hypnosis, we're merely hyperextending the normal memory faculties of the conscious mind beyond their current conditioning. In meditation, we're exercising the same memory process as we would use to recall an experience we had yesterday, or in childhood. By exercising this memory process, we develop a superior quality of memory. It's not just that memories come up, but they come up with clarity and acuity. Meditating every day, we get clearer and clearer about the roots of our consciousness. When there's a deepening of the roots of our consciousness, we are transformed in the here and now. It's like an adopted child finding his original birth certificate and discovering the roots of his true identity.

Another way to exercise our memory process is to keep a dream journal. We make mental notes to ourselves, or jot something down on a piece of paper to help us jar our memory; keeping a dream journal is a slightly more esoteric version of this principle. Dreams are the repository of psychic sources of transformation, so keeping a dream journal helps us to stimulate even deeper recall from the resources of the subconscious and the superconscious.

The major thing to understand is that this process of recalling either past lives or childhood experiences is a normal extension of memory. It is neither "supernatural" nor beyond the means of any individual who is reading this book. We use these memory techniques intuitively all the time, although most of the time we're not fully aware of it. When we find we've misplaced our car keys, for example, the first thing we do is take some deep breaths and try to calm down. Then we mentally retrace our steps. We know that if we can relax sufficiently, we'll remember where we put our keys. The hypnotherapist says, "Breathe deeply and remember." The swami says, "Relax, my son. Breathe deeply, and remember the divine inner resources." These procedures call up our memory processes.

We rely on our intuition in these matters all the time, because we are intuitive beings. For example, we can't really *prove* anything. Can you prove where your car is right now? You can't, can you? Your sense of where your car is parked is based on your feeling, your intuition, and your memory that it is there, but you can't *prove* it. Even something as tangible as knowing where our car is parked is based on the acuity of our memory.

This same function of memory allows for the process of personal transformation. The key to the transformative process is to draw on all these memory resources. If we have positive visions of who we will be in the future, we can bring those positive visions into the present and draw on them for inspiration and clarity. If we feel positive about our childhood and absolved of karma from past lives, we can draw on our positive feelings, bring them into the present, harness them, and thereby acknowledge ourselves as the unlimited beings we are.

Remembering the Future

There is a final point I would like to make about memory. Since time, space, and consciousness are synonymous in our model, we remember not only past lives but *the future*. When someone prognosticates events, he isn't really "seeing," or even creating, his future—he's *remembering* it. When a person has insights or dreams of events before they transpire, he is *remembering the future*.

The memory mechanism is the same whether we're recalling childhood events, past lives, or future events. For this reason, people who have been meditating or working with hypnotherapeutic techniques for a period of time, and thus have a greater ease of recall of past lives, may also find their predictive abilities enhanced. In reality, the past, present, and future are happening simultaneously. As I said earlier, time is just a state of mind, and mind is memory. Once the memory mechanism is adequately developed, memory can go in all directions. But remember—memory is enhanced by repetition. Since we're less familiar with future modes of transportation, architecture, and trends and fashions, it might take a little more effort to remember the future than to remember the past.

Predestiny, Destiny, and Free Will

Time can be looked at in many ways. Some people say that time is a river that flows forward and backward and eventually folds in on itself, and therefore the past and the future are moving away from each other and creating each other simultaneously. Other people see time as a linear progression. Personally, I think of time as a pool out of which we can pull the past, the present, and the future. According to this view, everything is instantaneous. We are infinite and unlimited beings because time and space don't exist in an absolute sense.

When we try to recall something that happened to us two years ago, the memory comes to us instantaneously. It doesn't take us two years to retrieve it. Since thought can be perceived as instantaneous, what happened to us two years ago is happening right now, inside our minds, creating our emotions, our feelings, and our future potentials. If I ask what you're going to do when you put down this book, you might say, "I'm going to sleep," and you would know that instantaneously. You wouldn't have to wait until you actually stopped reading to answer the question. If I ask you what you were doing in the early 1800s and you can see into your past lives, the answer will come to you instantaneously. This means that everything is happening simultaneously within us.

As constructs time and space are relevant for us only to a point. Once we extend our consciousness into the infinite, we literally transcend time and space. They no longer exist because they have no impact on us—just as when we get a clear emotional perspective on a childhood event, it no longer has impact on us. It no longer pushes our buttons and ceases to influence us, even though it is transpiring simultaneously within us. Therefore, time is a pool out of which we can pull up the past, the present, and the future; and time, mind, and consciousness are synonymous.

If past, present, and future are happening simultaneously within us at all times, this means that by examining our past lives, we should be able to see what our futures hold. But in truth, the future is not fixed. This is because through exercising our free will, or our ability to make choices, we have the capacity to re-create or renegotiate our future. Let's suppose, for example, that you're about to perform the role of Mark Antony in Shakespeare's play. Even though the lines are fixed, the characters are fixed, and the event in history is fixed, it is the way you interpret the character that actually determines your perception of the moment. You can portray Mark Antony as an extremely devious man who lusted after Caesar's power, or as a confused individual who really didn't know what he was doing, or as a brilliant politician who really loved Caesar and wanted to see his vision of the Empire move forward. It all depends on how you play the character.

Using this same principle, two people can attend the same performance and read into a character whatever they want, according to their free will and their ability to observe what is occurring in that moment. So, even if the future were fixed, it is still our free will, as well as our responsibility, to consciously interpret events. This is why Spirit has suggested, "Destiny isn't an event, it's how we *experience* the event."

The Concept of Karma

So far, we've been exploring the different levels of consciousness, or the dimensions of ourselves as beings of mind, body, and spirit. We've looked at how these functions of consciousness contribute to our sense of ourselves in the here and now, and how we can draw upon the mechanism of memory to transform our present circumstances. What we've been talking about, really, is transforming the human ego, or the human personality, which is what the trinity of mind, body, and spirit represents.

These same principles operate in Buddhist psychology as well, although they are stated a little differently. The Buddhist principle that in order to transform ourselves in the here and now we must eliminate our ego is clearly stated in the Buddhist Four Noble Truths:

> All life contains suffering.
> All suffering is based on desire.
> All desire arises out of the ego.
> The way to eliminate desire is to eliminate the ego.

According to the model we've been working with, as well as the Buddhist model, all of the events from childhood and past lives that contribute to our current circumstances are referred to as our "karma." When we talk about transforming ourselves, or transcending our limitations from childhood and past lives, we're talking about over-coming our karma, or eliminating our ego. Spirit once said that even as the events in our childhood shape our adult personalities, so in turn, events or karma from past lives shape entire lifetimes. Our past lives are merely the childhood of the soul.

We commonly think of karma as a system of rewards ("good karma") and punishments ("bad karma"). Most of us are more familiar than we wish to be with what we think of as bad karma. Bad karma is when your car breaks down on the freeway in rush hour, or when your paycheck bounces. Bad karma leads you to ask that one cosmic question, "Why me?" Consequently, it keeps you very close to your ego. It causes you to carefully review all your past actions to come up with clues to your present misfortune. On the other hand, "good karma" shines down on that lucky neighbor who just won $10 million on a lottery ticket, then went to Las Vegas and turned it into $100 million. Tomorrow she's leaving on a world cruise. "Who knows how these things happen," she ex-claims. "I guess I just have good karma."

Bad karma gives us very little freedom because it sets obstacles in our path. Good karma affords us lots of freedom because the road always seems wide open. But whether we're dealing with bad karma, and very little freedom, or good karma, and lots of freedom, we're still dealing in degrees of freedom. Enlightenment, or ulti-mate realization, is total liberation, total freedom. Bad karma and good karma both tie us to conditional mind because they cause us to judge ourselves. People with good karma can fall prey to thinking they're better than others. ("I have good karma, so therefore I must be special.") People with bad karma tend to have low self-esteem and see themselves as worse than others. ("My bad karma is punish-ment for being such a bad person.") This is the wrong perception. It's a form of divine behaviorism—condition and response. It's functioning from the basis of the ego.

To rise above this ball and chain, we have to eliminate the ego. The only way to eliminate the ego is to go outside of it. And what lies outside the ego is God. Karma has only one value—to increase our understanding of our true nature as children of God. Once we understand who we are, we don't need to create karma, either positive or negative. Once we understand who we are, karma is eliminated, because its only purpose is to increase our understanding. The reason for every experience in our lives is to increase our understanding. The fulfillment of karma is synonymous with enlightenment, and enlightenment is remembering who we are, remembering our own true nature.

So, transformation isn't a process of accumulating good karma or avoiding bad karma, it's a process of total liberation. It is rising above our relative judgments and dualistic thinking. And this total liberation can come only from one source, our inner authority, and by knowing who we are. This is why I suggest we include in the Four Noble Truths that all life contains "experience" rather than suffering. All life is a continuum of experience. Most experiences arise out of desire. "I want to experience this," "I can't wait to experience that." When we eliminate the *desire* to experience something, and just experience it and flow through it, our understanding is increased. As the desire for experience is eliminated, so are our attachments to good and bad karma and our value judgments of ourselves. The ego, or the conditional identity, is then transcended and we become what is left over, which is God.

This knowledge of ourselves as part of God is the only discipline we need. Discipline is cutting away what we don't need. The only thing left, once we cut away everything we don't need, is God. Then that energy can flow into us. When we're agonizing all the time over such mind-bogglers as "Who am I?" and "What's wrong with me?" we're not flowing in our God-realized selves. When we're agonizing over things, or, conversely, congratulating ourselves over our many accomplishments, we're not getting things done. Once we just dive into the flow of an experience and go for it, our anxieties seem a waste of energy. When we're empowered in ourselves and in our identities, we just experience what's there, because there's no ego involved.

The elimination of the ego isn't the suppression of who we are, it is the expansion of who we are, the *transformation* of who we are. We become altered in the light of this greater heritage, this greater belief about ourselves as unlimited beings. It is only we, ourselves, who hold to our current circumstances.

So, here is the key. We're not here to fulfill good karma or bad karma. We're not here to accumulate merit points or atone for past sins. Karma doesn't mean that we must endure a series of unchangeable circumstances because of things we've done in the past. We've created karma, or results of actions in past lives, for no other purpose but to increase our understanding. And understanding can ultimately transcend our karmic circumstances, which arose out of our ignorance.

The law of karma is the law of return. Anything we put out will return to us. If we do something negative, there's no sense guilt-tripping ourselves, because guilt only locks us into the action, and into the past. It's better simply to acknowledge our action and increase our understanding about it so that when it comes around again we can handle it more positively.

If we put out positive thoughts, they'll return to us, so it's worthwhile to do what we perceive as positive for one another. But we can't do it out of the motivation to ward off bad karma. The truly transformative principle is our understanding of who we are. Once we understand that we've created everything in our lives to increase our understanding of who we are, we then begin to fulfill our purpose. When we understand that karma exists strictly to increase our understanding, the karma itself is fulfilled. Out of our understanding, we realize that we're unlimited beings, that we are part of that being called God. And this is the human condition.

Chapter 2

¶ *The Godhead*

The three functions of human consciousness we've been examining—mind, body, and spirit, or conscious mind, subconscious mind, and superconscious mind—are a blueprint of the human ego. They *are* the human ego. Ego can be defined as all the conscious perimeters of the human condition, of mind, body, and spirit.

The human ego is conditioned mind. It is a condition *of* mind. This means that even the spiritual dimension of ourselves—the superconscious mind, which is the sum total of all of our past lives and future potentials—is part of the human ego. The human ego is made up of all the conditioning we've had in the earth plane. People have a tendency to think that we've reached true spirituality once we've developed our psychic perception to the point where we can see our past lives or future potentials. This isn't so. Psychic abilities can be a powerful tool for personal transformation, but they're not the true or final goal of transformation. They are still a condition of the ego. They are still part of the human condition.

Perhaps you're wondering how the superconsciousness, the spiritual dimension, which can access absolute past and absolute future, can still be part of the ego. Well, for those of you who may have had past-life readings, weren't you the least bit disappointed to learn you were a plumber or lumberjack in your past life rather than someone more grandiose, like Cleopatra, Napoleon, or Saint Francis? And haven't you fantasized, at times, about coming back in a future life as a great leader or humanitarian? All of this falls within the realm of human ego, or, more appropriately in this instance, "spiritual ego."

So, if mind, body, and spirit all lie within the dimensions of time and space, and if they are all part of the human ego, what lies beyond our subjective, conditioned experience of the earth plane? What is it that transcends time and space and governs the various levels of reality? Only one entity—the being we know as God. Someone once asked Spirit, "Doesn't eternity lie outside of time and space?" Spirit's response was, "Eternity governs all time and space, but only God governs all realities." So, only God lies totally outside of eternity and transcends all dimensions.

Just as our own nature is threefold, consisting of mind, body, and spirit, the nature of God represented as a trinity in many cultures and societies throughout the history of the world. For example, in Buddhism there are the "three kayas," or "three bodies," which represent the three aspects of Buddha—mind, body, and speech, or *dharmakaya, nirmanakaya,* and *sambhogakaya.* In the Vedic trinity, we have Brahma, Vishnu, and Shiva—the creator, the preserver, and the destroyer. In Huna, we find another trinity, *aumakua, uhane,* and *unihipili*—the superconscious, conscious, and subconscious. Similar trinities exist among Native Americans, Mayas, Incas, Aztecs, Toltecs, Olmecs, and many other cultures.

The model I work with incorporates the Judeo-Christian representation of the Godhead, which consists of the Father, the Son or Daughter (in deference to feminism), and the Holy Spirit, or the maternal aspect of the Godhead (not unlike the Father/Mother God referred to in Eastern philosophies). I use the Judeo-Christian model only because it is the one most of us are familiar with in the West. Quite honestly, I believe it is the same three aspects of consciousness taking on different names and appearances from one culture to the next. In other words, I believe that the concept of the threefold nature of God is an "archetype," or universal principle, as Carl Jung would define it. The Father, the Son or Daughter, and the Holy

Spirit are simply functions of consciousness, just as mind, body, and spirit are functions of consciousness. They are a memory process. But because human beings feel comfortable describing things in familiar terms, the trinity is represented as a family unit. Ultimately, God is a being of energy, androgynous in nature.

The Father

The first function of consciousness in this trinity is the Father. This is the idea that God is omnipotent, omnipresent, and all-knowing. God is in everything and is everywhere. The Father is the paternal aspect of the trinity, or universal intelligence. This is the function of consciousness that supersedes the limited perspective of time and space.

Consciousness isn't something contained within the physiological body, which then gives it permission to exist. As I've indicated, research in the field of parapsychology yields strong evidence that consciousness transcends physical form. The New York laboratories of the American Society for Psychical Research have contributed outstanding documentation in this area. In one very interesting experiment in the early 1970s, two psychics, Ingo Swann and Harold Sherman, were asked to leave their bodies (astral project) and travel to Mercury and Jupiter to observe the atmospheres of those two planets. Researchers hoped that the information the two psychics brought back would be corroborated by NASA's deep space probes, which had been sent to those planets and were due to orbit back within days. The intention of the experiment was to demonstrate "remote-viewing" capabilities, or the ability of human subjects to psychically observe an object at great distance, with pure consciousness, or pure mind, as the only means of observation available.

The data from the probes showed that both Swann and Sherman accurately described certain previously unknown characteristics of the planet Mercury. These findings certainly seem to verify remote-viewing capabilities. Even more important, however, is that the information was received "instantaneously." NASA's photos, which were broadcast over electromagnetic frequencies, took approximately 6.5 minutes to get from point A to point B. This means that even at the speed of light, there was a time delay. Ingo Swann and Harold Sherman experienced no such time delay because they were receiving their information at the speed of thought. This means that the speed of thought exceeds the speed of light. Whatever occurs at the speed of thought happens instantaneously. Consciousness, which travels at the speed of thought, is instantaneous, and hence omnipresent. Here again we have evidence that, as has been said throughout the ages, time and space are an illusion.

The Son or Daughter

The second function of consciousness, the Son or Daughter, is our ability to have an individual identity, or an individual expression of consciousness, within the all-encompassing consciousness that we call God. It is our free will within that all-encompassing consciousness. It is not unlike our national citizenship. In the same way as we are each an individual citizen of the United States, identifiable by name, parentage, and birth certificate, we also have a collective national identity, as in "We the people of the United States." The Son or Daughter function of consciousness allows us to be individual beings within the universal mind that we call God. It is our unique individuality. As John has said, we are individual thoughts in the mind of God.

The Holy Spirit (The Mother)

The third aspect of the trinity is the Holy Spirit, or the maternal aspect of God. This is an intuitive state of knowingness. It is our uncompromising knowingness of our oneness with universal consciousness. This knowingness entirely bypasses our logical, rational, and empirical processes. If this function of our consciousness is ever compromised, and we start to think of ourselves as less than who we are, we negate our full potential.

Someone once asked the poet Maya Angelou, who has had a profound impact on me, to define slavery. She responded that if we can convince a person that he or she is a little bit less than human, we have a slave. And if we ourselves can be convinced that a person is a little bit less than human, we are enslavers. In this same way, I believe that if we consider ourselves anything less than fully what we are, which is mind, body, and spirit, we are enslaved to ignorance, or unconsciousness. And when we aren't living up to our full potential as divine beings, society can't live up to its full potential.

So, the Holy Spirit, or the maternal aspect, is our uncompromising knowingness of our citizenship. If our rights or our knowledge of ourselves is compromised, anyone can dictate to us the quality of our citizenship. This function of consciousness is the intuitive or driving force that often inspires people, even if they have no intellectual concept of it, to feel that they are somehow linked with the divine. This knowingness doesn't come from psychic powers or from psychic awareness—it is intuitive. When we finally restore this element of knowingness within ourselves, we begin to realize our full potential.

Returning to Our Original Nature

These three principles of consciousness—the Father, the Son or Daughter, and the Holy Spirit, or the maternal aspect—taken together constitute the Godhead. The first principle is the universal or the omnipresent nature of consciousness. The second principle is the ability to have an individual and unique identity within that omnipresent consciousness. The third principle is our intuitive knowingness that it's impossible to lose that link with the divine or omnipresent consciousness. To lose this knowingness would be like a form of divine amnesia. We would lose our ability to maintain individual identity. The human soul is our ability to be an individual and unique being within an all-encompassing consciousness. Our human soul is the expression of consciousness we call God.

We are attempting to remember one thing and one thing only—that each of us is a soul. Buddhists refer to it as recalling our original nature. Taoists say that if we've lost our memory of the Tao, we've lost our memory of the Way. The truth is that we are conscious entities and our consciousness is independent of physical matter. We are beings who transcend time and space. We are souls. We are one with God. This is what Jesus implored us to remember—who we are. He said, "Why marvel when it is said that I am the Son of God? Does not our own Scripture say that ye are Gods? Anyone who believeth in me, indeed, may become as the Sons and Daughters of God." The Buddhists say it as well: "Remember who you are." That is what we're here to do.

When we finally embrace the knowledge of our own unlimitedness, that we are thought and thought is unlimited, and when we can hold this knowledge in the here and now, that is the fulfillment of our purpose. We are more than the sum of our past lives and future potentials, we are co-creators in the divine. We are not limited to the events of our childhood or to our current adult personality. We are developing all the time. We aren't our past lives and we're not even our future potentials. We are none of those limited events. We are co-creators with God. Everything comes from God and everything returns to God. God is love, and love is the innate harmony that holds together the cosmos.

Chapter 3

The Soul's Path

Our true nature is revealed in the human soul, which is our individual and unique identity in the all-encompassing consciousness we call God. It is that transcendental quality that exists in each of us—the essence and true root of our consciousness. It is our citizenship in the universe. Our souls allow us to have direct knowledge of who we are and distinguish us as children of the divine, or children of God. When we sojourn through our past lives and future potentials, whether in the dream state or in meditation, we recall that we are God. *This is the soul's path.*

An Esoteric History of Souls on the Earth Plane

This brief esoteric history lesson, drawn from the channelings of Edgar Cayce and Andrew Jackson Davis, as well as from Plato's *Atlantis* and my own channeled sources, will help explain how we came to incarnate on this plane of existence, and therefore into the human condition. I think you will find that it echoes themes that are common to many cultures.

In the words of a famous American astronomer, "billions and

billions of years ago" there was only one spirit. We call that spirit God. That perfect spirit, that universal mind, had three great creative and evolutionary acts.

The first great creative act of this perfect spirit, this omniscient observer, this omnipresent consciousness, without whom nothing could exist, was to move into perfect matter and set it expanding into motion, or what is known in physics as the Big Bang. It is unlikely that this expansion was thermonuclear in nature. It was probably a form of psychokinetic activity, or the ability of mind to move matter. The same force of mind that can open and close our hands can open and close the universe. In Hinduism, it is the idea that Brahma awakes and Brahma sleeps. So, in this moment, the universe awakened. After perfect spirit moved into matter, it expanded that matter and created worlds without number, unlimited solar furnaces we call stars, universes within universes, dimensions within dimensions. It created the physical universe, which is now governed by the natural laws of physics. Spirit once said, "Physics is but the shades of God's consciousness."

The second great creative act was to take inanimate matter and group it into very simple compounds known as amino acids. These amino acids became self-perpetuating and evolved into single-celled entities, and then multicelled entities living in colonies. Eventually, they evolved into various species, the various life forms. All the worlds without number were filled with the many creatures of the oceans and the various forms of beasts and fowl, and the planets were covered with the various forms of flora and fauna, the dimension we call biological life.

Finally, this perfect being called God, who doesn't have the capacity of selfishness, self, or ego, wished to share his creation. So, universal mind folded in upon itself and, in the third great creative act, gave birth or revelation to a new expression of beings called souls. These souls were entities who had individual identities within the all-embracing consciousness called God. Spirit has said that even as we have many thoughts yet only one mind, so in turn there are many souls yet only one God. And each of us is as a thought within the mind of God.

Souls were created as soul mates, in twos, neither one being truly masculine or feminine, nor positive or negative, but androgynous and complete in their own nature. They were created in twos so that they could give perfect witness to each other and not experience aloneness. They could be complements to each other, because it takes two observers to have the focus we call creation. These two conscious observers would then give consensus to further creation.

These souls, these omnipotent, unlimited beings, were one with the omnipresent consciousness, and yet they had individual and unique identities and they possessed free will. Spirit has defined free will as "the ability to be free within the unlimited will that is God." The souls were sent out to all sectors of time and space. Some of them went to the Andromeda system, some went to the Pleiades, and some went to a small backwater planet called Earth.

As some of those souls came in, they began to diversify various species of flora and fauna. Some of them began co-creating and diversifying the various species in the oceans' depths. Others continued to diversify across the land, while still others filled the atmospheres. At some point, certain of these souls moved too close to their creation and incurred the phenomenon we call incarnation. Rather than moving *through* their creations, they ended up incarnating *into* them. And once having incarnated, they lost their uncompromising consciousness of themselves as creators, and thus lost their knowingness of their oneness with God. They were like an artist who identifies too much with his canvas and loses the knowledge of himself as creator.

According to Edgar Cayce, these souls first entered into the lower primates. Then, slowly, through the natural forces of evolution over many, many aeons, and through the natural principles of reincarnation and karma, cycling from one incarnation to the next, they became the evolutionary force on this plane. These souls went from one embodiment to the next, drawing up and evolving from the lower primates, passing through the esoteric civilizations of Lemuria and Atlantis, then washing up onto the ancient civilizations of Egypt and the Far East. Next, reaching the current shores of history, they created a new species that had never existed on the earth plane before—human beings. Finally, they moved onto our own Western shores.

We *are* those souls who began their esoteric journey in the womb of the conscious entity that is God. We participated in the initial foundations of the creation of all the universes. Diversifying ourselves into the individual expressions that we call souls, with free will, we evolved life forms on this plane of existence. Having become attached to our creations, we merged with them, and at that point lost our higher consciousness. We developed "divine amnesia" in relation to the true source of our identity. Through reincarnation, however, we evolved the physical vehicles that we can now use to reclaim our higher consciousness.

The process of incarnation and reincarnation, and the evolutionary path that is ongoing in this very moment, looks something like this: The infinite, God, through the expression of souls, projected down into material embodiment, into the lower primates. Then, very slowly, over many millions of years, through the natural laws of evolution and the gradual expansion of intelligence (mind), souls drew themselves up from subconscious beings into conscious entities. They did this by evolving into the species called human beings, with physical forms through which they could reclaim consciousness of themselves as divine beings. They increased their conscious seats of intelligence by literally creating themselves on this plane of existence through one incarnation after another. With that higher intelligence, they began to examine their own nature and to recall past lives.

Perhaps these evolving souls had visions of the future and realized that they weren't just physical beings. They understood that they could transcend their physical appetites and that they indeed had a spiritual dimension. They began to question the nature of that spiritual dimension. Do humans reincarnate a certain number of times and then die? Does this transcendence of mundane time and space through increased consciousness imply an immortality to the human spirit? If souls do transcend time and space, what does this mean? These questions would inevitably have to be asked, because only when we, as souls, know the true origins of our consciousness can we restore to ourselves the ultimate expression and the knowledge of the beings we truly are.

Universal Life Purpose

The process of realizing, or self-actualizing, each soul's potential, or God-like nature, is what I refer to as "universal life purpose." The soul is the ability to have an individual and unique identity within God. It is our uncompromising knowingness of our link with the divine. It is the process of incarnation and reincarnation that leads us to insights about our spiritual nature. The soul is the integration of our knowledge of our link with the infinite into our circumstances in the here and now. It is the total dedication of mind, body, and spirit, of conscious, subconscious, and superconscious mind, to lead us to the insight and knowingness that we are one with the divine.

We are here to manifest and fulfill our knowledge of this indelible link with the divine. We are here to restore this aspect of our knowingness, to respect each individual spirit as a holy spirit, a divine spirit. According to the principles of psychology, we can transform our personalities by identifying the roots of our behavior; how much greater the transformation if we identify the ultimate roots of our consciousness as God. When an orphan or an adopted child is cut off from the root of his original identity, with no knowledge of his biological parents, that child will often begin an intense search for his parents. The child feels compelled to learn the roots of his identity. In many cultures, ancestral lineage contributes so much to one's identity that people spend much of their lives reestablishing those roots.

We are here on this planet to manifest this higher quality of our nature. If an event in childhood can totally transform an adult personality, the knowledge that we are one with the divine can transform entire lifetimes. Or, as Spirit has said, "Even as the events in our childhood shape our adult personality, our karma from past lives shapes entire lifetimes—and God shapes the whole." When we work with the knowledge that we are all a part of God, we begin to see the universal nature within all persons. We begin to transcend the difficulties that have plagued humankind. We return to the ultimate root of our identity. That is universal life purpose.

Progressing Toward God

There are times when we feel we're progressing in the fulfillment of our universal life purpose, and times when we feel we're definitely regressing. Because we have such long-standing habits of judging ourselves, we're always applying labels, such as "success" or "failure," "good" or "bad," to our spiritual development. We also tend to see God as "up there" and ourselves as "down here," rather than feeling our at-onement with that divine essence. In fact, our thought process often goes something like this:

> Day 1:
> I got my secret mantra and prayer beads this morning, and simultaneously started my juice fast. Also, I confirmed my flight to India for my visit with Maharishi. I'm progressing toward God today.

> Day 2:
> Didn't have time to meditate this morning. And couldn't hack that juice fast, so grabbed a burger and fries at Jack-in-the-Box. Also, I missed the deadline for enrolling in the training with Maharishi. I guess I'm no longer progressing toward God.

Ah, but don't panic, everything's okay, because on Day 3:

> I read a few chapters of Shirley MacLaine's new book before work this morning and sent in my deposit for Kevin Ryerson's Life Purpose seminar. Remembered to say my secret mantra one thousand times, so now I'm really progressing toward God.

We see ourselves on a perpetual roller coaster, continually moving closer to and farther from God. But this is just an illusion. What actually occurs is more like this:

> Day 1:
> Things are going well today. I finished Shirley MacLaine's book and feel inspired to start meditating. I also signed up

for a Tai Chi class and started a dream journal. I'm progressing toward God at the speed of light.

Day 2:
Didn't remember any of my dreams last night. Broke down and smoked a cigarette after an argument with my boss. Think I'll grab a cold beer from the fridge. I'm only progressing toward God at the speed of sound.

The point is that whether we're progressing toward God at the speed of light or the speed of sound, whether our consciousness is accelerated or decelerated, doesn't make any difference—we're still progressing toward God. We're *always* progressing toward God. There are no ups and downs, no moving toward or away from something that resides in the center of our own being. We are always progressing in our conscious awareness that the divine is within us.

At times we may feel that we're standing absolutely still when we're actually accelerating at the speed of light. Sometimes it seems that everyone around us is accelerating at the speed of light except ourselves. Then, when the proper moment arrives, everything falls into place and we become aware of just how rapid our own progress has been. When our awareness is finally expanded to the point that we can truly discern the speed at which we're traveling, we'll see ourselves at points of acceleration and deceleration rather than highs and lows, and we'll always know that we're progressing toward God.

At this point people invariably ask, "If we're all progressing toward God, how do you explain the lack of ethics in some people?" My answer is that a person behaves unethically when he senses that his own well-being hasn't been promoted. If we look into the background of any so-called criminal, for example, we'll inevitably find the roots of the incident that convoluted his thought process. Almost always these are acts of ignorance perpetrated by individuals who were significant in the criminal's early development. This has been thoroughly documented in the area of child abuse. The great majority of individuals who perpetuate crimes against children were themselves victims of abuse as children.

The cycle must be broken somewhere, and I can't think of any way to break it except through uncompromising love and respect for everyone's innate humanity. All we can do to improve the quality of life on our planet is to unconditionally see God in everyone. God, being unconditional love, doesn't judge our process. Of course, this opens up a Pandora's box, because the next question is always, "How do we love someone like Charles Manson?" It's hard for most of us to imagine someone like Manson, who seems the epitome of evil, as progressing toward God along with the rest of us. So, I'd like to briefly explore this problem of evil.

First of all, the word *evil* is emotionally charged. It instantly conjures up images of Satan, Adolph Hitler, and other classic villains. If we trace it to its Aramaic and Greek roots, however, *evil* actually means "that which isn't well for you." This could be anything from chain smoking to first-degree murder. Drawing on its original meaning, I consider evil more of a sin of omission than a sin of commission. Most of the time, "sinners" are people who feel that their own well-being was not promoted. Almost always, they bear deep scars on their psyches.

So, where do we break this cycle in human behavior? Do we just imprison child abusers, for example, and release them into society seven years later with no form of rehabilitation or reeducation? And if these are individuals who bear deep scars because their well-being was never promoted, don't we, as a society, have a responsibility to help them? The only solution I see, then, is to acknowledge the humanity in all of us and to promote well-being wherever we can. I'm not suggesting that we throw open the doors to all the prisons and let the Charlie Mansons go free. I don't think that would promote anyone's well-being. I'm suggesting that we open our minds and hearts to the source of the problem so that we can find a genuine solution.

I, personally, am unwilling to compromise individuals by calling them evil. And I question if the rest of us are really in a position to judge, especially when we consider, for example, that a massive protest on the part of the German people might have prevented Hitler from committing such atrocities. So, does the evil rest with Hitler, or with the masses of people who stood by and let the atrocities happen? Each time we abdicate our responsibility and say, "Those individuals are evil and there's nothing we can do about it," bad things happen. Evil happens when good people do nothing, when there's failure to recognize other people's humanity.

We are all in various stages of personal development. Our personal habits and emotions influence our rate of progress. The denser our personality, the more karmic obstacles we generate. A business tycoon who gets to the top of the heap by stepping on other people incurs a lot of bad karma on his way up. Although he may think he's moving along at a very brisk pace, he's probably progressing at the speed of a snail—but he *is* progressing.

Individual Life Purpose

Our universal life purpose is to manifest our own God-like nature. Using the principles of transformation already introduced, we can regain the knowledge or memory of ourselves as unlimited. It isn't the memory of our past lives and it isn't the memory of future potentials—it's the memory of *who we are*. So, whether we extend back into our childhood, or even further back into past lives, or into the future—we're always led to the center of our identity, where God resides.

Once we understand our own God-like nature, we're still left with the questions: "Where do I go from here?" and "What is my individual life purpose, my life's work?" It's like the immigrant who for many years dreams of moving to America, inspired by a vision of this country as a land of unlimited opportunity. But once this immigrant lands on our shores, the question becomes, "What next?" In that same way, once we become empowered by the knowledge that we are one with the divine, and that we are unlimited and loving beings, the question becomes, "What next?"

On the practical level, we are here to fulfill our God-realized nature by meeting our own human needs. When we meet our own needs first, we are then empowered to recognize and help others meet theirs. The Bible tells us to "Love the Lord God with all thy heart, soul, mind and strength and thy neighbor as thyself." If we're unable to identify and meet our own basic needs, we will suffer from low self-esteem and a poor self-image. Consequently, we will be harsh and unloving toward ourselves and will invariably treat others in the same way. In my opinion, this is powerful motivation to begin to identify and meet our needs as individuals.

The essential needs of human beings are clearly defined both in traditional psychology and in the various humanistic parapsychological and spiritual models of man. Spiritual models of our nature existed long before modern psychology defined us as physiological beings, products of our material environment. We are both transcendental *and* shaped by the events of our physical world, and our primary needs reflect this multidimensional nature.

In India, over twenty-five hundred years ago, Prince Siddhartha (later known as Gautama Buddha) identified the essential needs of human beings in the "Eightfold Noble Path." The needs he identified were: right understanding, right thought, right speech, right action, right livelihood, right effort, right mindfulness, and right meditation. Buddha taught that by sincerely practicing these principles, which establish a middle path between self-indulgence and severe asceticism, we could end our suffering and attain enlightenment, which is our deepest human need. These eight categories are similar, though not identical, to what Spirit has channeled through as the "eight primary human needs."

The belief that meeting basic human needs is essential to coming into greater realization is also reflected in the writings of the American psychologist Abraham Maslow. Maslow observed that even though Sigmund Freud's therapeutic methods often succeeded in identifying an individual's source of neurosis and even eliminating unadaptive behavior, patients treated within his model continued to suffer. Since Freud himself never identified the needs of healthy, happy, and self-fulfilled individuals, he was never able to guide patients into their higher potentials. His colossal mistake, then, according to Maslow, was to base his discoveries about the human psyche on severely neurotic patients and then generalize those findings to normal, healthy individuals.

Unlike Freud, Maslow based his studies of humanistic psychology on men and women with high self-esteem, achievers who experienced themselves as successful in meeting their life goals. The term *self-actualization* came out of these studies, reflecting Maslow's observation that when certain primary human needs were met, people could then self-actualize toward their higher goals. He identified a "need" as something that, when met, causes health and well-being, and when denied, causes illness. Maslow postulated that once we meet our basic survival needs for food, warmth, and shelter, we then enter into a more complex level of needs, such as culture, justice, and social order. Meeting these needs, we then extend into an even higher order. Even "beauty" was identified as a human need.

Eight Primary Human Needs

According to my own spirit sources, any blockage or obstacle along our path to self-actualization or enlightenment is the result of our ignoring one or more of the following essential human needs: right understanding, right labor, right diet, right fellowship, right expression, right prayer, right meditation, and right mind.

Some of these needs are extremely practical, such as right labor, right fellowship, and right diet; some are more spiritually oriented, such as right prayer and right meditation; and others are more subtle, such as right expression, right mind, and right understanding. But no one need takes precedence over any of the others, and, actually, each need helps to fulfill the others.

It bears repeating that this idea of first meeting our own needs before we can help others meet theirs is not disguised egotism or selfishness. If we base our experience of ourselves on true human need, we're acknowledging our own humanity. We take into account our own strengths and weaknesses. It's simple intellectual and spiritual honesty. It's, "Lord, give me the wisdom to change those things that I can change and to discern those things which I cannot." And it is only when we have acknowledged our own humanity that we can begin to acknowledge the humanity of others.

Now, let's look at each of the eight primary needs more closely.

Right Understanding

Right understanding comes from the absence of fear. Fear has a tendency to override our rational, intellectual, logical, and intuitive processes. All fear arises out of our uncertainty in the face of the unknown. Right understanding is the right to life without fear.

Perhaps the most prevalent example of unreasonable or irrational fear of the unknown is racism, which has historically deprived us of right understanding both as individuals and as a nation. When we fear our neighbors because they are of a different ethnic or racial background, we restrict the opportunities not only of those individuals but of society as a whole. With his inspired application of Gandhi's concept of "uncompromising truth," Martin Luther King, Jr., was able to help many people overcome their fear. By exercising, in our own lives, the principles for which Dr. King stood, we rid ourselves and society of prejudices and limitations. As the saying goes, "Conquer your passions and you conquer the world."

Right Labor

Right labor is the most pragmatic of the eight primary needs. In Buddhism, it is referred to as "right livelihood." Right labor is so important to us that it has a tendency to be overlooked. According to Spirit, right labor should arise out of our natural, God-given talents. By becoming aware of our talents, and then applying them to something we love to do, we fulfill our own needs and are then empowered to help others fulfill theirs.

The need for right labor arises out of common sense. If we're miserable in our work, we're of little value to ourselves or anyone else. When we're miserable, we're not manifesting our God-like nature, which is to be loving to ourselves and others. On the other hand, if we enjoy doing something, and we have the talent or skill to accomplish it, we're much closer to manifesting our God-like nature. Loving our work generally brings out our best qualities. We tend to be more giving, more patient, more energetic, and more enthusiastic about life generally.

For people who want to pursue a spiritual vocation, the issue of right labor is sticky at times. Many individuals feel it is wrong to receive financial remuneration for spiritual counseling or healing, so they take jobs that meet their financial, but not their spiritual, needs. This often compromises their spiritual development, because if an individual's energy is depleted in an inappropriate livelihood, he invariably has less energy to give to others. To that degree, such individuals are not living up to their highest potential as spiritual counselors and are not optimally sharing their gifts.

As a personal example, in my senior year in high school I was scheduled for several interviews with a vocational counselor. I was given a series of dexterity tests involving such complex tasks as transferring a series of washers from one pole to another. Having completed these tests, my counselor assured me with unabashed enthusiasm that my future in the industrial Midwest was secure. According to the results of the tests, I was eminently qualified to work as a dock foreman.

That came as somewhat of a shock to me, since being a dock foreman wasn't exactly the career I had envisioned for myself. I said, "Excuse me, but is there anything among those facts and figures about a career in graphic arts?" The counselor said, "We're terribly sorry, we don't test for that type of aptitude." Fortunately, I was confident about my artistic abilities, so the results of the tests didn't deter me, and I went on to pursue my appropriate livelihood.

And while we're on the topic, I've never been able to identify with the myth of the "suffering artist," or to understand why so many creative individuals have lived and died in poverty. There were so many ways they might have applied their talents—moonlighting as commercial artists, helping others develop their artistic skills, inspiring people in the use of color and form, and much more. Personally speaking, not only did becoming a commercial artist save me from working on the docks, it was a way of creatively interacting with other people. I could assist others in translating their ideas into artistic expression and inspire them to develop their own talents. It also left me with the time and energy to pursue my own art.

I made a similar choice when I set aside my graphics business to pursue trance channeling full-time. Trance channeling was something I loved to do and had a talent for, and I felt that my development as a channel would be quicker, and I would be of greater benefit to others, if I gave it my full attention.

So, developing our natural talents and pursuing things we love to do can be very fulfilling. Because I love my work, I feel great vitality and enthusiasm; these qualities in themselves help to promote the well-being of others.

Right Diet

Right diet is simple and pragmatic. Certain foods promote the body's well-being and others do not. In my opinion, the vegetarian diet is the most appropriate one. I don't practice it fully myself, but I hold it as the ideal.

Whenever I recommend a vegetarian diet, people ask, "If you're going to kill plants for food, why not cattle and other animals?" Well, by logical extension, why don't we all become cannibals? This is an extreme convolution of any logical principle. Clearly, we're not cutting down a whole tree to eat an apple. By picking the fruit, we're not destroying life, we're promoting it. In Genesis it says, "Behold, I have given thee every herb-bearing seed upon the face of all the earth, and trees which bear fruit-yielding seed; to thee it shall be for meat." The lacto-vegetarian diet, which allows the consumption of dairy products, on the other hand, promotes the well-being of animals that have been domesticated. It is far better to drink milk, and thereby promote the well-being of the animal, than to kill the animal for the meat it can provide. Such motivation is much closer to the principles and the practice of vegetarianism.

Spirit has often pointed out that when we rely on meat for our protein, we're getting it secondhand. Since the flesh animals we consume get their protein from vegetation, it seems illogical that we couldn't get ours in the same way.

Right diet promotes mental, physical, and spiritual well-being. It is a human need. When we consume too much sugar and other harmful substances, we poison not only our bodies but the well of our own psychology. Someone once said, "Take care of your body, because where else are you going to live?"

Right Fellowship

Right fellowship is keeping company with individuals who give us positive reinforcement for pursuing and fulfilling our life goals. It is people manifesting a loving heart, being nonjudgmental, and helping to promote our well-being. We all have a need for human fellowship, to be around creative, supportive people. None of us is an island, and we don't have to do the whole thing by ourselves.

Incorrect fellowship is keeping company with individuals who give us negative reinforcement, who don't promote us as positive and unlimited beings. At times we may find it easier to maintain these kinds of associations, particularly when we're feeling spiritually lazy, but then we don't progress as quickly and are often hampered in the fulfillment of our other needs as well.

Right Expression

Right expression is the ability to articulate clearly. If we know what we want to do but we can't express it to others, we probably won't get very far in life. If I apply for a job, for instance, and the resumé I submit is incomplete, as well as messy and smudged, I'm not "expressing" my talents and abilities appropriately. On the other hand, if I submit a professional-looking resumé, and perhaps a flattering photograph of myself, I am communicating my value much more appropriately.

A more profound example of right expression is the famous "I have a dream" speech given by Martin Luther King, Jr. Dr. King was able to articulate deep and urgent needs of humanity in words that ring true to this or any other generation. The life and works of Henry David Thoreau are another example of right expression. Thoreau's discourse on civil disobedience was the inspiration for the passive resistance movement of Mahatma Gandhi. As Winston Churchill (undoubtedly another individual who was skilled in right expression) admitted, "That thin little man in a loincloth is going to wreck our empire." It was Gandhi's theories of nonviolence that in turn inspired Dr. King.

Right Prayer

Most religions evolve their ethics and values in relation to a higher power. Historically, that higher power is called God. Prayer is dialogue with that higher source. It has been said that prayer is the time we spend speaking with God, and meditation is the time we spend listening. Right prayer is the ability to articulate our needs, simply and elegantly. It is the ability to dialogue with our inner resources, and to draw, from deep within, inspirations and insights that will quicken our intellect.

In his classic disagreement with Freud, Carl Jung said that God lies in the seat of the id. A familiar biblical quotation comes to mind, which I paraphrase: Behold, the mountains were moved out of place and I found not the Lord. Behold, a whirlwind, and I found not the Lord. Behold, a still small voice. Therein I found the Lord.

The Lord's Prayer is the simple acknowledgment that we don't live by bread alone ("Give us this day our daily bread, and forgive us our trespasses as we forgive those who trespass against us . . ."). It is an acknowledgment that as we fulfill our karmic responsibilities to one another, so in turn do we become enlightened to our own true nature. So perhaps we can say that right prayer is the ability of our inner dialogue to reveal our true nature.

Right Meditation

Right meditation is whatever aligns us in mind, body, and spirit. It is the relaxation of the body while the mind explores the full perimeters of itself. For me, right meditation involves hiking or my art. Some people practice hatha yoga (*yoga* means "the union of body and spirit") or sit in disciplined meditation. For others, jogging, dancing, or writing is their meditation. Spirit has often said that the best meditation for any of us is the one we're the most likely to practice.

In relaxing the mind, the body, and the spirit, we allow the essence of the divine to flow through us, and meditation is whatever allows us to enter that contemplative state. Meditation gives us greater clarity. It facilitates the healthy functioning of the body and reduces stress. Through meditation, we increase our consciousness of ourselves. Since we are ultimately God, every time we meditate, we're contemplating our own nature. We're exercising that memory function in reminding ourselves of who we are.

Whether we know it or not, we all meditate. Mild altered states of consciousness are part of the human condition. For example, we all daydream at one time or another. This occurs when, consciously or unconsciously, the body has relaxed to the point where the mind slips into a mild altered state. We often return from our daydreams with greater clarity, increased vitality, and an expanded sense of well-being.

Meditation is totally natural. It is a human need, just as sleep is. Spirit has channeled that even depression is a meditative state; it is "biologically induced meditation." All we're doing when we sit down to meditate is consciously harnessing those altered states. Meditation is the relaxation of the body while the mind explores the full perimeters of itself—usually through such techniques as conscious breathing, visualization, or reciting mantras.

Meditation is also a memory process. In hypnosis, we go into the subconscious to remember childhood events. In meditation, we recall the childhood of the soul. Meditation is not an escape from reality, as many people think. On the contrary, it is the path that leads us back to the reality of who we truly are—one with the divine.

Right Mind

Right mind is acknowledging that each of us has a particular way of thinking, and not judging those whose minds work differently from ours. Many apparently unresolvable human conflicts boil down to different methods of thinking. When we can respect the way another person thinks, and at the same time acknowledge and respect our own thought processes, the need for right mind is met. When people think differently from us, it doesn't mean that one or the other of us is flawed. Many times, we're just applying different, and often complementary, methods of thinking toward the same goal.

One of the best illustrations of right mind I've seen comes from the book *The Art of Thinking* (Berkley, 1982), by Allen Harrison and Robert Bramson. The book describes five basic styles of thinking: the synthesist, who can identify similarities where others see none; the idealist, who welcomes a broad range of views and seeks ideal solutions; the pragmatist, who will go for whatever works, and who typically seeks the shortest possible route to his goal; the analyst, who is interested in scientific solutions and tends to hold out for the one best way to resolve things; and the realist, who relies on fact and expert opinion, and who is interested only in what he considers "concrete results."

Science and intuition provide another example of contrasting methods of thought. Science is not the omnipotent body of knowledge many people take it to be; it is the exploration of those things that can be observed and measured by man. Intuition is simply another method. It is a "direct knowingness." Drawing on the example I used in an earlier chapter, no one knows where his car is parked right now. You can intuit where your car is, but you don't really know. For instance, if you say you know where your car is, I can simply say that I had it towed away. You couldn't really prove that I didn't without going to look at it. So, intuition is a method of direct knowing that isn't based on the five senses. And right mind is recognizing and respecting our own and other people's thinking processes.

The Interdependence of the Eight Human Needs

Although we often fulfill our more physical needs for right diet and right labor before moving on to our more subtle needs, this is not an absolute rule. Maslow observed many instances where individuals fulfilled more abstract needs before meeting their basic survival needs. The truth is that none of these needs is separate and discrete from the others, and meeting any one of them helps us to fulfill the others.

For example, a person who is engaged in right labor generally builds enough self-esteem to initiate appropriate fellowship. In my case, my family did not constitute right fellowship for me when I was starting out in graphic arts. My grandmother, who was the dominant parent figure in my family, once said that she wished I could conceive of my future beyond my father's paintbox. Her concern was that in pursuing graphic arts, I wasn't meeting some greater potential, although she never defined what she thought that potential was. So, my family did not constitute right fellowship for me as an artist. Fellowship with other artists, who would support me in what I knew to be my right labor, was more appropriate. This shows how meeting one need can help us to fulfill another.

Right diet is an obvious example of how one need affects all the others. If our diet is poor, our work productivity goes down, our thinking becomes lax, we're not motivated to spend time with others or to express ourselves, our prayers and meditations are not empowered, and we're more vulnerable to states of fear. Conversely, improving our diet can profoundly affect our ability to meet each of the other needs. Right meditation also assists us in meeting all of our needs, as it is a window into our inner nature. There is virtually no need that doesn't help meet the others. Right understanding, which is the absence of fear, helps us identify right fellowship, because we're no longer fearful of approaching people. Right fellowship helps us to overcome fear if we apply the ideal that all people are our brothers and sisters. As each need becomes fulfilled and integrated into our nature, it becomes effortless. It is absorbed into the stream of our consciousness and is no longer a struggle.

As long as we're clear in our understanding and aligned with our life purpose, each one of these needs begins to reveal the others. This then leads us to greater actualization, which is to manifest our God-like nature. We become aware of the loving and altruistic beings we are and can begin helping other people come to this understanding in their own way. It's a clear, simple way to keep the Golden Rule, which is, "Love the Lord God with all thy heart, soul, mind and strength . . . and thy neighbor as thyself," or, "Do unto others as ye would have them do unto you."

Desire Versus Embellished Need

Now arises the question, "How can I distinguish my true needs from my desires, fantasies, and illusions?" Defining our needs is fairly simple. A need is something we must fulfill in order to perpetuate our well-being and fulfill our highest potentials. A desire is more subtle. Its fulfillment may or may not perpetuate our well-being or help us to fulfill our potentials.

Desire is merely "embellished need." When one of our needs isn't being met, we amplify it so that it comes into the forefront of our consciousness. There it will absolutely demand to be heard. If we have emotional charges around food, for example, these issues become amplified. If we're not applying right diet, they become amplified into "I wish to be thin," or "I've got to start pumping up these muscles." These translate into desires and then, at times, into extreme imbalances, such as anorexia nervosa or bulimia. This is an obvious misapplication of right diet.

A desire, then, calls our attention to the fact that one or more of our eight primary needs aren't being met. Our imagination will blow this up out of all proportion on an emotional level, even to the point of obsession, until sooner or later we confront the issue. When we go deeply into it, at the center we find a pearl of great price, which is the knowledge that we are not meeting some of our basic needs. Once we identify which needs aren't being met, the desire or obsession falls away.

For example, you may think you "need" to quit your job in the city and move to the country. As time goes by, you become more and more obsessed with this need. Then one day some friends invite you to drive out to the country with them. Once you're out in nature, you realize that you don't really "need" to move to the country after all, that what you really need is to be out in nature more often. What you thought was a need to radically transform your lifestyle was really just an embellished desire based on your true need to get out into nature more often.

Identifying Our Individual Needs

Unless we can clearly define our needs, we can't fulfill them or communicate them to others. The best way to identify our needs is by meditating on them. If we calm ourselves and reflect deeply on the eight needs discussed above, any need that isn't being met will send off a little bell in our heads. For example, if you have difficulty articulating yourself, when you come to "right expression" you'll get a reaction to that. Or, if you're under too much stress at your job and have been sensing that it's time for a career change, a little bell will go off when you get to "right labor."

As a personal example, in my early days as a graphic artist, I noticed I was getting unusually fatigued. In one of my meditations it occurred to me that my fatigue might be a toxic reaction to the lead-based paints I was using. When I shifted to water-based paints, the fatigue went away. So, through right meditation I was able to solve the problem without missing a day's work or having to consult a doctor.

In our meditations we can ask ourselves specific questions pertaining to each of the eight primary needs. This can be of great assistance in identifying our needs, since, drawing on principles of inductive logic, if we can form a particular question, the answer is already present within us. Following are some possible questions we might ask.

Right understanding. Am I happy in what I'm doing? Do I feel comfortable meeting new people? Am I open to new experiences? Do I impose my prejudices on others? Do I have strong principles that guide me in my daily actions? Do I behave in ways that might be masking fear (for example, am I boastful or arrogant)? If so, what situations trigger this behavior, and what is the cause? Do I avoid situations where I might have to confront my fears?

Right labor. Am I happy in my work? Do I feel inspired and alive at my job? Does my work put undue stress on me? Is it serving myself and others in a way I can feel good about? Is it harnessing the full range of my talents? Are there talents I'm suppressing? Am I eager to return to work? Are my contributions appreciated? Does my job give me the flexibility to meet other needs in my life, or does it demand all of my time and energy? Am I preoccupied with other things when I'm at work? Do my co-workers constitute right fellowship for me? Do I feel clear and vital when I leave my workplace?

Right diet. Is my diet promoting my health and well-being? Is it vital? Does it meet my ethics and principles (i.e., vegetarianism, lacto-vegetarianism, and so on)? Do I have food allergies? Do I eat my meals leisurely, or do I bolt them down? Do I eat enough whole foods? Am I overly concerned about my weight or physical appearance? Should I be taking certain food supplements with my meals? Have I experienced any symptoms of imbalance in my diet, such as skin problems or a lack of energy?

Right fellowship. Are the people in my life promoting my well-being or are they holding me back from pursuing my goals? Would it be better if I had more friends? What kind of people am I drawn to? Is my thought process stimulated by the words of a particular individual, or by the association with certain people? Can I express the full range of my talents with the group of people who are currently active in my life? Do I have a high trust level with my current friends? Are the relationships in my life based on honesty and openness? Do my friends reflect my values and principles?

Right expression. Do I articulate myself well? Do I feel that people really hear and understand me? Am I talking *to* people or *at* them? Am I adequately communicating my needs to others? Am I saying one thing with my mouth and something else with my body? Does my style of dress express who I am? Am I too impulsive in my communications? Too measured? Am I afraid to express my true feelings to others? Does shyness or lack of confidence interfere with my self-expression?

Right prayer. Do I feel comfortable going into an inner presence? Do I take the time to have a deep communion with God? Do I remember to pray for others as well as for myself? Do my prayers seem to help in any way, or do they seem empty or unfulfilled? Do I feel the divine presence when I pray? Do I respect others' right to pray as they choose?

Right meditation. Is my meditation promoting my well-being? What is right meditation for me? In what circumstances do I feel closest to the divine? When do I feel the most inspired? What kind of meditation best aligns my mind, body, and spirit? Do I feel refreshed and revitalized after my meditation? Am I comfortable in the space in which I meditate? Do I feel more comfortable meditating alone or with others? Are my meditations deepest in the morning or at night? Do I meditate better outdoors?

Right mind. Can I identify the nature of my own thought process? Do I use it to my advantage? Do I recognize its limitations? Do I thrust onto other people my own method of arriving at solutions? Can I respect the thought processes of the people around me, even when they differ from my own? Do I always have to be right? Can I put myself into someone else's shoes to see things as they see them? Do I hold one method of thought to be superior to the others (e.g., analytical is superior to intuitive, or vice versa)?

Simply by asking these kinds of questions, we can learn a great deal about ourselves and discern how successful we've been at meeting our needs. This is why right meditation can be the key to helping us fulfill all the others. Pay attention to your dream states, as well. Frequently our dreams will try to tell us which of our needs aren't being met. For example, you might have a dream in which you fight with your boss and storm out of the office. This could indicate that you have pent-up frustrations concerning your work situation and need to "close the door on it." Many people dream that they're standing in front of an audience, naked. This often speaks of fears of being seen by, or expressing ourselves to, others. A dream that we're being chased by a ferocious animal yet we cannot run or scream could be speaking to a profound fear of the unknown. The best way to interpret what our dreams are saying to us is to examine them in a quiet meditative state and see what comes up. A dream journal is also quite helpful, since often we need a little distance from our dreams to see them clearly. After a passage of time, the symbols in our dreams have less of an emotional charge and can be easier to read. We might even see patterns or interrelationships between the dreams, which will give us a broader perspective.

Conclusion

We were in a state of grace at the beginning and, in many ways, we never lost it; we just don't recall it. Remembering our original state of grace restores us to what is already our own nature. If we had amnesia, and knowledge of our citizenship was temporarily lost to us, a process of reeducation would restore that knowledge. We've never lost our citizenship of the universe, we've merely forgotten it.

This is the soul's path. Our universal life purpose is to remember who we are. We are God, and God is love. We are here to manifest our own God-realized nature. We are here to actualize the spiritual dimensions of ourselves by the application of this intuition that we are God. The soul's path is a self-actualization process that leads us to this end. It is simply a process of memory. We have only to remember who we are. We are a loving entity, because God is love.

What is love? Love is the innate harmony that exists in all things. When we're in harmony with nature and its laws, our minds and our bodies function with greater harmony. The deeper the roots of our philosophy, the more profoundly we realize our spiritual dimensions, that we are sacred within the natural laws of God. This is the soul's path. It is what Buddhists call "remembering our original nature."

Our perception of God ultimately shapes how we see ourselves. If we think of God as angry, more than likely we'll be motivated by anger. If we think of God as loving, more than likely we'll be motivated by love. Either way, the roots of our consciousness lie not in our past lives or in some future millennium—the roots of our consciousness are with us in the here and now. God is omnipresent and is in each of us. That is the final transformative principle. Our life purpose is to manifest God in the uniqueness of our own being, to work with these edifying principles and thoughts, and give them reinforcement. All memory, even if it's a memory of ourselves as divine, is a matter of positive reinforcement. Positive thoughts and positive deeds *do* work. They are an expression of the harmony that is.

We have been on a journey of exploring our true nature. Our spiritual guides and teachers, whether they are incarnate or discarnate, are here to assist us in this exploration. The Buddhists speak of an "awakened heart and brilliant mind." If the awakened heart is one which expresses the truth that God is love, the brilliant mind is that mind which realizes its original nature, that indeed we are multidimensional beings of mind, body, and spirit. The soul's path is this process of awakening our hearts and allowing the natural brilliance of our minds to show through.

There is an old French saying that if a person loses a coin, he should look for it on the street that has the most light. The path we have chosen for ourselves is the path of light. It is the soul's path. For indeed, we have been here since the foundations of the world and have returned again and again, not only to cast more light on our own nature, but on one another's natures as well. The spirit is that light that reveals our inner path. We are God's expression on this plane of existence. We are humans—beings of light.

Part III

Spirit Communication:
The Ascendant Path

Chapter 1

❧ *The God Force*

God and Prayer

John

There are many descriptions of God, but only one that reveals that great being's true nature. God is love, and love is the altruism that exists in each and every one of you. It is the ability to give forth from yourselves as abundant beings. For if you are immortal, if you are a spirit, if you are the children of God, then you may give of yourself in no shallowness and in no hesitation. And you will then, in each act, transcend the mundaneness of the physical plane and become more and more the children of God. For this is the merger of the mind, the body, and the spirit in dedication and service to God.

In God, who is omnipresent and impersonal, we find slumber, we find sleep. In yourselves, as the children of light who are the co-creators with God in the universe, we find an awakenness. That which awakens awakens only for the purpose to return to slumber, yet that which slumbers slumbers only for the purpose to reawaken.

101

That which appears is only for the appearance to disappear. Ultimately, God is sleep. This is nirvana. The awakenness is the expression of your individuality within God and that uniqueness within self. So, it is through you that God perceives and expresses upon this plane. You are the eyes, the ears, and the senses of God upon this plane.

You are a personal being, so therefore God is personal. You are also a being of infinite resource, so therefore God is a being of infinite resource. There is a deep personal relationship between yourself and the divine. God is love. When you manifest a loving nature, you manifest the personal nature of God. God is the Father/Mother God that is neither male nor female. There is only oneness.

It has been said that none may see God, but you may feel, sense, and come into the presence. If by this it means that you see yourself more clearly, then perhaps you have seen God. If you have seen a loving act, you have seen God.

Man looks to God as though he has the power to cause change. There is no such thing as change, there is only movement. Movement may cause inspiration in the minds of men so that they may seek to achieve higher goals. God is love, so therefore, if you love your brothers and sisters on the earth plane, you are in harmony with them and you manifest God, or the power to cause movement.

God is love, and love is harmony. Manifest harmony within the self and you become the greatest healer of all, for through your personal example, others will desire to be drawn into the light, and it is better to light even a single candle than to curse the darkness.

Each of you is as a son or daughter of God, and each of you may be as lifted up, perhaps according to the personal example of the man Jesus, or of Buddha, or by your own consciousness. For it is the upliftment of the soul that concerns God.

You are a part of God in the state of unfoldment, seeking to understand the nature of God through personal example. As a part of God, you are already in a state of perfection. The soul knows nothing but perfection, for it is the son or daughter of God.

The outer darkness that you perceive in some persons is but ignorance of God. Abide with them in a state of patience but do not pour yourselves out nor cast your pearls before swine. Love the Lord

God with all your heart and mind and your neighbor as yourself. Keep this commandment and you can break no other. Be not burdened by laws, for laws were to give you the ability to itemize your progression, to give you measure of inner peace.

When you are loving, you give up your limited self and entertain the whole. You then see yourself and others in that higher light. Love your neighbor as yourself. In this you allow God to shape your nature, and you acknowledge that you are one with that higher order. That is the appropriate relationship. Love God with all your heart, mind, strength, and soul, and your neighbor as yourself.

The reason you have forgotten your relationship with the divine is that you have become more familiar with the activities of the earth plane. Memory is developed by a process of repetition. You focus upon conditions in this lifetime, hence they become the most familiar. But when you move beyond the mundane memories of this lifetime, you begin to recall and be inspired by the memory of God. The more you meditate and ponder this, the more you exercise memory, and the more you become familiar with the higher order. So thus, you begin to remember that you are part of God.

Ponder your true age, the make-up of your atoms. Are they not millions of years old? When you contemplate your nature, you are ancient. You spring forth from a vaster whole, even as a physical being. How much more ancient, how much more infinite in your nature, if you accept yourself as a spirit? For when you calm yourself, you will remember. And when you ask yourself what should you remember, remember that you are God.

Loving the Lord God with all your heart and mind is your commitment to the universe. Loving your neighbor as yourself is your commitment to God in this plane, for when you look to the one who sits next to you, this is your highest commitment, to love this individual as yourself. And even as you do unto the lesser of these, so do you do unto the greater.

Many seek truth in complex systems of thought, and mock the simplicity of love. Love means harmony. If you bring harmony to yourself, you may extend it to others. No matter what your system of reference, no matter what guidance you may receive, the final attributor unto all these things is the love that dwells within you, for this comes to you from God and is a gift that is given eternally unto you in an abundance that shall never run dry. These are the waters that you must partake of, that you never thirst again.

God gives to you abundantly. Look at your vast fields of grain, your vast resources. It is not the lack of food that causes starvation amongst your nations, it is the lack of the inner bread of life, the lack of love for one another, the ignorance of your true nature as sons and daughters of God.

Seek to evolve spiritually so that you become the spirit and the expression of God. God is love, and love is a twofold factor. It is the creation of harmony, but it is also the sensing of the separation of yourself from others. For it is when you sense that separation that you desire to move toward that from which you feel separate. And ultimately, when you merge with all things, even love itself must end. So therefore, the ultimate end of your spiritual evolution is the merger with all things, which is the ultimate act of love, the ultimate giving up of self.

You must be the vessel to create the void, to pour yourself out, to sacrifice all things, to sell all things to obtain the pearl of great price, which is the direct knowingness of your original nature, your original name, which is preserved in the Book of Life. For each of you is a word which has come forth from the mouth of the Father/Mother God. And each of you is a word in the Book of Life. Even as you have many thoughts yet only one mind, so in turn there are many souls and only one God. You are as a thought within the mind of God.

Bring forth balance within the self, for this is what God desires for you, for you are a portion of God. Even as your physical body has many cells yet still but one body, so in turn there are many souls, but only one God, and you are but as a corpuscle in the body of God—complete, unique, and individual. So, what is God? God is love, love is harmony, harmony begets peace, and peace is that which causes movement in all beings, to turn to one another that they may establish the final harmony, which is the collective whole of God, which is love.

Inspiration always comes from the Father. Give all praise to God, for it is he who loves you, above all others. Even as he loved the man Jesus,so in turn does he love you also, that you, too, may be lifted up upon the wings of harmony, that peace may be established within you.

Work within guidelines that inspire you. If there is inspiration in a name—as in the name of Jesus or Buddha or Mohammed or Brahma—and meditation upon such causes movement within, then it is wise to take that name as a point of focus. But remember that names are only points of focus. All the names of the Hebrews, Christians, Buddhists, Hindus, Essenes, and Muslims are but points of focus. It is God which gives them relevance. So, if you desire to focus yourselves upon God, work in the name of love, that you may manifest these properties.

How do your prayers work? If you are appealing to the whole, which is God, and you are then carrying on a dialogue to affect certain circumstances, it is merely that the added appeal from your own inner God-self would then influence those circumstances.

Be not as a hypocrite who prays before many, seeking the adoration of men and women. But go in secret into your living temple, into meditation; unite your mind, body, and spirit, which is the Christ principle itself, in service to the greater whole. But seek also to share in fellowship those things which come to you; for who is it who comes quietly to you in the night? It is simply God, who is love. And love begets harmony, which indeed is peace, whence all your thoughts would spring and from which you hold dear to each other.

Even as you would make your life a living sacrifice, so in turn you may make your life a prayer in itself, carrying this internally within your heart. It says to go in secret and pray, and God shall reward you openly. Be not as the hypocrite who stands upon the corner with long face and fasting. Men may extol their virtues, but ultimately, they have their reward. Moreso, go inward. If this be in the humbleness of your daily labors, so be it. If it be in structured meditation and you seek not the praises of man, then so be it. The manner of prayer is individual to the person, but it is always a dialogue or exchange with the highest force in the universe.

There are many philosophies, many systems of thought, but there is only one God. Philosophy seeks to express God upon humanitarian levels. Religion seeks to express God upon the mystical levels. God seeks to express himself in his personal love for each of you.

Now, look upon the face of the person who sits next to you, for herein is where you will find God. God is in each and every one of you and makes you all equal. To be God is not to have power over life and death, for death does not exist—there is only life unto life. And life is made up of your interactions with other persons. You live by every word that proceeds forth from the mouth of God, for in the beginning was the word, and each of you is as that word, making up a single paragraph in the book. But there is only one book. Each of you is an individual word, and it is by loving one another that you are bound up and made as one. And that one is God, which is love, harmony, and peace.

Tom MacPherson

Remember that you are God. That is your only purpose—although you may choose to go about remembering it in a unique way, in terms of occupation, talent, diet, prayer, meditation, and religion.

How do you visualize God? Every priest I know of down through the halls of time has been trying to bottle that one up. God is love, love is harmony, and, as John puts it, harmony begets peace.

There is starvation in the world not because God wants it, or because there is too much food in one place, but because there is a lack of God, or lack of a loving or altruistic nature. When someone comes along and blows the whistle on all of your politicians for being stingy, they start scrambling, feeling guilty, and wanting to explain. But actually, all that is needed is a free-flowing set of ideals and un-compromising recognition that all persons are human and all are worthy.

Atun-Re

What is God? God is the interlinking of yourself with the whole. It is from the whole that the inner light comes. So, if you are derogatory toward any of your brothers or sisters, then you are derogatory toward yourself, and that light grows dim, for you have disinherited a small portion of yourself. Therefore, your light grows brighter, much brighter, when you acknowledge your brother. Ah, but here is a mystery. The light also grows dim if you do not acknowledge yourself, for you are also a part of the whole, are you not?

Your prayers are the emptying out of your concerns. They are an appeal to a much more vital force. They are an appeal to the whole to serve the single individual or to serve a larger, but still focused, segment of the whole. Prayer is your witnessing, your testifying, of the worthiness of an individual, or your belief in the worthiness of that individual.

Keeping the higher law is dropping the barriers between yourself and all things, but still maintaining the integrity of your individuality. For that is what the soul is. It is the ability to be one with all things, and with God, and yet to maintain the integrity of its individuality. That is keeping the higher law. John says that love is harmony. This is the ability to negotiate a broader position for yourself. And love is also the sensing of the separation between yourself and another and the desire to merge with them. Then love becomes harmony and no longer exists in that original dimension of movement and merger. So the highest law is the exercising of love, which ultimately reveals all things merging with them.

The essence of existence is love. Love is not just an emotion. Nor is love even dimensional. Love is that which binds the dimensions together. Love is the ultimate context of God, it is that which, by binding everything together, creates a harmonious, understandable perceptual experience. It is personal but it is universal. It is the alpha, it is the omega. It exists and it does not exist. To love, you must reach out your hand and touch another person in the deepest sincerity that you can muster within your capacity to be sensitive and to feel. Love occupies all areas of emphasis of the human mind. God is love.

The Physical Universe and Its Laws

John

Originally there existed only pure consciousness and total materia, or matter. It was perfect consciousness, observing and penetrating perfect matter through a process of psychokinesis, which started the currently existing known physical universe.

The origin of the planet was a creation of the Father's works, using those laws of substance which you term the "laws of physics." For even as you have your own metabolism, so are the laws of physics the metabolism of God in the physical form. And even as you have conscious choice in the birthing of children, so in turn was it with God in the creation of the universe. It was the desire of the Father to cause movement in the physical plane, to give three-dimensional existence for personal expression.

In the beginning was the word. For the universe, upon its final levels of thought, is perception. All the things which govern your physical universe are in harmony with those things which are as yet unseen. For even as it is said that God is the unseen force, so in turn is it with your universe, that the final perceptions of the universe would have to unfold from a state of perception.

Those things which ultimately govern the laws of your universe are not so much beyond perception but beyond the physical limits of this physical universe, and hence are yet unmeasurable. The final yardstick of your reality upon this universe is that which you determine as the speed of light. But there are forces which go beyond the speed of light. It is not that you are limited to the speed of light, but moreso that you cannot perceive beyond it, for since your ability to observe is dependent upon the speed of light, or light itself, you cannot observe those things which dwell beyond it.

Light is not a by-product, it is an activator of the natural forces in your known universe. Man often perceives light as a by-product of activity upon the atomic level. This is incorrect. Light itself *is* the activator of all forms of activity, other than the primary force, which governs its own nature. Black holes are the focal point whence these activities proceed forth, or light proceeds forth from your sun, or it is drawn out from your sun by the greater force of the black hole. Black holes are a focal point for the pattern of those things which travel faster than light, as well as light itself.

Particles which travel far beyond the reaching of light have been termed, since ancient times, as the "ethers," or the unseen forces, for they are quite literally unseen. They are a pattern traveling in a frictionless state. Therefore, the qualities peculiar to light itself, such as its traveling in waves yet still having the appearance of particles, are unobservable to you, since you have no instrumentation at this time to perceive them and they have but a brief life in your time/space continuum.

These forces, which are instantaneous and beyond the speed of light, approximate that which you might term the "speed of thought." Even as you can recall instantaneously a decade or a thousand years past, so in turn is thought itself instantaneous, and thus beyond the measuring stick you term "light." It does not travel along the normal curvatures of time and space. The science you term "radionics" is perhaps the closest to understanding and documenting these things.

The universe is a system of calculus. It is the perfect balance between all things. Those particles which travel beyond the speed of light in a completely frictionless state are finer forms of energy. These particles travel not so much in waves but in a specific pattern. So the universe is not limited to the mass which you now perceive, but there are other levels of mass which bring balance to the system as a whole.

The universe is the physical body of God. Even as you have a soul or spirit, so in turn there is the spirit of God. The physical creation of the universe was for personal expression, so, to understand the universe, you must turn inward to begin to understand self. The universe is not a chaotic system of energies interacting with one another, shaping things of their own accord. There is harmony in the universe, for God is love and love is harmony.

These activities are not so much shaped by the laws governing light—because the speed of light is but the yardstick by which this physical universe is measured—they are shaped by the spirit within self. For there are those things which travel beyond the speed of light and shape your activities upon this plane, but since they travel in the frictionless state, they are as yet undetectable to you. So interlocked are they with your activities, you have yet to detect them. You still perceive upon the levels of the speed of light and continue to give credence to the idea that there is such a thing as time and space.

Time is merely God's way of keeping all events from transpiring at once. Time itself is part of the conscious process and is eliminated when you recall events from childhood instantaneously. Then, if you draw insight or prognostication from that recollection, you may utilize those energies to alter yourself in the present. We would say that the very overcoming of the illusion of time and space is synonymous with spiritual evolution, for God knows neither time nor space.

Even as you have discovered that there is linkage between man and the rays of the sun, so in turn will you find that you have linkage with all the universal forces. Man has often spoken of the mind of God as the soul, for the soul is immortal and is the center of your very being. When it leaves the physical body, the body becomes inactive. It is not that each of you is a biological creature dependent upon the earth plane and its interplays and forces. Moreso, each of you is a soul, and each of you is as a caretaker of universal forces. Even as you project, in your dream states, into the astral realms and the levels of the soul which lie beyond the God planes themselves, so in turn must you understand the physical body as the vehicle for the soul, as well as the projection of your energies in the extensions and interplays of your mind upon the universal levels.

Each of you is a shadow upon the surface of the universe, for the universe has its own system of thought, its own consciousness, and each of you is but a projection upon it.

There are many forms of life within your physical universe. Life is not so much a biological function but specific ongoing patterns of intelligence. These things have manifested, in part, upon other planes of existence as well as upon similar physical planes and solar systems. There are not only other forms of biological life, there are other patterns of existence wherein beings are but as states of pure energy.

All forms of biological life are a focal point for an activity known as "intelligence." Intelligence is but a pattern of energy which is completely self-contained and holds itself in its continuing form of perception. Therefore, any form of life is but a level of perception upon a specific plane of existence. There are other solar systems quite similar to your own in humanoid form.

Indeed, there are beings from other galaxies who monitor your technological advancements. They do not so much desire to quarantine the planet, but moreso they wish to see you align your technologies with spiritual values and respect for all beings. For if you cannot respect even your own planet, how could you be trusted with the stars themselves?

Many landings have already been sighted by private individuals who have made it their life's work to communicate their experiences. This information has been systematically suppressed by your government, but many documents are now beginning to be released. They ebb and flow with the consciousness of each country. These things occur in part to release man's ego from the perception of himself as the single most intelligent of beings in the universe.

Harmony, not chaos, rules your universe. The universe is the physical body of God in which he reveals himself unto you ever continuously. From the most minute of particles to the great whales which inhabit your seas, all of these things are interdependent, one upon the other, in a state of harmony. All of these things bind you up and make you whole. And it is this one energy, the love and harmony which is the true nature of God, that gives you your sense of purpose, well-being, and peace in your sojourn in the earth plane.

The Higher Laws

John

The law of karma is simply the law of return. That which you put forth will return unto you. This should prove to be a liberating influence, for each thought that you think, even as you think it, so in turn is it judged, and it returns unto you as karma only that you would gain understanding, not as punishment.

All actions originate out of karma, but all may be altered through consciousness. Karma may be the initiator of an event, but consciousness is that which brings it to its conclusion. Thus, as you become more and more conscious of yourself as a harmonious being, or as one with God, the results of karmically initiated actions may be entirely different than if you had but accepted yourself as a victim of karma.

Karma is simply actions taken in past lives. When the soul originally incarnated into the earth plane, it was out of ignorance, as you had forgotten yourselves as part of the divine. As you drew yourselves up to become conscious entities and you passed through many incarnations, your actions became more and more sophisticated, more and more conscious.

According to the degree to which you recall yourself as God, the fear of God is the beginning of wisdom. *Wisdom is simply applied knowledge.* Never confuse knowledge with the truth. The truth is simply that God is love. Eventually, all of your knowledge, all of your wisdom, all of your actions, be they positive or negative, must surrender to the truth, that you may indeed embrace all things with a wise nature. For there are many paths that may lead you to the truth, but never confuse the path with the truth itself, for it is the truth that shall set you free.

Do not so much attempt to will karma out of your existence but try instead to transcend it and thus alter your personal life circumstances. Although you often have a sense of predestiny, that predestiny is simply that all would eventually return to the truth. And the more you animate the truth in your life, the more you are liberated from mundane karmic predestiny. Thus, free will applies here. There are no accidents, there is only karma. But karma and understanding are synonymous, and if you have understanding, karma is transcended.

It is possible to have citizenship in other spheres of existence. There are those who travel between the spheres—you call these individuals "space beings." There are numbers of other fellow souls in the journey through the physical who are also your brethren. At times your soul has held fellowship in their planes, but in the omnipotent wisdom or objectivity of the soul, you will always return to fulfill your karma at the point of its origin.

The law of grace is perhaps the most delicate of the laws and is simple in its practice. The law of grace is that which dissolves the law of karma. It *transcends* the law of karma. The law of grace is summarized in, "Forgive us our debts as we forgive our debtors." That is—like begets like. As you forgive, which is the law of grace, so in turn are you forgiven, thus superseding the law of karma. For if you forgive an action against you, so in turn is action you have taken against others forgiven. Those who possess grace move smoothly through the earth plane.

It is the soul that is creating the physical body, not vice versa. For the soul has always been at one with the universe and never separate from it. When the soul chose to project its consciousness into the earth plane, it created you as being *under* the law. But you were not meant to be under the law, you came to *fulfill* the law— and that law is the law of grace, the law of karma.

At times you sense that you have positive or negative karma. Positive or good karma allows you great freedom and you need not contend with the issues of ego. Negative karma holds you close to the issues of ego, for it causes you to scrutinize yourself and have low self-esteem. It is the link to the ego that creates the circumstances of positive or negative karma. So thus, eliminate the ego and you are then free of all karma, free to do service, free to love one another. For this is truly the unconditional love that springs up eternally and shapes the foundations of your very being. And then, indeed, you become one with God and you are *in* the world but not *of* it.

Free will is your individuality in the spirit, so therefore, the oneness of the spirit has always existed with you, even as an individual soul. For the soul is but your individuality in the spirit, and free will is the ability to be free within that spirit. Ultimately, free will means to be free within the will of the Father, for you gain your greatest freedom within that will. This is not so much the ability to choose any one of several different directions, it is moreso to be free in the direction of the will of God, which is total harmony with all things.

Divine will is the revelation that you must apply yourself in the direction toward oneness and unity with the whole. Limited will, or will of mind, is perhaps but the direction or the course that you set for your life expression, such as occupation and diet, that you apply your will toward. These are simply the tools, whereas the master who uses the tools is the divine will.

Tom MacPherson

Karma is simply the actions you took in past lives. Just as your childhood events shape your adult life, your activities in past lives shape the broader events or circumstances of this lifetime. So therefore, they have meaning. But you are not here to labor out your karma. If anything, you can transcend your karma through being a loving person. That is what it means to "forgive us our debts as we forgive our debtors." You are not here to work out your karma, you are here to be loving beings and, if anything, to transcend your karma.

The wheel of karma is the idea that you must keep traveling in cycles of reincarnation due to actions you have taken in past lives. The way to break the wheel of karma is to roll with the wheel of dharma. The wheel of dharma is the wheel which turns 360 degrees without really turning. It is symbolic of ultimate liberation, because you can travel in all directions through service. You can break the wheel of karma, or cycles of incarnation, by refining your spiritual service and doing it well. And spiritual service does not mean that you necessarily become a priest or nun. (If it did, I don't think I ever would have made it.) It means spiritualizing your purposes. It means isolating your talents and doing them well, and being basically a loving person.

In spirit we have a broader overview, but actually, we learn through you. You see, there is really no getting rid of karma incurred in the earth plane unless you have a physical body. Karma incurred in the earth plane can usually be gotten rid of only in the earth plane. So, by observing your actions as physically incarnate persons, we can also burn off karma.

Criminals and murderers sometimes come back around to be murdered themselves, or perhaps to become a saint. For instance, Moses was a murderer. I do believe he killed in an act of self-defense, but still he was a murderer. He beat the fellow to death out of rage, which was not exactly the most ethical decision. But he went on to become a great intellect, a great law-giver, and is considered a saint by many people. So basically, you get many chances. Your karma is your system of judgment. There is justice.

There is great famine amongst those individuals who would turn their noses up at the starving people in Ethiopia and say, "It's their karma," because theirs is a famine of spirit, which is an even deeper famine.

You are here to transcend your karma by becoming God-like. And God is love.

Souls and Soul Mates

John

In the Beginning: A Poetic Rendering

In the beginning was the Word, and the Word was with God, and the Word was as God. Nothing was made apart from the Word. And the life of the world is, indeed, since then, for when it is said, "Where were you when I laid the foundations of the world?" the answer therein was, "At one."

At first there was the Void, and the Void was without form. There moved in those days only one spirit, one consciousness—the all that was nothing and the nothing that was all. Indeed, a state of perfection. If you roll back the rivers of time and space, and the fields which bind together the forces that hold the very atom, these self-same forces could crush all of creation and it could pass through the eye of a needle.

God did look out upon the Void and saw it was without form. Pouring self forth, perfect spirit entered into perfect matter, and mind, light, came forth. Illumination. A soundless sound that was the creation.

There was set forth in motion a dance, of which the dancer and the dance are one. Perfect mind entered into perfect incarnation, and the creation was conceived. All of creation then began to unfold like the fresh bloom of the lilies of the field, and the hand of the Father/Mother God did weave the mighty loom, casting stars to all quarters of time and space, interweaving universes within universes, creating worlds without number, and scattering them across the cosmos—creating the harmony that is all things, like so many gems from the treasures of Solomon, awesome in the movement.

In these days you study the laws of the creation, that which you call "the universe." Worlds without number were created by the force of mind. For consciousness is the evolutionary force. Mind precedes matter and contemplates itself. These things that you call physics, these laws of the cosmos, are but the shades of the Father/Mother God's consciousness as it passes by. This was then the completion of the first great creative act.

Flowing through the rivers of time and space, the worlds pooled and began to take form. Then stars, of which there are more than the grains of sand upon the beach. There were oceans, and pure sweet airs, yet still nothing moved in and of itself.

The perfection of mind, the perfection of spirit, that was, and is, God, moved into that moment and bound and rebound and weaved and intertwined to create a tapestry and a glory unimaginable. He set forth in motion a dance and a dancer, which again are one, to weave and interweave until the weaver and the loom became one, inseparable. There then was the binding together of simple and elegant forms, wherein form could replicate self, first into one, then into two. Then two became many.

There was the taking of simple forms and binding them into moments—that which you call "atoms," that which you then call "molecules"—chains and ribbons, spiraling upward in form until they possessed the consciousness to replicate themselves. Finally, they became bound in single cell form. Then union amongst those cells—colonies.

For aeons the weaver wove. With great patience and ever more abundant materials, the ancient weaver wove with richness and diversity. Aeons the weaver wove, for the creation of expression of a new dimension. For many species of beings crept across the terrain of many worlds, species that sprouted many limbs, wings to master winds, variances of limbs to master the liquid called "oceans." Diverse in number, elegant in form, this was the creation of the dimension called "biological life." And thus completed the second great creative act.

Moving in perfection, the Father/Mother God gave forth from all these things by force of mind, through consciousness as the evolutionary force, patiently, over aeons, thousands upon thousands of revolutions of the turn of your small sphere of existence about a lone star, ever progressing toward a unique moment that is relevant to you now. For there was a third great creative act, and this was the force and the thrust of a creation of a new expression of consciousness. For that perfection that was the spirit, that perfection which was perfect mind, the evolutionary force in all things, which binds the cosmos, in being perfect, in being perfection, could tolerate no imperfection. And so, thus motivated only by perfection, would create to express and to manifest the perfection so as to fulfill perfect self.

How so? By the development of no expression except that perfection, by moving and drawing upon the substance of the perfection that was the spirit and the mind of God, to contemplate the nature of the creation that had been set in motion. And thus there came to be born the phenomenon you call "souls."

Souls were created to be thoughts within the mind of God. For each was the perfection of thought within the universal mind. These souls were created in both male and female, positive and negative, in twos, as reflected in the creation, so that they may bear witness with each other. Created as "soul mates," they were without number, infinite, perfect, radiant in their being, for they were as light. They were the Word, every Word that flowed forth from the mouth of the Father. For in the beginning was the Word, and the Word was with God and the Word was as God. And no manner of things were created separate from them. For they were the same substance of the divine; they were the morning stars which once shouted as one. For indeed, they were messengers of the divine.

All came aborning at once. For it was their very perfection in their moment of time and space that was their oneness with the all.

They then began to flow forth with one simple commandment, to be that perfection that they are. For they were also given free will. And what is free will but to be free within the will of God? And they would then flow forth, going in pairs to be co-creators with the divine. For they were to diversify the creation.

They occupied all sectors of time and space, and they could explore the whole of the kingdom of heaven. For all the stars flowed below them and they could tread amongst the stars, which were as their home. These celestial beings were infinite, unlimited, but indeed, howso naïve—without experience, only knowingness. Without action, only knowingness. Without thought, only knowingness. Without mind, only knowingness. Yet they would come to know action, they would come to know thought, they would come to know mind, for they were the creators of its foundation.

So thus, these co-creators of God fell forth, for they spilled forth again as every Word from the mouth of the Father/Mother God. And they moved forward, oblivious to time and space, for they transcended it. They flowed forth from the omnipresent—unique and individual, yet bound, one to the other.

Wherein was the wisdom in creating them in twos? It is so the two would come to consensus for there to be creation between them. Between God and matter, they were two, which became then many. But the many yet still are one. For they contained all the elements of the perfection, and yet they were also given free will. So they moved in their knowingness to diversify the creation that had been set forth, co-creators in the cosmos. And they moved into the material dimensions of this physical level of existence you refer to as "earth."

In those ancient days, at what moment would these things be? Who can say? From the eyes of the Lord, one thousand years are but as a heartbeat, and a heartbeat is as a thousand years. But they moved into the affairs, into the creation.

And indeed, their knowingness was overwhelmed by the senses of this plane. Vast and diverse were the eddies and the currents of the creation. Vast and deep were the reservoirs of their own being. A fountainhead of sensations never experienced before. Almost enough to overwhelm any form of knowingness, and indeed it almost did so.

Initially they diversified the creation and succeeded well therein. For consciousness is the evolutionary force—not random circumstance. And is not infinite mind ultimately patient? Would not the concept of infinity which rules all time and space explain why the evolutionary force, and each movement upon the weaver's loom, would create and stretch a fabric that you call time and space? For infinity rules all time and space, but only God rules all realities. So thus these youthful weavers, even though they were aeons old, moved, created, diversified, through the natural laws, for indeed they were the law and they were one with it.

But as they moved forward, their senses became overwhelmed. For the first time, they developed sensation, and using free will they moved into their creation rather than through it. And they came into that which you would call "incarnation," incarnating primarily into the life forms that you would term "mammalian," or into the lower primates.

And it was at this moment, moving into their creations and focusing singularly, that they became as an artist who, in creating a clay pot, would focus so obsessively upon that one creation that he would identify with the creation instead of the fact, the knowledge, the knowing that the creator and the creation are one. So thus, moving from the infinite into the finite, moving into matter, moving into that which you would call the animal forms, they lost their knowledge of the divine. And that which once had been graceful, like a player's fingers on harpstrings, ceased. But the perfection that is, the process of perfection, continued, for that which is perfect remains perfect, even when the illusion of imperfection is present.

These souls, these co-creators, then went through and set in motion a cycle, the law of karma, which is simply the law of return. Everything comes from God, everything returns to God. With infinite patience and infinite skill, these weavers sought to draw up a form of embodiment from the dust of the earth itself, a form of life, a new expression, a species of being elegant in form.

Early Civilization

First, in a form reflecting the singularity of their own androgynous nature, being neither masculine nor feminine, they drew up seats and centers of an awareness while yet still physically embodied, to fulfill and complete their actions that they had set in motion so many aeons past. They lived and dwelled in the land that is now but memory. You call it "myth." They lived in a shimmering landscape that men and women still call Eden, and some call Lemuria.

They lived in crystalline cities that spread like jewels across an emerald landscape. They mastered technologies and tilled not the earth with a blade, but indeed drew forth the fruit of the field by pure force of mind. They mastered the tools of sound and light and all things were bent to their will. And they lived many aeons in perfection, both masculine and feminine, in one form. For according to all the legends, they were the Adamite race, Anelius, the first people, the first humans.

Luminous beings were they, for they sought to master the expressions of luminosity. Not judging one another by their grosser physical forms, but seeing the light shining about each and every one. But wishing to bring a greater perfection, and not wishing to remain the self-centered expression, and with the rise of other colonies, there came the days of another moment, that in the collective myth, in the collective unconscious of humankind, there rose up another civil expression called Atlantis.

In Atlantis, they sought to master not so much luminosity and mind and align themselves with the divine, but sought moreso to master the material, to bend it to their will, to meet all need through the material, seeking resolution in the material rather than in their spirit. So their light grew dim. But for the first time in the human experience they brought into manifestation, or at least brought the opportunity, to divide self into two expressions, masculine and feminine. This was the birth of Adam and Eve, the first man and the first woman, of new experience and new sensations never experienced by souls before. Two genders scattered amongst seven races to bring the perfection, and to have two to make a witness.

As this species of beings continued their experiments in awareness, and as the eddies and flows in the currents of time and space moved them forward, and as Lemuria and Atlantis entered into the myths and mists of time and space, and history flowed forward as a relentless tide under the fullness of mother moon, washing and lapping upon the shores of your current histories, upon your current awareness, these souls had shaped for themselves the physical embodiment, the living temple that allows you to be human beings.

These human beings came from light. They never truly entered into darkness, but need only to reclaim that which makes them human—the fullness and the richness of their spirit. To reclaim the journey of the soul. To reclaim the richness and the heritage that is their own.

If the histories that we have mentioned are perceived as a myth, there is still the seed of the truth that resides within them, and can illumine the mind. For you are those souls. You are that perfection. And this is your heritage. It is the oneness that is.

The Roots of Consciousness

To understand the soul, you must first understand the workings of the divine spirit you call God, for in the beginning there was but that one spirit, and that spirit folded in upon itself, creating the beings who became known as souls. They were created in polarities, male and female, yet were androgynous in nature. These were known as "soul mates."

Soul mates are individual souls with whom you were created many aeons past, for the one spirit that is God did not wish his children to be alone, but rather created you in pairs to give witness to each other's existence. Thus, soul mates were created and given charge and command to be "co-creators" with God. This is the purpose and function of souls, to be co-creators within the physical universe you know and see, as well as throughout all the dimensions and orders of time and space, and even beyond those levels into the projections of consciousness itself.

Soul mates were given charge to be co-creators with God, to create two polarities from which there would then come the creation, that which you call "the laws of physics." These were recorded in the Book of Enoch, where it is said, "Behold, I saw all the angels attended unto all the machinations of the sun." This was the activities of souls making their sojourns through the ethers which dwell beyond the speed of light. The by-product of their creation and movement is those laws of physics which you observe in these days.

Souls then took upon themselves individual identities, which became the personal reflection of God upon this plane. For God can be considered the life force and the soul of the soul itself, the focus which encompasses the whole. But the souls, also being children of God, reflect the nature of God and occupy all sectors of time and space and all the dimensions, penetrating into consciousness itself.

So, thus, souls were created. Entering into their activities as soul mates, they were given dominion over the many planes and levels of existence, then coming to the dimension that you call the earth plane, projecting down from the levels of the ninth dimension, through the seven that you measure with your current technologies, then moving perfectly through the first dimension and circularly back to the ninth. Thus souls moved to create the physical universe and became the time flow and the law itself, or the causal force upon the earth plane.

The great spirit called God had already created the physical universe, traceable to that which you term, in your laws of physics, the "Big Bang." There was then the creation of the biological dimension you call life. It was here that souls began to diversify their creation, diversify the species, for they were given commandments to subdue the earth and make it their own. And in this they diversified the life forms, moving through all biological dimensions, and all the sensations of the higher realms of consciousness were theirs to command.

But as souls moved forth, they concentrated more and more of their energies in the levels of the third dimension, and the intense focus of their energy set in motion the beginnings of the foundations of mind, mind being the by-product of the soul's sojourn through the physical. Thus, mind rather than pure consciousness came to be the builder and the active force upon this physical plane.

Mind came to be elevated above the impersonal and nonmental aspects, which are the true divine attributes of the soul, to levels of personal emphasis, covetousness and special creations upon the earth plane. So thus the inexperience of the souls began the creation of the ego and the emotions. Out of this grew both a competitive order and the beginnings of emotional attachment. These forces slowly drew more and more of the soul's energy, taxing the natural laws of equal displacement of hydromechanical fluidiums upon which the soul functions, and the plasmalike state of the soul crystallized into the three dimensions of self that you currently acknowledge.

From the third dimension, then, came the creation of ego. This is why there are three primary points of focus, referred to in the Vedas as the "three knots," in which the central aspects of the ego must be broken up by a superior force known as the kundalini. As in other systems of thought, these became the "three permanent atoms." Souls could liberate themselves from all aspects upon all dimensions except the third dimension, in which they came to be concentrated. They could distill their essence even to the level of pure ethers, except for the three permanent atoms upon which their attachments as personal entities became bound upon this plane.

It was the continuous cycling of these three atoms through the species, to which there was a natural magnetic attraction, that set in motion the law of karma. And thus souls fell. Rather than being *as* the law and the causal force upon this plane, they came *under* the law, responsible for their actions in the third dimension—and with greater emphasis, since they were attached in their ether fields through the three permanent atoms.

The three permanent atoms at first had their centers in the three baser chakras. They existed in pre-man as just that—three baser chakras. These related to the grounding of the soul in the physical, the sexual forces, and the primitive emotional constructs. These imprisoned the souls, or bound them there. Then, a second wave of souls came into the earth plane to fill the void that had been left by the souls who had physically incarnated and become imprisoned in the various diverse animal, vegetable, and mineral kingdoms.

This second wave of souls became the angelic and devic orders. They immediately began to set right the natural laws and order of things by speeding up evolution and beginning to clear from the planet all life forms that would be threatening to the primitively constructed prehumanoid forms. Thus there was the extinction of many species, as great concentrations of the odic force, or the life force, were necessary for the rapid evolution from the levels of pre-man to that which is now known as the humanoid form.

Also, new portals were needed for the influx of this life force. It was decided that perhaps the most superior form would be a primitive lower primate, from which all the souls would eventually build up the redemptive humanoid vehicle. Many other humanoid and semihumanoid forms, known as the demigods of Greek mythology, were lifted up too, so that you were a multispecies society in those days.

Next came the development of the etheric body to tend to the primary elements of human evolution, and then the emotional body. The etheric and the emotional bodies were the first two created. Originally there were no emotions upon the plane. Each being was according to its own nature. There were no emotional constructs, no personal attachments, for emotions are a merger of the physical and consciousness and a construct of the ego.

Next came the mental body, which was the beginning of the first realization of a peculiar and unique nature. Then came the astral body, necessary for keeping specialized the lessons that the souls would have to learn in actualizing themselves back toward God. But it was not until there arose a multispecies society that the activities of the spiritual body came into being. Here then we find the spiritual and the causal bodies, the beginnings of the link with a planetary consciousness. The sense of oneness with the planet then activated the principle of the soul body and the linkage with the higher consciousness.

With the creation of each of these evolving subtle anatomies came new portals that found their seats in what would be known as the chakras. These were found, particularly in prehuman form, in the testicles in the male and the ovaries in the female, in the adrenals, in the spleen, in the thymus, the dominant thyroid, and then the primitive, reptilian skeletal brain—the pituitary and the pineal.

The development of these chakras was the key to the development of the right- and left-brain hemispheres. For as the life force began to pour in, it was necessary to store the energy in quantities so that consciousness could be measured upon the plane. Thus the right- and left-brain hemispheres began to develop; and thus the logical and intuitive concepts of man also began to develop, so that men and women could meditate and ponder their acts upon this plane and would become conscious beings.

With the slow development of the right- and left-brain faculties came the greatest creation of the soul on this plane—the human personality. The physical body became the storehouse of all those things unrealized in the being. It was also at this time that the permanent atoms began to find new seats of consciousness within individuals, moving from the baser chakras into the heart, and in some, into the thyroid and the pineal. In others, into the *hara*, the heart, the pineal, and the pituitary.

The new positions of the three permanent atoms shifted the pouring in of the life force to the belly point of the physical body and forced its evolution upward, for the life force was also concentrated in the pituitary and the pineal. This caused rapid and massive swellings of the neurological activities, finding their climax in Cro-Magnon man during the Lemurian and Atlantean periods. At this time, the heart, the thymus, and the muscular tissues of the heart became critical to the health and well-being of the individual, with the thymus forming the very foundations of the biological personality in the first seven years of life. It has been this way from the time periods of Atlantis into your current recorded history.

In the early days, humankind was under the direct order of the angels and had no will of its own, save to draw up the redemptive humanoid vehicle. Then there began to be races to achieve higher levels of consciousness, for again the beast—the ego—was rampant. This led to the jealousies of gods, and also drew in that second wave of angels, who entered into those competitions rather than remaining in the divine. This spoke of the second wave of incarnation.

The second wave of incarnation contributed greatly to the creation of a higher level of consciousness. And this second wave of angels was also catalytic in finally drawing up the Adamite race in Lemuria, which then became the Garden of Eden. This was for the final restoration of free will upon the physical plane, which was the first step in restoring humankind to the divine.

Then, in Lemuria, came the completion of the seven chakras and the origin of the seven rays, giving souls pure consciousness of themselves upon this plane so that they would begin slowly to uplift themselves to no longer be *under* the law but to be *as* the law itself. When the will is weak in these areas, individuals withdraw into the three baser chakras. These become the origins of sorcerous natures that seek to manipulate higher forces to preserve the personal will rather than the divine will, which is to spiritualize the self.

The forces known as the seven rays link you to higher forms by coordinating with the chakric centers for the drawing of the life force from the higher dimensions, the oneness with the universe. This allows personal direction of the soul's force upon this plane and greater manipulation of the permanent atoms that bond souls here. It also allows the physical body to become a naturally restored unit of energy, with its ability to be *focused* on the plane rather than *bound* here.

The original bond of the soul to this plane became the mythological concept of angels bound in pits and tormented night and day by the angels of God. This was but the calling up of those souls from that abyss in the ancient, ancestral, and racial memory of mankind, of the knowledge of yourselves as divine beings and sons and daughters of God.

The rays reveal the activities and the emphasis the soul desires in the personality, the yet-remaining spiritual lessons. So, study of the chakras and the rays reveals the unspiritualized or unrealized aspects of the subconscious, which is the physical body. So thus the drawing up in same.

Having obtained many levels of perfection, there was a final gathering of souls and archangels in both the incarnate and discarnate state. It was desired that the perfection be tested one final time, for the oneness obtained in Lemuria had not yet been tested; and indeed, this would not only be testing, but to see if the light could survive in the new form. Thus, the single androgynous form of the Lemurians came to be divided into male and female so as to create intimacy and sharing between two beings of like need, like temperament, and like consciousness. This would be the final testing of the egos. And this indeed has been the testing of men and women ever since.

With these activities, there was the drawing of the individual lessons back into the lower chakras, bringing forth issues of sexuality. For indeed, it is the churches of the lower chakras that seek to test the prophets and often find them wanting. This is not to say that it is only concepts of sexuality which are critical to advancement, but that each individual would realize he is more than a physical being and that the physical is simply his focus and emphasis for the lessons upon this plane.

Even today you are having the testings of androgyny, where each individual is coming to understand that he has a personal relationship with God. Androgyny is the ability to be both male and female and to act out the natural constructs of these things in altruism. This is so that no individual would judge the other according to his sexuality or sexual expression. Thus, the issue of a balance between male and female and the final order of establishment. For the issues of male and female and the human expressions of intimacy cut across all racial, social, and economic lines.

The testing then is to achieve balance—not simply the restoration of equal relationship between male and female but the equality of all who find expression in the human form. So the testing is the final drawing up of energies from the lower chakras into the higher, where they may be made divine and you would serve one another without prejudgment, without prejudice, with unconditional love for one another and the desire to create harmony in all things.

Know that your soul is bound to the physical body not as a slave but to experience revelation that may come from the personality. For the personality is but a memory to the soul, and you have had many lives, so therefore many memories for the soul. Even as you have memories from your childhood that still shape you though you are no longer a child, so it is with the soul, that eventually you shall mature in the soul from the personality.

The soul is bound up as a commitment to the physical body not so much as a slave but moreso as a servant, that each may serve the other for the revelation of God in this plane of existence.

The soul is your individuality with God. The more you manifest this presence, the more you begin to manifest the presence of God within your personal activities.

There are many methods by which the soul reveals itself to you, for you are the soul. And the more you integrate that phenomenon into your own nature, the closer you move to fully remembering who you are. And indeed, you are gods.

The soul actually knits itself within the mother's womb; the needles which it chooses to knit the framework and the tapestry of the physical body are your parents.

The soul is the conscious entity that makes you uniquely a human being. Upon birth, and the first drawing in of the breath, the soul's consciousness begins to be conditioned, and the conscious mind and conscious identity are formed. As the will becomes fixated upon the world, the infant, a fully conscious being, simulates and adapts the framework of mind to the reference points of the lessons that are to be learned. Slowly but surely, the veil of forgetfulness is drawn so that the soul may have total focus in the earth plane.

Exploring the phenomenon of the soul is synonymous with exploring your own nature. The soul is that portion of you which is indelibly at one with God, never changing, always constant. It is the idea that there is a constant in the way of things—not rigid, not fixed, always moving, yet always at rest. It is the alpha, it is the omega; it is the divine that is within, ever-flowing and ever-moving. The all that is nothing and the nothing that is all.

Not only is the soul one with God, you *are* the soul, and the soul is one with all things. In this vastness and oneness that is God, that is the soul, so in turn are you contained. Ultimately, it is the creation of your own reality, for there is nothing that is outside of God. And therefore there is nothing outside the phenomena of your personal reality. For ultimately you would extend yourself and become as the soul.

The soul is immortal and can never be "lost," though it may at times wander from its true path or purpose in this plane. But no soul is ever lost or perishes; perhaps it dwells for a time in darkness until it comes home into the light.

Tom MacPherson

Originally, you were all born in the spirit and had a common origin. You are all just as old as one another. New souls are created only according to their relative experience in different portions of the universe. You are the children of light because you came from light. There was basically a wave of you that got caught in the bog of the earth plane, so to say, and were drawn into various physical forms; and then there was a new wave of angels who came in, planning a rescue that was about as effective as your flight over Tehran a few years ago. They were sucked down into this plane through actual intercourse with your ancestors. They materialized physical forms, made a bit of whoopee, and got stuck in the emotional barriers. However, there were archangels watching the whole show, and, having an understanding of these activities, they didn't have the capacity to fall. You are the children of light because you have an awareness of these things and can draw other moths to the flame—not so they will get burned, but so they can see themselves in that same position that you are attempting to hold and maintain. You are trying to light other candles.

New souls are those wonderfully happy little beasties that appear to see and hear no evil. They are your perpetual optimists. It is usually such a person of whom it is said, "That bloody fool stands on the corner singing merrily, no matter what misery crosses his path."

As to the phenomenon of "walk-ins," we have a slightly different view as to what that might be. One theory is that you have a soul up here who incarnates as a certain individual, travels along, something traumatic happens—such as a buggy wreck or something—that person leaves his body, comes over here, and makes a deal with another soul to take over his body. The original soul gets off scot-free, while the second soul gets a body to do some great work. That is how many define a walk-in. We disagree with this model. In our terms, what occurs is that a soul will incarnate, travel along, and then experience something traumatic. He leaves his body for a while and perhaps encounters some master soul, or perhaps his own soul on an expanded level. That master soul says, "You better bloody well get back down there because your work isn't done." And I can assure you that after a tongue lashing from Moses, Jesus, or Buddha, or even your own oversoul, you are no longer the same person you were before. And after your near-death experience, people will swear up and down you are not the same person you were before and will assume you are someone else.

So, with "walk-ins," it is not that one soul incarnates and another disincarnates, it is that the soul is so completely transformed, and the personality functions are so radically altered that the soul's karma no longer applies to its original intent and purpose and it takes on higher karmic purpose and depth, almost to the point of a complete soul identity incarnating in the physical form. So, it is not one soul coming in and one soul exiting, it is the complete transformation of the personality, so it is no longer accurate to describe it as the same being.

It is extremely rare that two souls would occupy the same body in a single lifetime, if it occurs at all. With a few Tibetan lamas and a few mystics perhaps, but it is usually only that the party is temporarily communicating through that soul's own psychic force, the same way I temporarily communicate through this instrument. The instrument is always here, but there is usually only one soul to each body.

Soul mates are not persons whom you meet and marry and have children with; they are beings with whom you were co-created to keep you from becoming egocentric, because your creation was dependent only on yourself, you could become too egocentric. But then, by having a soul mate with whom you are a co-creator, this is a reminder of your commitment to other beings in the universe. Identical twins are usually soul mates.

So, a soul mate is not someone you incarnate with to make whoopee. It doesn't work that way at all. A soul mate is someone who was created for you by God, back when souls were originally being made. God was a bit lonely, you might say, so he sort of rippled himself, made a bit of movement, and created souls. And not to make the same mistake with the children, lest they be lonely also, he created soul mates. He created them two by two, in positive and negative polarity, or the duality you work with on this plane.

Although you have only one soul mate, you have many twin souls. These are souls with whom you have had many incarnations. For instance, you both like to play tennis, you are both left-handed, you both hate spiders, and you both like French restaurants. This is because you lived together in the court of Louis XVI, and both of you studied under Leonardo da Vinci, who was left-handed. Usually when you fall in love with someone like that it is because your cycles of lifetimes are identical. You were both feeling the influence of your Louis XVI lifetime when you met in a French restaurant. But a year later or so, your mate may go into his Leonardo da Vinci lifetime, while you are still in your Louis XVI cycle.

Soul mates are beings with whom you were created many billions of years ago. They are not people you were predestined to meet and with whom you fall romantically in love. If anything, soul mates are simultaneously incarnate only in the case of identical twins or in great historical acts, such as Anwar Sadat and Moshe Dayan, who were soul mates. However, there are twin souls, souls with whom you have had many incarnations and share much common karma and service. Those are persons with whom you are highly compatible and whom you may meet and marry—and if you wish to romantically call them your "cute little soul mate," you can use it as a term of endearment.

The reason you are experiencing a bit of a baby boom recently is that there is such a broad amount of experience available on the plane these days. For instance, in the days of Atlantis, all you had was a homogeneous, advanced culture. Nowadays, you have an advanced culture—scientifically speaking, that is—as well as persons still living in your so-called Stone Age, although probably more spiritually advanced than your own society. So, there is a broad variety.

It is sort of like the planet is a bit of a lively pub nowadays that souls wish to come in and experience.

Atun-Re

Ah, Atun-Re would come to speak to you. You ask how we would define an "old soul"? We say, in humor, that an old soul is but a slow learner. The designation of an old soul is strictly relative to the experience of the soul in a particular plane of existence where you perceive time and space. The very word *old* itself implies the concept of time and lengthy experience. So therefore, a soul that began to have experience upon your earth plane perhaps five hundred thousand years past and continues in cycles of reincarnation would be an old soul upon this plane, with many lifetimes of experience. A soul beyond the sector and experience of this particular plane that would come in within your last few centuries would be a new soul to this plane, creating a new reality. But all those souls were created simultaneously, many billions of your years past. So your five hundred thousand years becomes but a drop in the ocean of the total experience of the soul.

To understand soul mates, you must understand yourself strictly as a spirit. First, you were created by God and you were created in God's image. God is a spirit, so therefore you were created as a soul. God did not wish souls to be alone, but neither did he wish them to become too heady. Therefore, he created them in perfect polarities of male and female; and those polarities could be reversed, of female and male. So therefore, the souls are androgynous and yet they have mates. For in order to create their reality, they were to be in a continuous oscillation, so that they could then have movement. This was not to bind them or chain them, it was to give them perfect individuality within all the dimensions of perfect sensitivity and at-onement. So they were individual, yet it took two to create, two to make a single witness of the reality they observed.

So that is your true soul mate, one with whom you are a co-creator of universal forces. Occasionally, you may meet your soul mate on the earth plane, but this is usually in the form of identical twins. It is very rare that soul mates meet and marry. But you have many soul twins. These are souls with whom you have common experience in many incarnations and are usually members of your soul group. So therefore, they become your soul twin, with whom you are highly compatible and you may marry. Soul twins have shared so many incarnations, so much similar service, and so many similar actions—or identical karma—that they are your twins relative to your spiritual growth.

The soul mate is a consciousness with whom you were created long before the birth of the gods, when there was only one great God, one great spirit. For you were created as soul mates so you would always have another consciousness to bear witness to your reality, so you would not be alone, and so you would not have too much ego and would always be one with the divine.

Spirit Guides and Teachers

John

Each of you has a specific band or spectrum of spirit guides and teachers who are with you. Fluctuations in your states of spiritual growth determine which entities you attract. There are guides and teachers who seek to bring you laughter and joy. They usually appear as children, or as those who are gentle and sentimental.

There are those who desire to impart wisdom. Perhaps since childhood you have held certain images of how a person of wisdom would look. Often, this is not so much your imagination, but a literal communication from a particular spirit guide or teacher.

There are guides and teachers who give you wisdom and philosophical direction, those who give you guidance in mundane and practical affairs, and those who guide you in specific areas of study. Your various spirit guides and teachers are with you to bring you comfort, joy, and wisdom, but above all else, to familiarize you with the sense of yourself as a spirit, which you truly are. For it is from the levels of the soul that your final learnings come. You begin to understand yourself as a portion of God, active in his wisdom, and that you, too, are a soul, you, too, are a spirit. In this way shall you gain greater understanding and clarity, for your final witness must always be within the self.

Your spirit guides and teachers are usually of a higher vibration or higher consciousness and dispense understanding of both a spiritual and philosophical nature while you are in the earth plane. All of you are souls who have been in experience since the foundations of the world, and all of you are sons and daughters of God. It is in this right that God's messengers minister unto you and try to guide you back to your truer nature.

The purpose of spirit guides and teachers is to provide guidance in specific areas of thought. It is not that the spirit entities who work with you in these realms are earthbound, but rather that, since there is no progression in this plane of existence without a physical body, they desire to fulfill karmic patterns through empathy with you, because you have a physical body.

The physical body is your temple, and each of you is as a spirit. The guidance that your guides and teachers give unto you is to bring forth understanding of yourselves as a spirit, as they dwell in those realms already. And as you are lifted up, so in turn are they. In this way there is progression for all.

The phenomenon that you call "spirit communication" is little more than a dialogue with entities identical to yourself. As you progress, so in turn do the spirit guides and teachers about you progress. Above all else, you promote one another's well-being.

They are usually members of your soul group, but in the discarnate state.

Spirit guides and teachers are not infallible in the information they give. Advice from them should be taken as just that—advice or counseling from one who perhaps has a broader spectrum of life experience.

Prognostication from such entities should be tempered with free will. That is, any prognostication can be altered, so advice that is given to you is to be taken as inspirational and directional, with the understanding that you may alter it with your own free will. This is not to undermine your confidence in prognostications, it is so that you would know yourself to be as spirit also. The final decisions all lie with the individual in the affairs of the spirit.

Individuals always have the ability of free will and can alter any predictions made for them. We encourage you to scrutinize all information received from any channeled source to know that you make the final decisions in all of your life affairs.

Rapport that you possess with a guide or teacher is based upon a familiarity, a knowingness, and a bond that needs no explanation. It is an intuitive condition. So in turn is the bond with your guides and teachers. For, in expressing your humanity, both of you expand the wings of the intellect to where it becomes as clothed in the atmospheres of the spirit, and both of you soar in such a rapport.

The relationship between yourselves and your spirit guides and teachers is best described as friendship, or a bond between individuals. Perhaps you knew them in lives past, or when you were discarnate and they incarnate, for there have been lifetimes when you have been discarnate and have given guidance from the other side through the trance state. That is, you have been spirit guides in your own past lives. In this way, the relationship parallels your relationships upon this plane. If you permit individuals of a derogatory nature on your own plane of existence to guide you, so too will you attract such entities from beyond your plane.

Can you be influenced in a negative way by your guides and teachers? Only if your own consciousness permits it. That which you term "negativity" is but ignorance. So therefore, even as you may receive negative counsel from one who is incarnate, but it is your free will which must activate it, so in turn is it with any guidance you would receive from those of an ignorant nature upon the ethereal planes.

An unillumined personality structure seeking to give guidance may attune only with those levels of consciousness that you permit. So, you would first begin to manifest such a pattern in your own personality, and they would but take it as opportunity to affirm that negativity which already lies within you. The responsibility of the creation is your own, either for your upliftment or for your obsession in the areas in which you are as yet unillumined.

You ask, "Can we trust that our guides and teachers are good and not evil?" First, there is neither good nor evil, there is only wisdom and ignorance. Just as there are individuals among you who you feel are not physically or mentally developed, or those you would term as retarded in their ability to learn, and yet you do not fear them, among the realms of discarnate beings there are similar personalities or souls which still manifest a lack of development. These are not so much evil as ignorant.

The relationship between yourselves and the spirit guides and teachers you attract is one of free will. There is no such thing as "possession." Possession is but obsession with a particular level of thought. You can attract nothing higher or lower than that which you already are, in your own consciousness. So therefore, the relationship is that of free will.

So, it is not a matter of good or evil, it is moreso a matter of enlightenment and darkness, or enlightenment and ignorance. Since you can attract nothing that is higher or lower than that which you already are, any information you receive should motivate you to examine the level upon which you perceive yourself. If the information is what you would term "lower level," this should inspire examination of self so as to accept or reject that information.

To gain knowledge of a guide or teacher, isolate those areas of past-life knowledge you may already possess. These may come through talents, repeated or specialized cycles in your life pattern, and attractions to individuals of different ethnic, national, and cultural backgrounds and varying time periods. Meditate upon those locations and time periods. Construct them in the mind's eye before falling into the state of slumber. In doing this, you not only increase your chances of establishing communication, but you deepen your rapport with such communication as well.

Seek to learn the name of your spirit guide or teacher, as this will give you various clues to the cultural background of that particular entity. Once the name has been given, seek to develop a point of contact with that guide or teacher, perhaps in the form of a symbol. Often omens or "touch-ins" are given forth from a guide or teacher in your daily affairs.

Some individuals contact their spirit guides and teachers through automatic writing. This is where you set aside or relax your own consciousness and allow a message to flow forth from your pen, upon papyrus. The message is often not in your own script, but bears the ledger of the guide or teacher whom you contact. This is one of the simpler forms of contact to develop and can be accomplished in the following way: Meditate briefly upon the name you have obtained from meditation or from another source. Allow the hand to flow freely upon papyrus. Then, seek to receive the formulation of various word structures within the mind, writing them down. The flow of words usually comes quickly. Guidance may be clearly given through this particular tool.

The predominant sources of communication are through meditation and the dream state. By keeping a dream journal, you may gain higher access to those beings who give you guidance. By meditating, which is merely the alignment of mind, body, and spirit in contemplation, you may deepen that rapport.

The various disciples of the man Jesus used psychic faculties and spoke in what was known as "the tongue of angels," or "in tongues." This was various spirit guides and teachers speaking through them, for they spoke the tongues of many languages and cultural backgrounds. "Mediumship" is but a term for the focusing of spirit through the individual, above and beyond the range of his or her own conscious faculties. Each of you has this faculty already within, and your meditations shall bring it nearer to you. It is your spirit guides and teachers who communicate with you and have dialogue. But remember, pray only unto God. Acknowledge the Father who is in heaven so that he may send a messenger unto you. And if you perceive God as love, this is the master you will serve.

Meditation is the cornerstone to any form of contact or dialogue with spirit guides and teachers. Meditation is but taking time to be with yourself and God, to think or express in prayer that which you desire to be answered. I would say to pray only unto God, and he may send unto you a messenger as one of your spirit guides or teachers. You may have dialogue with your guides and teachers, but never pray to them, for there is only one God, one spirit, and one revelation. Guides or teachers shall reveal to you, within your own time, the learning that is necessary for you. If you are intuitive, there need not even be contact upon the mental or personal level with guides and teachers. Many bypass teachers with personality structures and go on to the order of the angels.

Angels are different from guides and teachers. Angels are beings who have never incarnated and still dwell in states of perfection. In contrast, spirit guides and teachers appear to you with personalities from lives past to give you a focus of identity, so that you, being incarnate, may express to them and may learn from their philosophy, insight, and the context of their cultural understanding. For they desire to project understanding of an empathic nature.

Pray to God for a revelation concerning a particular aspect of spiritual growth, or perhaps the need for enhancement in the personality to bring about peace within the self. Pray directly to God. God has many names but only one spirit. God is love. So thus, pray in love and this is what you shall receive. Do not pray for the revelation of a spirit guide or teacher, pray for the revelation of God, perhaps *through* a guide or teacher. In this way God shall reveal the chosen one. It may be a guide or teacher, or perhaps even one of the angelic order. It is up to the vibration of the individual, and in accord with free will and God's own time, that these things are revealed in your meditations and you are receptive to them.

The channel speaking dwells upon certain levels of light which are moreso illumination—not so much thought or mind, but illumination and attunement with various forces, seeking to give forth crystallization of various forms of light. For a crystal is perhaps the perfect prism through which light may pass for illumination. It would be as an individual who has lit many candles and meditated upon them with eyes open. Then, turning away, he could still hold the pattern of those many candles within his visualization, and he would then reside in a deep sleep and have naught but dreams of the candles; and each illumination would have a specific meaning for him while in that state of sleep.

The source of knowledge of the channel speaking is said to be expressed from the God within. For you are not incarnate in the physical body, you are incarnate in the human condition. Embodiment, mind, and spirit are just the human condition. The channel speaking's very words are but an expression of a vocabulary that is the human personality. The channel speaking seeks to be of the presence of the divine and may comment intelligently upon many things by coming from that pure knowingness.

From you who are incarnate, we who dwell outside of physical time and space learn such things as caring, love, and patience. Each individual learns from the others, for indeed, you do not inhabit the physical body, you inhabit the human personality, which is the by-product of the sojourn of both the spirit and the soul through the material planes.

To facilitate communication with the spirit realms, first you must remember the many dialogues you have with us already, through dreams. Indeed, there are no steps you must take, you must simply remember. Who among you has not lost an object and then, upon relaxing your mind, remembered where that lost object was placed? Your meditations and dreams come when you relax the physical body and allow the mind to explore the full perimeters of itself—mind, body, and spirit. Simply remember your dreams. Meditate deeply and then remember. Draw in even breaths. Relax the body and allow the mind to remember. If the memory process works to recall the lost object or the lost event in childhood that shapes your adult personality, it can recall your former selves and all of your future potentials, and inspire you. For ultimately, all that has value is that which inspires you.

Meditate and remember your original nature, that which makes you human. Your original nature is that you are children of light, children of God, being neither male nor female and transcending all. Meditate and remember that all things come from God, and all things return to God. Simply remember. Your dialogues with those upon the spirit planes transpire at all times. We speak with you in the most edifying of manners and yet you do not recall these things because of your conditioning in this world. Be in the world but not of it. Simply remember.

The ability to interface with spirit beings or any other form is but an aspect of recalling your own nature, and as you become more aware of your own deeper resources of consciousness, so in turn will you carry on deeper dialogues with levels of spirit. There is ultimately only one spirit, and that is the spirit you call God. It is from that level that you manifest your highest nature, although you learn of that nature perhaps through dialogue with other spirit presences. The more you come into that presence, the more easily you flow in the language and tongue of angels, in the language and tongue of spirits, in the language and tongue of saints. So therefore, it is but as a sojourn within yourself.

Above all else, the dialogues you carry on with the channel speaking or any other incarnate spirit have value only if you love each other. Your dreams, your meditations—these are your recall. Simply remember. This is all you must do. Meditate, draw on your breath, relax, and expand the mental dimensions. For mind has only one gift—to remember. When you merge the mind, the body, and the spirit, you remember the divine, from which you come and to which you return.

Tom MacPherson

Spirit guides try to inspire you to see a particular perspective. It is not that we lay out dictates for you, but that we try to give you insights into what your life is all about, which is that you are primarily a spirit. Teachers try to teach you that, guides try to guide you to that. Guides usually deal with emotions, while teachers usually deal with your ethics. Ultimately, your best source of guidance is your own inner divine.

If you are emotionally upset, a guide takes priority. If you are going through a career decision, a teacher takes priority. If you are emotionally upset and it is blocking your career, the guide takes precedence. But it is strictly relative to the experience of the individual. Guides and teachers are equally important. Both contribute to your spiritual development.

How many guides and teachers do you have? You don't have the Light Brigade or anything to that effect working with you. We usually suggest you attempt no more than three direct levels of communication. Otherwise it becomes a bit like too many chefs spoiling the broth—and when you're the broth, that's something to be concerned about. There are usually half a dozen guides who work with you—it's relative to each individual. I would say to study the most pertinent issues currently with you, those which are the most urgent and topical, and there is probably a guide who coordinates with those needs.

Generally, your guides and teachers attempt to give you insights rather than a general pattern or blueprint. The communication is usually through a series of synchronicities. Your own consciousness has an outreach of several days, weeks, and months in advance that sets up a series of events that will attract appropriate individuals, or attract you to appropriate locations where you will experience the collective culmination of information and persons that then become significant.

The best method for contacting your guides and teachers is meditation. Merely learn to put yourself into a light meditative state and be open to the communication. Relatively quickly an omen or a sign may come through. One of my favorites is to work with your Shamrock dairy trucks. It is very easy to arrange for a dairy truck to go by the restaurant you're sitting in just when you're wondering where your next meal may be coming from. The Shamrock truck goes roaring by and that's a quick assurance; it's Tom MacPherson communicating, "Don't panic—something's being worked out."

The only thing to fear when you try to contact a spirit guide or teacher is yourself, because you attract to yourself only what lies in the sphere of your own consciousness. And if, upon occasion, the so-called boogeyman comes along, perhaps it is only because of your own inner light. They may wish to learn something, receive a blessing, and then go on to a higher order. The only thing to be concerned about, really, is ignorance and fear, which are synonymous with superstition.

I would describe existing in the realms of spirit more like a state of knowingness. It's a very secure state. It's also a very objective state. You don't have fears or issues of mortality or stress. You do have feelings. Occasionally you even slip into a bit of emotionalism—more like frustration. It's a very human state actually, without its higher optimums.

It's not at all strange not to have a body. We have a tremendous sense of focus here. We can experience things just as spatially as you. We're not just floating around.

As I perceive this room, for instance, it has the appearance of a friendly old English pub. The gentlemen are sitting about in clothing appropriate to their consciousness as they would have been in that day. Some of the ladies are sitting about in shamefully low-cut dresses appropriate to whatever daring level of consciousness they had achieved in that day. Other ladies are sitting around buttoned up tighter than a drum. Your attire and appearance is adjusted so I don't suffer a culture shock in speaking with you. Your lamps are replaced with candles and copper-backed reflectors; fluids and beverages that did not exist in my day adapt to being ale. This perceptual reality assists me in my communication so I can work with you logistically.

There is another level that I can adjust to rather quickly, where the lot of you are little more than illumination, pure light. Depending on how far into the planes I go, eventually it all becomes white light, with perceptions of movement and greater and lesser luminosity, where all things are accessed instantaneously—rather like when you spin a color wheel with all the colors and it eventually goes to white. It is light, pure illumination, passing through various tunnels and corridors, but all in states of illumination. Strictly light. Close your eyes once and look toward an illumination and you get a slight perception of what it's like. Look away from the light and it will get darker. Look toward it, you'll see more. Press on the surface of your eyes and you'll see sparkles. It's very similar to that.

I often joke that, as a good Irishman, I haven't incarnated over the last four hundred years or so because with the British empire all over the planet, I couldn't find a decent place to come in. But I will incarnate probably in the next fifty to seventy-five years, because at that time your society will be more advanced spiritually and technologically. Most of my karma was picked up in Atlantis, and the correct social and cultural context would be there about that time.

I've chosen not to incarnate because the instrument [Kevin] is doing the work for me and I'm frightfully lazy! If I were to incarnate, I might have to become a trance channel, only to discover the same things the instrument is revealing to you this evening that I was able to place in his path so effortlessly. But actually, it is not quite my time to incarnate, and since we don't just take a number and wait four hundred years, I wish to be active and dialogue with you, as we are all just human beings and can share a common dialogue with one another.

I have personally progressed in my exposure to all of you by gaining an update of the current cultural circumstances. In fact, some of my own growth is reflected in the degree to which your society has managed to let go of some of its prejudices. It is only small parts of your society that still hold on to these various prejudices, and only lazy segments that don't let go altogether. I'd say that, overall, I've cleaned up my personality mostly through the dropping of prejudices. (Though it may be hard to believe, if you wish to know the truth, I've also dropped my prejudice against the British. I keep it on tap only as a matter of national pride and for an occasional good twist of humor.)

When I'm not busy channeling, I just sit around singing songs and telling jokes about the English. No, just kidding again. I have quite a social agenda and am quite popular nowadays, thanks to Ms. MacLaine's work. I go bopping about the planes trying to give insights where I may—not unlike the way you do down here. There have been times when some of you were on the other side, in my position, giving guidance. In other words, there were times when you were rattling chains and rapping on walls trying to get attention.

And as to whether I meditate—I raise a tankard of ale or two, yes. Most definitely, I meditate. Meditation is merely contemplation of your own higher nature. I don't have a body, so I don't meditate the same way you do, but I contemplate and access higher levels of myself, which is what meditation really is.

As well as I would say that I, too, most definitely have guides and teachers. John acts as a guide to me. It's an escalating system of things, but there's no hierarchy.

We are often asked if guides and teachers communicate with one another when we're not in physical form. Absolutely. We get together for our little parties. They can be just as exciting or just as boring as the ones you hold down here. We communicate, but it's more like light or sensitivity. We sense one another more than dialogue.

Occasionally we hear a person mumble from the audience, "By God, I don't really believe in spirits." Well, we assure you that over here it's quite as difficult for us to believe in you upon occasion. But we are over here and we are here to help you, however you like. And if you don't feel you need help, that's quite all right. It's up to your free will, whatever you want to do with it.

So there's really no mystery. We're over here. We have personalities. We don't spy on you or peek in your shower or anything. And if you grow bored with us, you can just shut us off. In fact, believe it or not, it's a lot easier for you to tune us out than it is for us to tune you out. So pity poor us!

If you wish to become a channel yourself, the best thing to do would be to isolate a single guide and develop a rapport with him—learn his name, his physical appearance, and the area he gives you guidance in. Then attempt to set up a meeting with him in a meditation, perhaps just before falling into slumber, and keep track of your dream state.

Spirit guides and teachers do not enter your body, they merely "overshadow" you. How I function through this instrument is I can wiggle fingers and thumb my nose at the British—whatever I care to do—by simply telepathically communicating information to his body. But I assure you, the young man is still in control.

Now, are you willing to dedicate as much as one-third of your life to this work? Good for you, because you are already doing so when you sleep at night. Sleep is a sensitive state where you can receive visits from your guides and teachers. Eventually, as you continue to meditate and isolate which particular entities you work with, perhaps through writing, and you've become familiar with your guides, their words will sometimes pop into the flow of your own dialogue, though not without your permission. Eventually you will deepen your meditation to where they can speak through completely.

The Inner Teacher

John
_____

The true student, the true initiate, also becomes a teacher unto others, for the continuous dialogue and expression is just that—teacher to teacher. It is by calming the self in mind, body, and spirit, through the process of meditation, that you would hear another, that you would hear, with a deeper sense, words that are given unto you, and allow yourself to be taught. Then, the one who has poured himself out unto you readies himself to become again the student, that he may go on to a higher expression. And ultimately this is but for the rediscovery of the point of the focus which indeed dwells within the self, which is God.

The ultimate expression is the dialogue with self, for ultimately you exist in order to allow God to quicken your intellect and shape your activities. This comes forth not from any words stored in volumes—for words are poor conveyors of that which the spirit seeks to reveal—but that you would come to full knowledge of yourself through your personal expression and your personal experience. When you keep the higher law you are liberated, for then you are no longer *under* the law, but become *as* the law, and that law is love.

The impersonal aspect of self, which is God, never judges. It is always present, seeking to draw each of you up to the higher dimension of self. It is in that higher dimension of self that you ultimately express that perfection in this plane. It is actualizing yourself above and beyond the dimensions of the plane, to where you become the whole being, the whole expression. In this there is joy. For even as you look upon past behaviors that were originally embarrassing and you later see those behaviors in a wiser, older light and draw mirth from them, so in turn is it with the soul's present, of continuous joy, when you see things from that level. Everything is continuously new, but at the same time older than time and space, which do not exist.

Study the expressions of those who give forth love abundantly, for the environment around them becomes transformed. Those who study alchemy know that, ultimately, the work is not the transmutation of elements, but the transmutation of self, and that the "philosopher's stone" is the consciousness they achieve, since it is through consciousness that all things become transformed.

It is said: "I am the alpha, I am the omega. I appear only to disappear. I am love, which is and gives the illusion of the creation of the void. I am that which is omnipresent. I am that which is nothing. I am light. I am the void. I hold the keys to heaven and the keys to the abyss. I am the alpha. I am the omega. I am that I am. Be still and know that I am God. Be still and know that I am. Be still. Be."

This is the voice of the inner teacher. This is the mighty double-edged sword of truth, which cuts both ways. This is the inner thinking. This is the dimension of yourself that is one with God in the presence that will never forsake you. This is that which is welled up in all persons and collectively dwells in the midst of all peoples, drawing you permanently into enlightenment. This is the awareness that seeks acknowledgment that the illumination is within. This is the inner teacher, the inner master, which is love, and which binds you and makes you all one.

Tom MacPherson

All information is assimilated through various personal models. Gurus, for example, claim they can show the personal experience of God. They do this from one of two positions—they are either sneaky devils who just want a big following, or they are legitimately of that experience and take it upon themselves to suffer public harassment, as well as the dividends of a great deal of affection from their various followers.

Guru simply means "teacher." But everyone is a teacher. You may come to God realization by the look in the eye of the sweet little old lady down the street. She is a teacher. She is a guru. She is showing you an experience of God. The little old lady is just a freelancer, while the others advertise. In my view, a professional is just someone who makes a living at it. It doesn't mean they're better than anyone else.

Atun-Re

Each of you is a portal. You are a window upon the Akasha, the all-knowing. Collectively, you are the consciousness of this planet and you are portals through which light streams forth and illumines this plane. You are the eyes and the ears and the manifestation of God upon this plane. You are the perceivers. You are the teachers. For it is your interactions with one another that convince you that you exist.

But how foolish of you not to know this, so therefore you are also students. Teachers and students—all in one convenient package— meeting in the temple. You do not have to travel to Egypt, to the pyramids. That is simply an enhancer of what is already contained within you. The Pyramid contains everything that man knows, everything that woman knows, all the wisdom of the ages. And yet, how old are you? Before the pyramids you were. Here, in this temple, in your own physical body, do you meet your inner master.

Your personality is the student, and the Christ is where you meet your teacher within the temple, where you take your mind and calm it. You must go within the temple, within those innermost chambers, and meet the holy of holies, the higher self. For the higher self continuously animates your physical being. It fills your temple with light, and then, when you come back from those states, you seek to remember that which you already are—that is, light.

That which was known as "the Brotherhood" was a bunch of old fools who thought they understood things that were worthy of preservation. So, they invented something called "writing" to produce a bunch of foolish books and pass them on to other generations, who probably sat about trying to convince themselves of their own importance. But in the meantime, these books provide a marvelous service of continuing to inspire individuals and remind them that they are part of a greater whole, rather than just the limitations of those schools.

The ultimate value each school provided was that the person would eventually get bored with the school and then move beyond it, or at least suspect that there must be something that lies beyond these old doddering idiots, talking amongst themselves about this and that. And yet I also speak in jest. Because, of course, the schools are fellowships. They enable individuals to share with one another and to preserve a certain level of manifestation of that which was understood as God. But eventually, each school must drop its perimeters and merge with other schools. This is a continuous process of actualization, as school means simply "perimeter of knowledge."

So whatever school you find yourself studying within, realize that the true goal is not so much to learn everything that the school contains, but to reach to the ultimate act, which is the dropping of those perimeters to merge with the whole. The principle of letting go of the identity is what you learn from any school of thought.

Acknowledging the collective consciousness helps you acknowledge that you are more than just yourself. So, you attach yourself to a school of thought and take upon yourself the identity of that school. You say, "Now I am with like-minded persons, so therefore I am better received. I've expanded my area of influence." But ultimately, you must take upon yourself the identity of God, which will take you above and beyond all schools of thought.

The Masters

John

Masters are simply those who teach and express their understanding of their relationship with the universal whole. As each of you becomes a teacher, you begin to express the mastery that is within you, and life itself becomes the expression for all forms of teaching and association with one another. So, you are master teachers when you express to one another that which you feel in kinship with God. Ultimately there is but one expression, and that is the spiritual dimension that is within each of you.

It has been said that anything which is worth learning comes directly from experience, and all that is not worth learning is stored in books. We would say that contained in the pages of books are two-dimensional images, and from those flat surfaces, thoughts become stimulated. Thoughts then become activators which draw the experience of the individual from the ethers and unto the self. You are then drawn up, for you become aligned with all the dimensions of yourself in mind, body, and spirit, and even unto the Godhead itself.

It is in life, the great activator, the great principle, that you find true mastery. Those who would become masters of life should not so much seek to exercise control over others, for that rapidly fades, and it is foolish to sit upon a throne which eventually, in your wisdom, you would abdicate; instead, you must realize that he who seeks to conquer the world must first conquer himself, for each experience comes from the self.

Masters work through the spirit or by lifting you up to that level of existence. They often visit you in your most fitful moments of emotional experience, or when you are close to fatigue because your emotions are pulling you to the earth. Drawing upon that experience, a master may then reconstruct an aspect of your personality by transforming your emotions. For the personality is woven from the tapestry of your emotions, which are those unrealized dimensions of self in this plane from past experiences that you seek to uplift and eventually transform through the Christ principle.

As you seek to understand the concept of masters, always seek that which is deep within, for the true master is within the self. You will find this pattern in other masters, in Jesus, Buddha, Krishna, Mohammed, and all the others who have ascended to higher levels of consciousness in their service to reveal God upon this plane. For originally you were souls, created in the divine and in perfection, and, as souls, you range from the heavenly host to the various masters in your own right.

The master within the self is the Christ, and the Christ is the merger of the mind, body, and spirit in service to God. In this you become as revelations to one another, you become as teachers to one another, you become as inspirations to one another. For mastery is your own revelations that you share with one another. And as you join and become one in your spirit, then in turn you become strengthened.

This is more than a philosophy—it is that you would become the causal force upon this plane. It is more than a thought, it is that you are the causal force in the creation upon this plane. It is more than an activity of meditation, it is that you become the causal force upon this plane—the causal force, the creator, from which all reality extends forth, that you would live life as a master.

Life is the tapestry that you weave between one another, each of you working upon the loom of creation. And life is your interactivity with one another as you continue to create and have greater knowledge of these activities upon this plane. When you look to the masters, look to the weavers of fate, whom you are. When you look to the masters, look to those who are the causal force upon this plane. Look within. But also, look upon the eyes of the individual who sits next to you, for the eyes are the mirror of the soul, and in this you would find reflected the nature of God. If, within, you see love for your brother and your sister, herein you find the whole, that with which you would merge and become one. For herein you would find the gathering of the masters, within self and in your expression to one another.

All are equal in God's eyes, for God is no respecter of persons, of either master or student. Even as you do unto the lesser, so is it done unto the Father/Mother God, who is the Revelator, who gave all of you birth in the unique expression of the divine that you must kindle and let burn brightly so it is a revelation unto all.

Tom MacPherson

Each master is a mandala to be meditated upon to reveal some inner aspect of your own self. If you were to arrange all the masters in their hierarchical form, you would find a mandala quite similar to the mandala that represents the sound of the OM.

Each master is a process of self-actualization. It is rather like you create a mandala with precious stones, and each master would be represented by a precious jewel, with God being at the top of the heap. Depending on your own consciousness, you can take quantum leaps in your own schooling. It's merely something you can choose to measure yourself against, or choose not to.

Atun-Re

So, the children wish to learn things from masters. Indeed, it is the wise master or teacher who always seeks to guide you toward your own inner light, otherwise you are led upon the path of deception. But you must be careful not to deceive yourselves as well, for the light that comes from within you is a gift, a gift from God.

Is this not called "An Evening of Masters"? Haven't the children come to learn about mastery? Well, we have tricked you then, because *you* are the masters who are gathered here. For it is an evening of masters even without this old one's presence, isn't it? You see, it is *you* who create this evening, it is *you* who learn from one another, for without you there would be no focus, there would be no counsel, there would be no old Atun-Re. You give one another permission to live, and it is because you are giving that permission that each of you is a master. So, a master comes that you may have life and live it abundantly, and that is what each of you do when you observe one another. You convince one another that you are here. Ultimately, when you leave this room, you would have no way to prove that it happened. So therefore, you give one another permission to have life, and to the degree that you are masters, you allow one another to live life abundantly.

To reveal your masters is to say *God,* and to say to you that your master is and must be *love.* For I cannot perform a disservice to you by giving you any less than that, and to demand of you that you serve that master only, because that demand arises from the needs of this old one also—to serve that master. But the servant, as John would say, is also worthy of his hire, so you would also receive that love, but only by pouring yourselves out. For the value of the vessel, if you wish to contain it, is in its emptiness, so it can be filled again. Clean the vessel, for that is your physical instrument. Pour it out, for that is your mind. Fill it to the brim with waters that nourish, for that is your spirit.

Chapter 2

The Earth Plane

The Temple of the Soul

John

The physical body is a temple in which the soul resides, and is thus its vehicle for experience upon this plane. The mind is the priest that dwells therein and seeks to contemplate the nature of God, and the spirit is the presence that links you with the divine.

You are not encased in the physical body as a place of imprisonment, you are here out of choice, for the purpose of experience and revelation. The physical body is the ability of the soul to have focus in time and space. It is the natural extension of the soul's force in the earth plane and is given to its natural laws and dynamics. You are here to *fulfill* the law, not to be *under* it.

As men and women, you are a portion of spirit, a fine attunement of mind, body, and soul. The merging of mind, body, and soul is what you know as "personality." You are not a limited personality shaped simply by parental or environmental in-

151

fluences; moreso, you are a personality shaped by all the cosmic influences.

For many thousands of years mystics have known of the physical body's true energy patterns, as well as the illuminations which surround the physical body, or the "aura." It is only recently that your sciences have begun to document these things. In part, science is the scribe who documents that which God already knows. Indeed, the physical body has direct linkage with the universe itself, as reflected in the ancient science of astrology.

The physical body is the temple wherein the soul, which is the portion of God within you, has chosen to reside. So therefore, the soul is your linkage with the universe, and the physical body is but an expression of that soul on this plane. The physical body carries within it all the unique patterns of your past lives. It is shaped by the soul to perhaps even institute further physical body patterns through your children for further incarnations of that soul at a later point in time.

The flesh brain is a physical vehicle for storing the mind. It extends itself to other portions of the physical body through the nervous system. Picture the entire physical body as a reasoning faculty or as a physical organ for the expression of the soul. Then picture the patterns of individual thought extending along the body's various meridians. In this way, the soul's thoughts are extended into the physical body and manifest in specific properties within the various organs.

The soul is in a state of perfection, yet the illumination that it may give to this particular plane comes through your physical body and is therefore filtered through your experiences on this plane, which is your karma. Each organ into which the soul's thoughts are extended has a specific function and is reflective of a certain aspect of your personality. As your personality is manifested in the physical body through the filtrations of the soul's karmic patterns, disease is perhaps disharmony from a past life, which is regulated by the life force, which is the soul's thoughts and ponderance upon the physical body in this plane.

It is not so much that each organ bears a form of intelligence, it is moreso that each organ bears a system of consciousness. Even as you have discovered certain electromagnetic fields about the physical body, so in turn does each organ, by its very molecular existence and vibration, give forth specific patterns of energy that may be perceived, studied, measured, and understood. Each of you is already an instrument for these measurements upon the subconscious levels, for each of these patterns activates the natural intelligence which resides in the cranial area.

Intelligence is but the ability to perceive, retain, and apply. It is the intelligence which measures the energy pattern or the consciousness of each specific organ, for consciousness is but a collection of a body of specific information. Consciousness is not so much an intelligence, or a reasoning, or even a state of mind, it is but a collective body of facts that must be activated and applied by intelligence. So therefore, it is the natural intelligence of the level of the soul, or the ability to perceive knowledge and apply it, that gives forth the illusion of intelligence in the physical body. But it is moreso a state of consciousness that is perceived and utilized by the natural intelligence of the mind itself. It is the mind which calculates each of these forms of resonance and therefore gives instruction to either limit, or to allow, its own natural abundance.

Various karmic patterns stored within the physical body have the capacity upon the level of the soul to shape the physical body after the fourth month of conception. Since stored within the genetic structure are also certain karmic patterns, this often determines the shape of the physical body—to act out karmic patterns from past lives. Ultimately, however, the soul shapes the physical body through its reflection of the personality. For the personality and the mind extend deep into the physical body, like the roots of trees extending deep into the earth.

The mind is the pattern of the entire physical body. It is separate from the physical body yet grounded to it physiologically and through the personality. The conscious mind can perhaps be said to be the personality, but not the total substance of mind, which includes the superconscious, conscious, and subconscious mind functioning in attunement with the higher levels of the soul. So, since the soul itself is immortal, the mind has the ability to rejuvenate the body, which is its current vehicle, even to the levels of physical immortality. But immortality is moreso a property of the soul than a direct function of the mind.

The life force is the direct pattern of the soul's expression in the physical body. It travels along the various meridians. When there is blockage within the mind, there is corresponding blockage within the personality, which is the reflective instrument of the soul. So the mind is the builder. It is the architect of the physical body and the architect of your existence. Hence you can truthfully say that, as a man thinketh in his heart, so is he also in all those things which he does.

The life force does not travel by capillary action, but is a completely independent system of energy. It travels through the blood, within the hemoglobin, which is rich in iron, and its very flow generates a mild magnetic field. Also, the electrical properties of the nervous system, particularly the sympathetic nervous system, generate a similar mild magnetic flow. The life force, which extends forth from the soul, travels along these magnetic flows to various portions of the physical body. Its linkage with the soul is like individual streams of light which flow forth from the sun—the light is not the sun itself; it is but a portion of its energies.

A spirit is a particular focus. When it says, "Ye are as a spirit," it means that you are a point of inspiration on this plane within the spirit of the Father. But as a soul, you gain a greater sense of attunement with all levels of thought. The soul gains the breath of life from the spirit of the Father, but its individuality is that which gives it unique life patterns.

The soul knows neither time nor space, so it knows neither good nor evil. But as it experiences the immediacy of the time flow in these dimensions, the soul continuously arranges itself in acts and motivations throughout time and space. As these acts or memories continuously rearrange themselves into dimensions you call the personality, or the conscious mind, they give themselves meaning in the context of known history, but eventually they must become realized within God.

The spirit is the all-encompassing knowledge that is the Father. It is a body of knowledge and substance that all have access to. For this is what a spirit is—a body of information that activates certain points of inspiration within the focus of the mind. Since the Father is universal mind, and you possess mind as a soul, so do you possess the spirit which is the Father. But the soul is your individuality within the all-encompassing spirit.

Men and women were created in spirit since the foundations of the world. You incarnated into the physical plane for experience and revelation. By this we do not mean learning in the ordinary sense, as there is no such thing as learning—there is only revelation. For each of you is a portion of God, a portion of spirit, a portion of universal mind, which knows all things to begin with.

Revelation comes to you by a process of remembrance, for if all things are a portion of the truer self, which is the soul, then they are only forgotten and must be revealed unto you. Just as you may lose a particular object of great price and recover it through remembering, how much moreso would you seek to remember the kingdom that is already your own?

Those faculties which are termed the "higher self," or which you term "psychic," are the various gifts of prophecy—speaking in tongues, divination, clairvoyance, telepathy. All these things are but remembrance from the levels of the soul.

Your various sciences and psychologies study the mind and the various hormones of man in search of the biological personality and the linkage of mind and body within your species. Unfortunately, man rarely goes beyond those regions. He limits his studies to the mind and body, ignoring the influence of the levels of the soul.

It is peculiar that the human race identifies itself so much with the lower primates, that you have drawn all of your evolutionary models and sense of yourselves from rats. Consider the current state of your society and imagine what lessons have been learned. It would be wiser to study the higher primates, the higher mammalian forms, such as dolphins, and you will see intercooperation in a more appropriate environment, a highly fluid environment. For your own true environment is mind, which is as fluid as the ocean itself. It is feeling, as fluid as the ocean itself. Study these aspects of the animal kingdom and you will learn more of self and higher evolutionary patterns to emulate.

Currently, parapsychology has begun to explore the concept of past lives, or reincarnation, which is sometimes considered a key to the soul. But still most of your society continues to cling to ideas of genetic or racial memory which see man as only the physical body, and the personality as conditioned only by the earth plane. Your truer nature is in heaven, and is moreso a state of consciousness. For you are but shadows of the universe, and even as a shadow cannot exist without light and without the physical body, so in turn there is no existence without the mind, the body, and the soul. Your reality is made up of consciousness.

You are not incarnate in the physical body, you are incarnate in the human personality. As long as the ego dominates, as long as the ego clings and you focus upon it rather than spiritualize it, then you have not fully remembered who you are. You must activate the memory of the true source of your nature. That memory must *become* your nature. It is possible to be in the earth plane yet not be of it. It is possible to be physically incarnate in the human condition yet with full knowledge of your truly loving nature. Then you hold it in full sway in heaven and on earth—as above, so below.

Your responsibility on this plane is to so spiritualize the personality, and so integrate it with the levels of the soul, that when the hour of your passing comes, you may actually maintain and inhabit the personality that you have now, that the personality you inhabit be worthy as a garment to encase the soul, perhaps for a sojourn again into another similar pattern.

The soul "wears" a personality as you would a garment. The personality, being such a garment, is eventually shed and goes as a memory unto the level of the soul. It is not so much that you would pass away and lose all identity, for when you perceive yourself as a soul in this plane, you become as one living.

The soul is always in total illumination; it is the personality, which is but a memory, that seems to dwell in confusion. Even as your memory and your mind continuously wander from affairs you desire to be focused upon, so in turn is it with the personality as a whole. For the personality is made up totally of mind, and it is only when it becomes integrated with the levels of the soul that it makes its truer advancements.

Man has often spoken of the soul as the mind of God, for the soul is immortal. It is the very center of man's being, and when it leaves the physical body, the physical body becomes inactive. For it is not that you are biological creatures, dependent only upon the earth plane and its interplay and forces. Moreso, each of you is as a soul, and each of you is as a caretaker of universal forces themselves. In your dream states you project into the astral realms and into the levels of the soul, which lie even beyond the God planes. In this you must understand the physical body as the vehicle of the soul as well as the projection of your energies upon the universal planes.

Your superconscious mind, which is synonymous with the spirit, is the sum total of all your past lives and all your future potentials. It is a vast ocean of cosmic consciousness that all of you are one with. When you incarnate, or when this consciousness focuses itself through the physical body at your birth, then, collectively, the events in this lifetime are the sum total and expression of all of your past lives and all of your future lives transpiring simultaneously.

The same way that all of your childhood events create your adult personality, yet this is not the sum total of your being, so in turn the spirit, which is the sum total of all of your past lives and all of your future potentials on the earth plane, is still not the whole essence, the true self, or the true nature. It is but the soul's sojourn through the physical. For indeed, to move beyond the issues of life and death, you must be children of light. You must express yourselves as children of God. For if you are immortal in your spirit, or if your thought may survive for the briefest moments beyond the realms of the physical body, then indeed, you are a spirit, you are an energy that can neither be created nor destroyed.

To be human is to be of mind, body, and spirit. To be human is not only to err, but to forgive error, because you are spirit, and spirit transcends error. Try not to dwell too much upon the limited versus the infinite, which you are. Even as you have increased your mental resources and have passed through various schools of thought in forming your adult personality, how much moreso when your mind enters into the threshold of the spirit? Even as you have misplaced an object and found it through recall, so in turn, now recall yourselves as part of that infinite sea in an ocean of consciousness. Your actions must be shaped by love. Love is your only ethic.

Understand, then, that the universe itself is the physical body of God. Your own physical body is your capacity to have focus in this plane. The physical body is your temple and all those things which you take into the temple you put upon the altar of God, and even as the universe itself is God's expression, so in turn is your own physical body your expression unto God.

This is not to say that there must be a perfect anatomical form.

Moreso, it is how you utilize it as a teaching expression unto one another. The physical body is not a curse upon you. It is your capacity to have expression in this plane. For without the physical body, there is no progression. In this way, each of you has been given a focus in this plane of your own choosing from the levels of the soul.

Acknowledging the physical body as a vehicle of expression on the earth plane is to cause you to seek to the levels of the soul for your true nature, for each of you is as a soul, and the physical body, again being a focal point, gives you flexibility in this plane. It gives you the ability to be creative in this plane. Above all, it is a temple unto the one living God, of whom you are all sons and daughters.

So do not feel that the physical body is a burden upon you, for no matter what its capacity, it is to bring into focus manifestation of your true nature as God. The physical body that you have been given, no matter what its shape or capacity, is not so much to be an instrument of suffering, it is to give you focus. Each of you must look upon the other, for you are your brother's keeper and your sister's keeper upon this plane.

Each of you has within you true freedom. Extend yourselves unto the regions of the astral, where you would travel into greater understanding. But moreso, serve the love that is in each and every one of you, for the capacity of the soul is the one true master which you must all serve, and that is the love within you.

Love is harmony. Look to the universe and you shall find harmony. It is not a system of chaos. It is a system of harmony. It is the music of the spheres that extends into your planes that the physical body hears and records and perhaps knows not. For although you hear the wind and know not from where it comes, or where it goes, so in turn you know there is but one atmosphere from which you draw the very breath of life. So it is with the spirit. There is only one spirit, one God, one love, one harmony, which gives you life and gives you the only sense of true value and worth, the only sense of true measurement whereby you may measure your sojourn in the earth plane. So, while you are incarnate, the physical body is your expression. It is your temple unto the living God, of which each of you is a part.

Tom MacPherson

The higher self is your collective higher goals achieved in past lives, the same way your subsconscious mind contains your suppressed activities from this lifetime and past lives. When they merge, they become the unique being called you.

As long as you function from the ego, or just your limited physical perspective or sense of yourself, you're not fully acknowledging who you are. When you fully acknowledge yourselves as mind, body, and spirit, you acknowledge your full nature, so therefore transcend and transform who you perceive yourself to be. You thus have better relationships with others. As John points out, love God, and your neighbor as yourself, and you can't break any of the other rules.

The ego is basically your systems of preconditions and prejudices based on mundane experience and a certain unwillingness to go beyond your experience, because you think you have achieved clarity with it. However, the person who is willing to venture beyond and expand his nature eliminates the ego.

This plane came about, with all of you stumbling around down here, because the soul could travel wherever it wanted to. Time is totally irrelevant to the levels of the soul, so everything that's going on down here is just a drop in the bucket. Rather than looking at your entire life as one big stumbling block, remember that to the soul it's merely a drop in the bucket. The soul is in a state of perfection already—you just have the opportunity to prove it down here.

When you have a physical body, things are much more personal. You have the opportunity to demonstrate what is called "personal reality," where the whole experience is more intimate and less relative. And, even when you're in the physical body, you still have access to astral projection, soul projection, near-death experience, and all the other abilities that you call psychic. Psychic means "of the mind and of the soul." So you must not think of being in the body as being limited. It is merely an extra dimension to your growth that we, in the spirit, can only experience if we do it along with you.

The earth plane was created more or less as a body for God to express himself through. The soul that wishes to manifest here must enter into a dense level and then begin the ascent up through the laws of this plane. You're very fortunate to have a body, you know. After all, if you were an angel, or if you were perfect, all you could be is good, better, or best of all. It would be a bit boring. You have a little contrast down here, a bit of variety. And, after all, variety is the spice of life.

Since God helps those who help themselves, you should make positive affirmations on what you would like to accomplish, and then make yourself available to it. Making yourself available means going through all the paces and doing the necessary learning, with the confidence or faith that eventually you will see results. Usually your solutions will come through other individuals, often quite spontaneously and almost mystically. However, it is no mystery. Your telepathic alert attracts the people, and therefore the opportunities, to you. God does not work *for* you; God works *through* you.

You must remember that matter follows thought. In other words, it's the mind that closes the hand, not the hand that closes the mind.

You'll make it through, most definitely. After all, there is a thousand years of brotherhood prophesized. When it speaks of the end of the world, it means the end of the world as *you know it*. Currently, the muddle the world is in, I think it would be a rather wonderful thing to terminate.

Atun-Re

Again, Atun-Re would come and speak to the children. In my speaking with you, I would remind you that all aspects of divinity are natural to your personality, that each of you is a living act of alchemy, which is the merger of spirit to transform your personality so that you can come into a much higher alignment with the personal forces that are already contained within you. The philosopher's stone that was sought so long by the alchemists in Egypt, Atlantis, and Babylon, and amongst the kings in the farthermost reaches of the East and West, is your own consciousness. Yes, my children, the philosopher's stone is your own consciousness. You are masters of control over the body. You can make it walk, you can make it talk—all of these things are the mind's mastery over the body's chemistry, or its alchemy.

You accept that the mind can create disease, but can you also accept that it creates health, it creates well-being, it creates each of your waking moments. The mind is an architect. It helps you perceive and desire, and can help you redesign your temple, your physical expression, your body. For your body is the stage where you act out things. And it is the soul projecting down into the body that creates the mind, so the mind is a divine thing; it is the philosopher's stone.

The mind is the canvas of your consciousness. It is an inspiration. You should treat it well. Allow the emotions to soothe and anoint it, but don't let it get out of hand, because then it becomes ego and does not serve you well. Each of you must remember who you are. You are children of God, God who is all things. Your mind is blessed when you align with the divine will, which is that you are to love one another. There is nothing else worthy of you. Settle for nothing else but to love one another. Then you are set free. Then your mind can play, it can heal, it can create. It is the tool that aligns the chakras. Where would you be without your mind—out of it? It is the philosopher's stone.

Consciousness—that is your philosopher's stone. It builds the pyramids. If it can build the pyramids, it can rebuild you. It conceived Rome, so it can conceive and re-create you. Life is more eternal than the pyramids themselves. For all men like to reproduce themselves. It allows to each generation a precious gift, a heritage of the collective knowledge that your minds have perceived. Even that which the mind perceives as false still serves its victims. It allows each individual to overcome his own obstacle, to seek for the truth for himself. No one can give you the truth. That comes only from within. The truth is expressed—but if you reject it, if you do not believe, that is your choice. It can only be offered to you. It is you who must accept. That is a choice of mind.

As long as you function from the ego, or from your limited physical perspective or sense of yourself, you're not fully acknowledging the being who you are. When you fully acknowledge your mind, body, and spirit, you acknowledge your full nature, so therefore you transcend and transform who you perceive yourself to be.

You thus have better relationships with all others. As John has pointed out, if you love God, and your neighbor as yourself, you can break no other laws.

Human Emotions

John

Emotions are the substance that binds you to the earth plane. They are the malleable material from lives past that make up the substance of karma itself.

Emotions are stored in the subconscious mind. The conscious mind is anchored to the physical plane through the emotional commitments made there. When those emotional commitments are examined upon the higher levels, they become a fine-tuned sensitivity. It is not that you become impersonal, it is moreso that you become "sensitive." Your emotions then begin to ground and spiritualize the personality. They become the sensitive conductors that ground the higher light into the subconscious and therefore transform the whole.

But you must understand that, in the highest sense of the word, emotions do not exist. Rather, within the self are varying degrees of the one true energy, which is love. Love in itself is not an emotion, but it is felt *in* the emotions. The emotions are but the strings on a finely tuned instrument, like a harp or a lyre, but love is the instrument as a whole. The strings of the harp give off many tunes and harmonies, creating the illusion that they themselves are making music, but moreso it is the entire instrument and its attunement that is responsible for the melodies.

Also, there is no such thing as anger, there is only frustration. What you experience as anger is but the blockage of love, so in the true sense of the word, anger does not exist. It is only the lack of love. It is love that has substance, and anger is but the focal point of the frustration. Therefore, when you are angry with an individual, or you identify the emotion of anger, do not express it. Do not even be concerned with it. Moreso, ask the question, "Why am I frustrated with this set of circumstances? Why do I feel unloving toward this

individual?" Then examine your feelings objectively, from the true
state of consciousness and the one true energy which heals all
things, which is love. Love restores harmony because love *is* harmony. Also, you activate God in your life, for God is love.

Nor is there such a thing as hate. Men and women do not have
the capacity to hate, for they were created of God and are a portion
of God, and God does not have the capacity to hate. So, what, then,
is that emotion you identify as hate? Hate is the true void wherein
there is the lack of love. Anger is the blockage of love. That which
you perceive as hate is the void that follows. But since nothing may
give birth to nothing, and like begets like, and hate does not exist, it
has no power of its own. It is merely that you cause a frustration in
others for the lack of the flow of loving energy within you.

All emotions stem from the lack of love or harmony within the
self. Even certain states of love can be traced to the lack of harmony.
You must be totally loving, because when you love discriminately,
and only by various degrees, or conditionally, you are not coming
from your total being. To be a total being, you must love indiscrimi-
nately, or at least desire harmony within all, which is the beginning
of love.

The emotion you identify as fear is but lack of knowledge, or
dread of the unknown. Looking directly into the heart of ignorance is
looking directly into the heart of the unknown. There is nothing that
burdens the human spirit more than ignorance. The only thing you
can be ignorant of is God in the shaping of your actions. For all
there is to know is God, and all things are expressed within God.
When you are ignorant of this, stirring up your feelings and looking deep into the heart of the unknown may be fearful, but since
all there is to know is God, the fear of God is the beginning of
wisdom.

If the fear of God is the beginning of wisdom, then pain is but the
activation of knowledge. So in turn is it upon the physiological
levels. Pain, when removed in the proper manner, is but the activation of knowledge within the individual. This can be done in a
loving manner. Love is restoring harmony to the physical body.
Although at times this may be considered painful, joy quickly ensues
after the release of the pain.

Many migraines are but tension in the muscular structure pulling on the cranium or cranial plates or the lower muscular structure in and about the area of the medulla oblongata. Those things which you identify as anger and frustration bring about such critical states.

Violence is not the suppression of emotions, moreso it is the storage of emotions within the self and then the desire to release them upon the physical levels in a violent act. Note the violent contortions of the physical body when an individual becomes violent due to the frustrations stored within the self. To overcome violent emotions, you should meditate regularly. Rather than seeking to suppress your emotions, study them and the feelings they bring forth, and then release them to God through prayer and faith.

Neuroses are voids or gaps in the flow of love within you, which travels along the meridian points and the nervous system. When there are gaps in the energy flows, there is confusion, and confusion is but a void, a darkness or ignorance, which begets fears and neuroses. Eventually this mounts into paranoia.

Neurosis is activity which is stored within the physical body and is slowly released so that you can deal with it in your own time. That is, you are still in a state of relative balance. Schizophrenia, on the other hand, is when the mind has extended itself deep into the levels of the physical body and continuously activates neurosis, sometimes causing splits in the cellular structure itself. The body is then shaped or imprisoned by its own biochemical activities.

Schizophrenia can come from trauma to an individual before the ego is well developed or it can evolve over periods of time when the ego is in a state of weakness. The ego is self-confidence in its finer forms. It is the fine line between self and selfishness. In a healthy individual, the ego may be used as a shield—not so much to protect you, but moreso to keep you in alignment through self-confidence in your expression on this plane.

All of these things are stored in the muscular structure. When the physical body's energies are correctly aligned and there are no gaps or voids, the muscular structure is correct and in tact. But when there are voids in the emotional structure, or blockages of harmony in the physical body, there is slippage in the muscular structure, both upon the physiological and physical levels, and even misalignment of the muscle tendons themselves.

So, within the physical body is a specific pattern of varying resonances of energy generated by the conscious activities of emotions. When there is a true flow of energy, you jar loose these blockages and restore the necessary synapses. This is how energy heals. Just as a break or short circuit in the flow of electricity may cause tensions and even the generation of heat (and the bursting into fire, which is disharmony within that system), so in turn is it with the meridians of the physical body.

Above all else, be patient with your emotions, for there is also no such thing as time. Time, or the sense of time, ages the physical body chronologically, for *chronos* means "time." But if you have patience, you slow the metabolism to its correct alignment, not so much within the time/space continuum about you, but moreso with the love, the one true energy that binds all things together, which is the original harmony. And then time has no impact upon you— whether upon the metabolic level, the physiological level, the physical level, or the emotional level.

It is often said that time heals all things. This is incorrect. Moreso, true healing can come only from the restoration of harmony with the universe itself, which requires patience. Abide in patience between experiences. There is experience, patience, then experience. For when you are amidst an experience, you have no sense of time. It is only when you are in between experiences that the emotional strains, as you term them, begin to hamper you. So therefore, master patience, and in this way you begin to master the sense of time, or chronos, which takes its toll upon the metabolic levels. Abide all individuals in patience. But do this from a meditative state, to generate peace within self, which illumines you with love, removes all the blockages from the physical body, and truly restores health.

With regard to the effects of emotions on the particular organs of the body, we give some brief suggestions—moreso the symbolic ones. The heart is of the loving nature. The throat chakra is of the expressive nature, the lower chakras are the creative force, and the abdominal area is perhaps the storing of unpleasant emotions. The storing of negativity, of course, produces ulcers. The lack of love or the inability to receive love manifests in heart disease and heart ailments.

Study the meridians and various emotions stored in the organs of the physical body and the tensions therein. For instance, it is well known that emotions of an upsetting nature are stored in the abdominal area. It is also known that feelings of love are experienced in the heart chakra, and communication in the throat. In the lower chakra, many tensions concerning sexuality and its expressions are stored. Treatment of the body's meridians through such techniques as acupuncture, acupressure, jin shin do, and jin shin jitsu would restore emotional balance to the individual. Those therapies which are gentle and which engender tenderness and love between the therapist and client are of the highest accord.

Of all your therapies, the most effective for resolving emotional blockages is the receiving of the Christ within self, the knowledge that you are part of God, and that God desires you to have joy. Herein is why faith heals all things. Faith is evidence of things unseen. Even within your church structures, many find joy in emotional release—although the dogmas of those organizations project certain negativities which ultimately bring about states of imbalance. But faith within the self, and faith in the scope of your own healing abilities, is the highest property, perhaps descending from the nature of God as the greatest form of healing, for God is love.

If you render all things unto God, the emotions do not exist, for all that would exist would be the love that is within you. So render these things unto God and he shall handle them, for if God is love and you offer these things up in love, they shall be brought into alignment.

Tom MacPherson

Do I still have emotional attachments? Well, as an Irishman, until the British let go of Ireland, I have attachments. Anyone who has a human personality has attachments. That is what is so sticky about the ego, you see. Attachments are merely what your karma is all about; they are the notions that bond you into the physical body to start with. But here's the catch. Those emotions can become your very sensitivities when you identify with one another as human beings. So they are not negative, they are merely opportunities to grow.

I would say the best remedy for blocked energies is prunes. Oh, I beg your pardon. I can never resist that one. But actually, humor helps. What it boils down to is that it's better not to take life too seriously. Also, when you become blocked, you're probably holding on to an event that appears to be blocking your spiritual progress, or carrying around the ballast of events, versus truly being spiritual and knowing that your spirit should carry you over the course of events.

Also, deepen your meditations and fellowship, and discuss the blockages with other persons. It's not that you must keep entirely to yourself and muscle your way through it. Talk it over with others. Also, balance the chakras. A massage often helps as well.

You can overcome frustration by realizing how it limits you. I overcame my own frustration by looking at what I was frustrated about and then deciding it wasn't worth it. For instance, I often jest that I didn't incarnate for the last four hundred years because, with the British empire all over the planet, I couldn't find a decent place to incarnate. Now that's silly, because ultimately the British are having their revenge by keeping old Tom out of the body and from coming down here and possibly straightening them out, so to say. Now, that's certainly limiting, isn't it? So, when you realize that your frustrations limit your freedom, eventually you decide to get over them.

Each of you needs practical experience in joy. As an Irishman, I've had a bit of personal experience with wakes, which are supposedly a time of great grief. But all we did was just slam the lid down and send the old boy on his way. What could be a better way of going about it than that? After all, you celebrate when you come into this world, you spend about seventy miserable years here, and then you mourn when someone gets the opportunity to leave. That's a very grim joke if I've ever heard one!

Sexuality and Human Relationships

John

Human sexuality and human relationships are practically synonymous, in that human sexuality is not to be found in the sexual act
itself, but is a continuous energy with each and every individual.
The purpose of human sexuality is to draw persons into levels of
intimacy. It was not intended as a barrier which would create self-
consciousness; it was designed to bring individuals into human relationships. For human relationship is where you have negotiated levels
of intimacy, and negotiated and open intimacy are the very cornerstones
of your interactivity with one another, which is life itself.

Human sexuality is more than an attraction between persons; it is
part of the character and make-up of the human identity. Esoteri-
cally, sexuality finds its seat of consciousness in the second chakra.
Here, in both male and female, we find the foundations of both the
personal identity and of society itself.

The separation of sexual roles into positions dictated by society is
one of the ways in which human sexuality has been used to divide
the race. There is only one race, the *human race*. These arbitrary
sexual divisions within your various cultures are but one instance of
the denial of total human freedom. Indeed, in the struggle of humankind, the first great oppression is that of sexuality. The kindling of
the stronger human instincts—the desire to have intimacy, to nurture
and reproduce—translates into powerful and tangible political and
social forces.

To understand human sexuality, you must become at one with
your own sexuality. The way to do this is not by dividing yourselves
into roles of male and female, but by merging those roles totally
within the self. It is only when you achieve the androgynous state,
accepting self as both male and female, that the self and everything
about the self becomes liberated. It is only when each person becomes androgynous and nonjudgmental of other persons' sexuality
and its expression (as long as it is consented to by both parties) that
all the diversifications of human sexuality merge and find a common
path that is both liberating and unifying. To be androgynous is to be

neither male nor female in the personality, but to become at one, where they balance.

The origins of human sexuality date back to the esoteric civilization of Lemuria, where the physical body was both male and female contained in one, or androgynous. Lemurians reproduced at will after deep meditative acts. The mammary glands were not prominent until birthing, wherein the individual took on the appearance of a female as you understand this today; but before birthing, they had the appearance moreso of the male. It was only later, in the esoteric civilization of Atlantis, that there was a division into male and female. For although prejudices of race and place of origin had been overcome in Lemuria, a final testing was needed to assure the perfection of human consciousness. Thus the division into male and female, wherein the true knowledge of self as spirit could be tested in its final state of androgyny, regardless of which of the physical forms of polarity the spirit occupied.

In Atlantean times, then, you find the beginning of the creation of the cultural conditions you now experience—of men dominating women. For although upon the levels of the soul, or upon the God planes as such, men and women have always been treated as equal, in the manifestation of the earth plane, man, having the stronger physical body and being the hunter amongst the primitive tribes after the sinking of Atlantis, came to dominate woman. Also, after the sinking of Atlantis, many tribes reverted to the lower forms you term as "primitives," particularly in the form of Cro-Magnon. This explains their highly developed art forms, for they were the caretakers of the knowledge of Atlantis, rather than direct practitioners. Eventually their practices were integrated into the higher cultures of Egypt, Greece, Babylon, and the others. Herein you find the roots of the relationships between men and women.

This is not to say that the testing was only between male and female, for indeed it was between female and female, and male and male as well, to integrate these activities into a whole. Thus there was the origin of, and necessity for, tantric practices, wherein human sexuality was used both to negotiate relationships and to integrate the faculties of mind, body, and spirit more fully. New emotions and concepts rushed in upon individuals who did not initiate these practices. Suppression of sexuality gave rise to the various phobias and hysterias that still plague your society in these days. Promiscuous sexuality led to imbalances, aggressions, and embarrassments, and the need to justify those behaviors.

In the tantric rituals, first there was the opening of the chakras and then foreplay involving the various erogenous zones in the physical body. Finally—and these are in the most simplistic of terms—there was the copulative act. Various positions assumed in the initial foreplay were not unlike the positions used by the students of yoga. These not only enhanced pleasure but were used specifically to regulate blood flows, and therefore flows of consciousness, from the different seats of consciousness in the physical body to the internal organs. Ultimately, foreplay always incorporates some principles of a tantric nature. The stimulation of each partner based upon the pleasure principle itself stimulates the blood flows to the varying portions of the physical body, particularly during orgasm.

In exploring their partner's physical body, individuals find certain areas of sensitivity; you have come to term these "erogenous zones." If studied carefully, these areas of sensitivity, particularly those of a highly concentrated nature, would show a pattern along the meridian flows of the physical body. If carefully mapped, a knowledgeable individual would find that stimulations of blood flows to those areas, or stimulation of those meridians by the erogenous act, would begin to create a blueprint of the consciousness in the individual; that by the mapping of the erogenous zones on the physical body and comparing meridian points, a blueprint of the personality of the individual is obtained. This is because the stimulation of the erogenous areas on the physical body sends the necessary blood flows to those seats of consciousness, activating them in the personality.

Thus the sexual act is not only the release of tensions; in even the most simple manners of foreplay, which is a tantric act in itself, there are actual alterations in the personality. If this principle is knowledgeably applied, those who share the intimacies of the sexual act advance, enhance, and spiritualize the personality by increasing the life force through the flow of meridians and allowing the blood flows greater ease when there are stresses released from the physical body after orgasm.

The kundalini is the awakening of the spiritual forces within the self. Sexuality is often one of the more powerful seats or centers to open the kundalini and the seats of consciousness therein. It is wise to open the kundalini in the natural and intimate sharing of the sexual act, perhaps through the suggested means of foreplay, and then entering into sexual intimacy. The orgasm itself can cause all the chakras and seats of consciousness to open if, after the sexual act, meditation ensues to hold the energy within the physical body. This energy, which is closed within the system, then opens the kundalini naturally, having balanced and grounded the emotional sensitivities in the sexual act itself.

The opening of the kundalini is the merger of the meridians, the neurological tissues, the blood flows, the muscular tissues, the skeletal structure, and all the other functions of mind, body, and spirit into a single focus of consciousness. This allows the individual to be in a continuous state of awareness.

It has been said that in the sexual act there is a drain of energy, particularly in ejaculation, from the male to the female. What actually transpires is a reversal of polarities. After the sexual act, passivity often comes upon the male and activity to the female. If both these states were consolidated within both individuals and meditated upon, the androgynous state would be attained, and thus the total enhancement and closure of the energy. But there is no loss of energy to either the male or the female.

The sexual act results in a reversal of polarities, thus creating an androgynous state within the individuals. The stimulation of the sexual act is comparable to that of acupuncture, acupressure, and other forces which work with the meridians of the physical body. This allows the personality to flow along the natural lines of sexuality and to attract individuals it has consciously chosen in this lifetime. This then becomes the balance point from which the individuality flows forth.

These principles serve to evolve human relationships, for higher understanding of the true purpose of sexuality allows for a deepening of relations between persons. But also, human sexuality is a magnetic fluidium that flows forth from all persons and acts as an attractive force, not only upon a biological level but upon a literal magnetic principle as well, creating a continuous force to draw individuals into human relationships.

Sexuality is the attraction between two like-minded individuals according to certain karmic patterns, both upon the level of the soul and upon the mental, which is the personality (that is, the personality as shaped by the immediate environment of this particular lifetime). So thus there is the principle of reincarnation—that sexuality is, in many rights, shaped by past lives.

Sexuality is the dialogue between two bodies. If the bodies are attracted to each other, then all exchanges of body language, the nurturing of the sexual act through whatever means, and the various manipulations of sensitivities of the two bodies in the sexual act are in themselves a dialogue in which the persons discover, upon subliminal levels, the releasing or increasing of tensions, according to how the conscious mind perceives the experience.

The biological orgasm is the culmination of all these dialogues. It is the measurement of the success of the dialogues presented earlier. It is the driving force to draw men and women into, not so much physical contact with each other, but communication upon the spiritual and emotional levels as well.

Sexuality, whether homosexual or heterosexual, is the exploring of the personalities of yourselves as incarnate beings, or as a spirit inhabiting the flesh. An individual's sexual preference should be viewed as neither good nor evil—such preferences are but the functioning of the body's dialogue to and with another.

Homosexuality, or sex between male and male or female and female, is but the sharing of intimacy. The division into male and female created human sexuality, crossing all lines of the experience— including heterosexuality, homosexuality, and bisexuality. Each pattern is equal in the lesson that, in the sexual expression and in the intimacies of human relationship, each individual should be balanced, loving, and altruistic.

Biblically, homosexuality was considered a form of birth prevention—in particular, affecting direct male lineage. The Hebrew people, in order to survive as a nomadic tribe, had to have continuous births due to the high mortality amongst children. These things applied mostly in the days of Moses, though they appeared also in the teachings of Paul, as he was still studying Mosaic law, as well as the New Testament of the master known as Jesus.

The biblical interpretation of this is that all things are in a state of evolution. Most of the emphasis in the Bible is placed upon

lust, wherein it says that "they burned with lust and unclean passions for each other." Lust is forceful or violent. It says "the women
turned from the natural uses of their bodies and burned with lust for
each other." This is not so much a comment on homosexual practices but moreso on the lustful manner in which individuals were
manifesting the physical body's dialogues. Thus the emphasis is
placed upon lust, which is being selfish, self-centered, or egotistical,
not on the desire for either companionship or balance for the soul's
experience, which comes through reincarnation. So therefore, it is
moreso the interpretation of the Bible, rather than the Bible itself, that
is oddly peculiar in these days.

Know, then, that sexuality is but the magnetic fluidium to draw
you into intimacy, so that you may then develop relationships. For it
is by your witnesses with one another that you have life and live it
abundantly. Life *is* your interactivities with one another, which allow
you to give expression to that which God is. God is love, love is
harmony, and harmony begets peace. You should come with love
into all your relationships.

At times you seek to understand sexuality through your various
moral structures. But as you continue to discover that these things
are all determined upon the levels of the soul, you understand that,
in Christ, there is neither male nor female. God does not judge you
in the sense of male and female, or on the nature of your sexuality. If
there is any true judgment, it is only upon the level of your understanding and to what degree you manifest the commandment to love
the Lord God with all your heart and mind and your neighbor as
yourself. There are no divisions in God; there is neither male nor
female. There is only one God, one love, which is harmony. And
harmony is that which must be established among all humankind.

Atun-Re

Ah, Atun-Re would speak with the children. Blessings to you. You
have asked about celibacy. How many know that experience volun-
tarily? The practice of celibacy should not be suppression, it should
be the channeling of the energy, by conscious choice, to the higher
states. It is looking upon each person gently and intimately, not to

suppress that which may be natural, but to allow that which is natural to flow throughout the whole of the physical form.

Celibacy should be utilized with sensitivity, in meditation. You may use that energy to flow evenly and to be a totally dedicated student to the spiritual path. Even the practice of celibacy in patterns of ebbs and flows adds to the health and the well-being of the individual, to educate you to the needs of your physical form.

Some of you dodder about, going, "I have gone too long without. I am so stressed." Then you throw yourself at the mercy of anyone. This is a sad state of human affairs. If you were to channel that energy, you would add well-being to your own physical body. You would reshape it. You would make it appealing. And you would create an even flow of energy about you, a more relaxed flow, with less anxiety, and less putting off of persons with whom you would desire to negotiate intimacy. For each person is a temple, and each temple should be respected with reverence.

The true practitioner of celibacy allows relaxation to come to the physical body so that he or she is not dominated by sex. For human sexuality needs to flow naturally from the individual and just to be channeled. Then there is relaxation in the physical form, as well as the actual altering of the features of the individual. At times, a new luxuriousness comes to them, or additional height, or a correction of difficulties in the flow and movement of the physical form. And if used wisely and with discretion, celibacy can enhance one's relationship to God. This is not to say that celibacy is the only practice—it is but a single practice, comparable to meditation or prayer.

The choice between active sexuality and celibacy is up to each individual. They are both disciplines. Undisciplined sexuality can be just as punitive as the strictly enforced celibacy of various cultures and religions. Sexuality and celibacy have equal value if practiced with consciousness.

If a person negotiates properly and tantrically, if he or she goes into the sexual act with a consenting individual and a loving heart and practices tantra with negotiated intimacy, then, indeed, benefits come to the individual.

Tantra is the channeling of the sexual energy for spiritual well-being. You should be no less cautious when practicing tantric techniques than you would be in other aspects of your life. You must treat everything not with caution, but with *sensitivity*. You may abuse yourself sexually by plunging into relationships where there is no satisfaction. You may abuse yourself physically by denying your body its proper nutrients. The kundalini is no different. It is not something to be feared, it is something to be treated with sensitivity. Caution implies an already-present danger. I would say danger arises only from lack of sensitivity.

It is through sensitivity that you may approach any form. Meditation and breath are the two forms which would be most beneficial to practice. Do not go into them arrogantly, for this may break up emotional patterns necessary for you to be balanced and deal with the world. If you go into anything with arrogance rather than sensitivity, you open yourself to dangers. The kundalini acts only upon that which you take to it. In itself it is impersonal.

The purpose of tantra is to raise the consciousness of the individuals so that they become more aware of themselves in all areas, not just in the context of the relationship. We recommend the model that John offered—the simplest of foreplay involving the stimulation of the physical body, culminating in the intimacy of the sexual act. This model in itself is tantric. But if you wish to practice tantra, realize that it may also be practiced in celibacy, through meditation, by channeling your celibate energies into the higher dimensions of your physical form. You may wish to increase your knowledge of these matters from those Eastern systems of thought that have organized the information into manuscripts in which they speak of a natural flow of love and erotica and its stimulation of consciousness.

Individuals should sit down, meditate, and then negotiate what they truly want from one another before entering into, or ending, a relationship. This is the very beginning point of the spiritualizing process. When a couple can no longer be honest with each other, then the relationship has no more growth. A couple who is honest with each other will always find more growth in their relationship.

The difficulty with adultery, as you term it, is that one of the partners has secreted himself away without the knowledge of the other, often bringing the third party back into bed with them, by envisioning, and this can be sensed by the astute lover. What effect does this have? It is more the party's dishonesty than the act itself that gives rise to any negative energy, through a process of internalizing rather than being totally open and creating that space within the relationship. For it is possible, even for individuals who have taken vows of monogamy, to be open and honest, to say they wish to explore their feelings for other persons. Then, perhaps they could set up separate households to explore these things, yet still preserve the uniqueness of their relationship. So, the key word is *honesty.* Honesty is not the spilling out of personal emotions, but presenting one's feelings and being willing to hear the other person's, and then negotiating from there.

There are no damages if there is honesty, if there is openness. The only damage is that which is internalized, because the person who internalizes at times feels vibrationally suspicious, which becomes stress, and an acid that may eat away at the character of the individual.

Sexual energy, properly balanced and channeled throughout the body, can be used as the magnetic force to attract in appropriate individuals to your life circumstances. The reduction of stress in the physical form, through sexuality, also becomes life-regenerating. Sexuality is the key element, the key energy through which you may work consciously to negotiate the levels of intimacy that you desire with persons.

We would recommend that you not apply sexuality in a promiscuous manner; avoid being like gibbons bounding through the trees. It is wiser to apply consciousness and sincerity to relationships. This is not to say you should withdraw or constantly protect yourselves in long robes as you go about your streets. No, we encourage you to work with meditation to reduce stress and, above all else, to rid yourself of fear in your relationships. Also, expand your holistic knowledge of the various sexually transmitted diseases, for there are dietary means to alleviate them. But above all else, meditation would be a key here—to merge, to make it the tantric act, with deep respect on the part of each party.

Actually, your venereal diseases usually come from the suppression or abuse of the creativity of the individual. It has little to do with sexuality or morality itself, since it can be picked up in only one sexual act, and usually when the individual is under heightened degrees of stress. In relation to sexuality, we would say that suppressed sexuality is suppressed creativity.

Abortion, we would say, is the conscious choice of an individual who does not feel mature enough to bring a soul into the world. Spontaneous abortion is found in nature and is considered an act of God. In certain cultures, it is a punitive act, to crush the individual into a social role. In these days, certain medicines and procedures make abortion available to females and give them a conscious choice. I would say that since spontaneous abortion does occur in nature, it may indeed be used consciously by individuals. To this old one, however, birthing is also noble, and if taken to full term, perhaps that precious bundle of the fully incarnated soul could go to those who could give nurturance and love. But mind you, if both parties, male and female, had been sensitive to begin with, then neither abortion nor adoption would be an issue.

Of rape, we would say that its negative effects may be seen in the trauma that the individual experiences, the scars that are left on the psyche, and the images which become imprinted upon the person. These may be alleviated through meditation and cleansing of the soul of the individual to restore their self-esteem and realize it is not they who stimulated this act, but a brutalized and incomplete individual. We would say that rape is karmic but not punitive.

In the spirit realms, there is a continuous exchange of sexuality between those who hold any level of human personality. There is practice of human sexuality in exchanges both of information and of energy. There are those who have learned much through the sexual act and, if they so desire, can still engage in that act in the disembodied state, through visualization. For true embodiment is in the human personality. You are not truly incarnate in a human body, you are incarnate in a human personality. And since it is the personality from which human sexuality arises, human sexuality is still practiced in the disembodied state and could be visualized as a form of sexual copulation according to the consciousness of the individual. But usually, it is more in forms of energy exchange.

It is said that man and woman were once in a single form and that you lived in round bodies. You became so powerful and so arrogant that you threatened to roll up the mountains and challenge the gods themselves. And so the Goddess of Love came to the conclusion, "Let us divide them in half, and then they will be so busy bickering amongst themselves, they will never bother us again." How successful the gods have been!

The Divine Healer

John

To be a healer means to restore harmony. The true healer channels divine and loving energy. You may speak softly to a person and heal him of mind and spirit and often the physical body will follow, for matter follows thought. Such healers are so filled with the divine energy that they transfer these harmonics directly to the person.

Healing is the highest gift of the spirit, for it is the restoration of harmony to all things within the self. As applied to the physical body, it is bringing harmony to the internal organs.

There is controversy amongst your current medical systems. Your traditional medical practitioners hold to the idea that healing involves the isolation of various diseases and the treatment of specific symptoms through the destruction of the cells, or the virus, or bacterial infection that appears to be the cause of imbalance in the physical body. The more natural or holistic therapies seek to restore the body and its various tissues and organs to their correct balance, and to their fullest capacity, by using the body's own natural states of immunity.

Modern medicine seeks to duplicate the body's natural properties by studying its biology. Observations are then documented and synthesized, and certain substances are derived to treat the body through injection or inoculation. Often those substances contain toxins which cause damage to the various internal organs, particularly in the cleansing tracts—the kidneys, the liver, the lymphatic systems, and even the blood itself. However, as is noted by your naturalistic practitioners, the physical body contains all the necessary chemical elements within it already. Stimulating the body by using natural therapies and providing it with selected natural foods, in their pure and organic state rather than tampered with by man, the physical body can assimilate and synthesize all of its own needs.

The physical body is an instrument of the mind, and not vice versa. The physical body is the temple. The health of the physical body is a state of harmony with the mind. Certain yogic diets and postures, and various exercises to expand the consciousness, will bring forth balance within the physical body itself.

The physical body can be treated and restored to balance upon its denser levels, but it also possesses etheric levels. Until recently, your traditional sciences have denied the existence of any form of auric or etheric energy field, but recently they have begun to record measurements of energy fields, auric fields, and even electromagnetic fields around the body. These electromagnetic fields are actually the final force that governs the physical body on a molecular level. The very chemical properties that make up the physical body are bound together by yin/yang energy forces upon the molecular level. And it is the vibrations of this molecular structure that make up the final etheric definitions of the physical body. For each of you is a being of light, each of you is energy, and so therefore, the physical body can be treated and restored to states of harmony on many levels.

Healing can be based upon vibrational principles as well as upon nutrition, knowledge of anatomy, massage (for stimulation of the body's natural biochemical forces), and many other methods. Modern science is in a position to document these various dimensions in the physical body, in order to refine them. All of your sciences and systems of healing may eventually evolve and integrate. They do not have to make war upon one another, but may all serve a useful purpose. All may heal in turn.

But perhaps the greatest blockage to healing is the mind itself, for the mind is the architect of your existence on this plane. It is the portal through which the soul may manifest itself upon certain levels. For contained within the physical body you are just that— mind, body, and soul, totally integrated into a single unit.

Mind is the builder in that it is the crucible. Even as you have a crucible to hold mortar for the making of bricks, and even as you have a crucible to hold the bricks themselves, and even as you must have the builder, who is the crucible for the knowledge to build the structure, so too is the mind the crucible wherein all these elements are contained, and thus is as the builder, the architect of all the things which you build within the self. As you perceive God, the personality is shaped and extends unto the regions of the physical body in healing. The mind is the architect of the physical body.

Man often associates himself as mind and body, denying the existence of the soul, but the soul is that perfect state of harmony that exists on all levels—from the etheric, then extending into the denser levels of the physical body through the chakras, or the seats of consciousness within the physical body. These chakra points correspond to the various glands—the testicles (in men) and the ovaries (in women), the spleen, the abdominal area of the stomach, the thymus or the heart, the thyroid, the pituitary, and finally the pineal gland. These are the portals through which the soul manifests itself in the physical. The master glands—the pineal, the pituitary, and the thymus—are critical to the immune system and to the development of the biochemical personality. The spleen is responsible for the production of many white cells, the testicles and ovaries for procreation, and the stomach for the absorption of nutritional needs and the production of many enzymes.

Herein you may find many examples of how the physical body integrates back upon the denser and upon the etheric levels, even extending to the levels of the soul itself. But the mind is the linkage between them all, for the mind is shaped by behavioral modification through the activation of the chakras, and tensions stored within the mind can cause blockage along the meridians or acupuncture points, thus causing and eventually manifesting disease within the organism itself. So therefore, healing is the integrated process of mind, body, and soul.

But above all, the soul is the harmonious point that exists within you at all times, for each of you is as a soul, and all forms of healing are directly for the expression of the soul itself. The soul is the portion of you that is the Father/Mother God, who dwells within all of you. Each one of you was created equally in that selfsame spirit. For even though you are an integrated being, and even though in this plane you manifest the mind, the body, and the soul as a three-dimensional state of existence, it is but a temporary state. Eventually you will evolve beyond that. To have true healing, you must integrate mind, body, and soul, and manifest the Christ consciousness, for you are strangers in the earth and are not of this plane.

You must eventually evolve to healing on the levels of the Godhead itself, for all of you are sons and daughters of God. And ultimately, all forms of healing of the physical body are but by-products of the soul's learning. In this way you must achieve the higher learning, the highest gift of the spirit, the highest healing of all, which is to manifest the perfection that is within you, or the love that dwells within.

The soul is a state of perfection already. It is the very vibrational foundation upon which all systems of thought, philosophy, and healing function. It is the very force that shapes the molecular structure that eventually evolves into the spiral DNA, which itself eventually evolves the genes that shape the very foundations of the physical body itself. It is the force that holds that intelligent pattern.

The mind and body may at times bring about dramatic forms of healing in themselves, but unless such healing is felt upon the levels of the soul, the affliction often returns. It is the soul which establishes harmony in man. It is the soul which activates the personality of the mind. So therefore, draw upon the harmony of the soul to give peace to the mind, which can then extend healing to the physical body.

The manner of healing of the man Jesus was through his own physical body, which was a perfect pattern. As he extended healing to others, and they were willing to accept it, they received the information from him telepathically, by being present in his aura. Their afflictions or diseased bodies would then have a correct pattern upon vibrational, molecular, and genetic levels so as to begin to rebuild themselves. For their conscious minds, which shape most of the activities of the physical body, had forgotten, through lack of faith, their own ability to heal themselves. Therefore, their physical bodies did not hold the pattern for the correct state of health. But when their physical bodies, or their minds, had faith in one who walked close to that perfection, called God, then they could reactivate that memory from the subconscious or collective unconscious or collective subconscious level. The physical body would then assimilate that pattern within itself and begin to rebuild itself, first upon the vibrational and etheric levels, then the molecular, then the genetic, then healing the organism as a whole. All was accomplished from the level of love, which is the soul.

The true healer is the soul, which is your individuality within God. The soul resides within the physical body, which is the temple, and desires that it be made whole and clean.

The soul has direct linkage with the physical body through the mind, so the mind is little more than the crucible or the vehicle which manifests the levels and the perceptions of the soul. Mind, body, and soul are a single functioning unit, independent of one another, yet dependent on one another. Therefore, there is a continuous linkage. For the physical body has its own consciousness also. Just as your body was evolved from the lower primates, who have consciousness but not a soul, so in turn the physical body has a consciousness, and the mind is the reflective point halfway between the soul, which is all-knowing since it is a portion of God, and the levels and instincts known as the physical body.

The study of animal behavior to gain knowledge of man's intelligence is incorrect. Moreso, you should study the activities of intelligence or mind itself—then in turn you find the linkages with the existence of the higher self. For even as man has discovered the subconscious mind, eventually he shall discover the higher self, or the superconscious mind, which is as the reflection of the soul in the earth plane.

The higher self is not so much the true, all-encompassing portion of the soul, it is but the top of a funnel wherein all the activities would filter down to this particular plane. For the soul is in a state of perfection, and for any form of healing, you have but to manifest that perfection within the mind, as the crucible, for then it will be manifested in the physical body.

Disease is but the breaking down of a specific area in the physical body that allows for the habitation of unnecessary life forms therein. Therefore, the disease is an affliction within the body, and not so much an attack from an outer organism. If you desire to manifest perfection in the soul, which is love, which is harmony, so in turn does that harmony then begin to restore the physical body from within.

Any form of affliction within the physical body is incentive for the mind to bring itself into harmony. With the asking of the question, "Why has this disease come to me?" you set in motion an incentive for improvement within the self, whether or not you are consciously knowledgeable of the activities of the soul. You may look to the mind for the answer, or to the levels of the soul, but it is the asking of the question itself that stimulates incentive for you to bring about progression within yourself, upon whatever level your belief system would manifest.

The conscious mind is but the doorway through which the soul reflects on this plane. It is a doorway which may be closed or thrown wide open, or it can have certain leakages of light coming through it even when it is thought to be sealed. The conscious mind is the doorway through which the light of the soul must shine. The door may be thrown wide open at any time and you may enter therein and dwell in the realms and regions of the soul. And since the soul is in a state of perfection, any who would open his mind to this concept would begin to manifest the natural properties of the light within himself. But it must eventually filter down to the denser levels of the physical body as a whole, which is why the healing process seems at times to be slow.

There are four principles that, if mastered, would establish harmony in your life—fasting, patience, correct diet, and correct communication with the levels of the soul, or God. The one tool which is the cornerstone to all of this, and indeed to thy spiritual growth as a whole, is *meditation*. Meditation draws on each of the above four principles for its proper practice and application. For, in order to meditate, you must have patience, correct diet, fasting (for the cleansing of the physical body and to enhance the meditative state), and correct dialogue or prayer with God at the soul levels, which is the central focus of the meditation. Indeed, meditation *is* the dialogue with the levels of the soul or with God, however you may perceive that being, and expecting and waiting for a response within the same time period. If the response does not come, then patience must be used as a tool until the desired communication ensues.

The first principle is fasting, which gives individuals the ability to travel for great lengths of time without sustenance, and allows freedom from interference from the grosser levels of the physical body during meditation. It also works well as a tool for the cleansing of the body.

Fasting allows the entire anatomy of the physical body to assimilate energy. Indeed, you could live solely upon that which is known as prana, and this pranic force would aid in complete tissue regeneration. For the physical body is actually a conductor of energy, of that which is known as prana, or the life force. It has been demonstrated that electrical fluidiums, or electrical currents, may cause tissue regeneration, and that when the low voltage of the neurological tissues flows unbroken to the cell tissues, they are more rapidly regenerated. How much moreso during a fast, when the physical body is no longer turned toward a biochemical process through the assimilation of foodstuffs? Fasting allows the physical body to turn the engines of the cell tissues toward being clearer conductors of energy and allows more rapid alignment of the chakras.

But do not confuse fasting with starvation, for fasting is merely abstaining from that which is not appropriate, and this can be achieved first through a vegetarian diet, rich in proteins to maintain proper health for the cell tissues, but protein from more appropriate sources. Fasting is the cleansing of the physical body, not the denial of foods.

In attempting a fast for the purposes of cleansing the physical body, or to prepare it for an intensive state of meditation, you must fast a minimum of three days for it to have any impact upon the denser levels. This is because it takes at least three days to rid the physical body of all unnecessary food tissues from the intestinal tract. Preferably, there would be a fourth day of fasting to allow for the tearing down of unnecessary tissues. For once the body has nothing in it to digest, it turns in upon itself, drawing upon its own natural reservoirs. But the last thing the physical body will digest is its own vital organs, which is why fasting can oftentimes heal cancerous conditions, as it begins to ingest afflicted tissues and eliminate them naturally. Fasting should be approached with the idea that it is cleansing the physical body for a specific purpose, either for meditation or for healing, or for the cleansing in its own right.

During a fast, great quantities of fluid should be taken into the system to continuously flush out unnecessary tissues. In this way, there is no strain placed upon the kidneys and lymphatic system, the liver, and the intestinal tract as a whole. Celery juices, cucumber juices, and other vegetable juices will neutralize the toxins which are released as a result of the fast, and hence eliminate nausea.

During the cleansing process, there is also the drawing up of old habit patterns, including indulgences of the flesh. Many of these patterns are stored within the cellular memory itself, so when you begin the cleansing process, you are not only preparing room within the physical self, but are also cleansing the subconscious mind. This is why individuals will often experience nightmares during a fast. The urge to resume eating at these times is often the desire to seal off these subconscious flows and engage the physical body in activities with which it is more familiar, such as the ingestion of food at the physical levels.

Correct diet allows individuals to go into any environment and partake of those foods which are natural to that area, and therefore to integrate themselves within the environment. Preferably, the correct diet would be of a vegetarian nature, rather than the partaking of blood meats or any form of flesh meats at all, including fish and fowl. The channel speaking recommends foods which are preferably steamed, boiled, or prepared in a wok, over low heat. Meats are to be used strictly as medicine, for instance when there is the need for certain forms of proteins to rehabilitate the body over a shortened time period.

All healings may come through obeying God's laws. Obeying God's laws means, "Thou shalt not kill." This is why it is, in part, wise to maintain a vegetarian diet. There are those who say that vegetarianism involves the slaying of plant life and hence violates the same principles, but this is not true. For the body of the plant is but to fertilize the next generation of seedlings, and if you compost human waste, you fulfill this karmic pattern. Thus there is not the slaying of individuality as there is in the slaying of animals.

Patience is the mastery of the element of time, which does not exist. Neither time nor space exists. There is only experience, then patience, then experience. Patience is that which exists in a tangible form between experiences. For when you are amidst an experience, particularly if there is great joy or intense preoccupation, the physical body does not age. Only impatience ages the physical body, for it gives the sense of time, and time ages the physical body. Time is also a doorway for disease.

Patience both heals and maintains the structure of the pattern as a whole. Patience is the correct pattern. It is the tangible substance of harmony as a pattern, manifesting within the self. Patience is not the suppression of aggressions or frustrations, it is knowledge of them and understanding that they are unnecessary to the system.

system. It is their removal and the correct restoration of the one true energy. In other words, patience is the ability to manifest the one true energy, which is love.

When active in an experience you perceive as healthy, you have no perception of time. You may even become so preoccupied with the experience that you are late for an engagement. Perhaps it could be said, then, that "you have no sense of time." In such instances, time has no bearing on you. For time exists perhaps as energy, but not as a tangible substance, although it may act upon you physically. Patience gives you the mastery over time and space, which do not exist when patience exists.

From the levels of the soul, which extend into the mind and then into the physical body, meditate upon the perfection that is the soul. Discover the OM, or the perfect word, or the perfect harmony that is within each of you. This comes through meditation. This is the preparatory state of all healers, to discover the perfection and the harmony that lies within, to remove from themselves any forms of emotional static and to dedicate themselves to the harmony that they desire to restore to others, for harmony in the physical body is healing.

Tom MacPherson

It is a common misconception that vegetarians have difficulty obtaining sufficient protein to maintain optimum health. There is an Aztec grain known as amaranth that is making a comeback these days. It is a more complete protein than many of your meats. As a vegetarian, if you were to assimilate tofu, with brown rice and beans, you would have a complete protein. Replace your one-pound steak with that and you'll be perfectly fine. Also, I believe you are discovering you need much less protein than the tables of your medical charts currently reveal. If you wish to know who created those charts, I do believe it was your meat packers, so the charts are a bit self-serving.

Dairy products are ethically a good source of protein—certainly better than killing the cow. But they are still a less superior source. It is getting your nutrition secondhand. If the cow can eat the grass and get all the protein it needs, and it is certainly much larger than you, why should you get your protein secondhand? Go directly to the source.

And I would not tolerate the old excuse that if you pick a pumpkin off the vine, you might as well go out and kill a cow. It is not the same. When you eat an apple, you are merely consuming the part of the plant that is prepared for the seed anyway. And as long as you compost the seed and return it to the earth, it is accomplishing its natural cycle. So you are not killing the tree, you are partaking of the fruit which was prepared for food, and thus you are in harmony with the higher laws and sustain a balanced state of nutrition for optimum health.

The spiritualization process places few demands on the physical body. Where the body is overly in demand is in too much digestion of unnecessary foodstuffs, which causes imbalances in the entire system. There is also a real demand placed upon the mind to not partake of compulsive eating. Both eating less and fasting are part of the spiritualization of the physical body because the mind is allowed to have a fuller integration with the body and a much higher degree of consciousness. And the more the physical and mental merge, the more you are in the superconscious states. Yoga is a demonstration of this in the sense that the superconscious has its final focus in the physical body.

While the body is busy grinding up unnecessary proteins, it is only functioning as a biological being. When it is well-nourished and sustained, it then becomes a vehicle and portal for the spirit. The mind can then spread itself thin along the grid of the physical body, which is an antenna or conductor for higher energy, and hence can maintain a state of superior health.

Seeking Personal Power

John

To understand the nature of personal power, you must understand the nature of power in its own right. Power is a focal point not so much for change—for there is no such thing as change—but moreso to cause movement in a system or structure. Since movement gives the illusion of change, man wastes much time in seeking power to change things. Moreso, if you seek to have movement, which is inspiration, then you have the key to personal power.

The nature of personal power, then, is not so much to bring about change or the utilization of force of will, but moreso to bring about movement in a set of affairs or circumstances which will eventually lead to end results that may or may not be material. It is the foolish man who seeks power from material gains. It is foolishness to say, "Money is power," for money can purchase only material things. True personal power is the ability to have influence. Perhaps the words *power* and *influence* translate literally into each other, not unlike love and harmony which are one and the same.

There is no good; there is no evil—there is only man and his systems of judgment. And when you realize there is no such thing as change, but only movement, then you will understand that rather than seeking to change those things which afflict you, you should attempt to move from them into a greater and higher consciousness, in love and wisdom.

It is the wise man who would seek influence in the affairs of things as they exist, as well as understanding of those things which are yet to exist. This is dipping into the future, which is, in its own right, a power.

Inspiration is a higher form of power. In each man and each woman is a desire to have inspiration or direction kindled within. One who understands the true nature and use of personal power will seek to bring about inspiration.

Inspiration comes from one source, and that is harmony. It is through personal example that men and women are inspired, and thus there is the gaining of personal power. Harmony within self, which is love, is personal power. So therefore, if you seek to establish harmony within self, then these things will cause influence within others through inspiration.

People use the word *power* because they desire change. If they thought more in terms of "movement" rather than "change," they would use the word *inspiration*. For inspiration is the ability to cause movement within the self. Therefore, power, movement, and inspiration are synonymous. The only power that one needs is the inspiration within self, which is the movement of the spirit.

There are no such things as structures or organizations, there is only the influence of people. Therefore, the wise man will seek to have influence rather than power to bring about direct change. People do not change. There is nothing new under the sun. Rather, seek to influence those things which already exist. Seek the cornerstone of influence, which is inspiration.

There is no such thing as change. Change is but man seeking rearrangement of circumstances that shall always be with him. The poor you shall always have with you, but poverty is relative to the consciousness of the individual. There are many who lead monklike existences yet are wealthy in that they own all things, having detached themselves from all things. There are also those who desire to be a focus for the flow of money. They are as a prism for these activities and allow it to pass through them, transmuted into many colors.

Power is but the ability to establish harmony within self, which then gives the ability to inspire others. For if the mind is filled with chaos, you then desire peace. And it is the attainment of this peace, this harmony, that would give you the ability to have influence—not so much over others, but with others.

Never seek to dominate in the use of personal power; moreso, seek to work with your power. In this right, you gain the greatest influence. Create a void and God shall fill it. Create the need and then, not so much create the desire within others to fulfill that need, but allow them to perceive that need within themselves, that they may then minister unto you. And in this balance, each serves the other, and there is the creation of perfect harmony, which is perfect inspiration, and so therefore perfect power.

So, once again, what is the nature of personal power? It is the ability to cause inspiration, to cause movement in a set of influences that already exists, wherein the end results may be material, but this should not be the pursuit in its own right.

Materialization is a direct gift from God and is not a result of personal power. Personal power is within the realm of the physical, and materialization lies in the realm of the mental, or perhaps upon its highest level, as the projection of one object to another. These are in the realms of spirit, which are the realms of God. Personal power does not come from the extension of the ego, but moreso from following God's laws correctly, through prayer and education. And the final influences are as one would act them out upon the levels of the physical. Materialization is direct visualization and the direct manifestation of God-like abilities.

All things must be built upon the one true energy, which is love. For if you love something, you have thorough understanding of it, and then it may, in turn, serve you.

To gain personal power, you must gain inspiration. To have that, first you must meditate. Meditation is prayer unto God, which is inspiration in its own right. In meditation, center yourself upon that which you desire to manifest through the nature of power. For perhaps the greatest truth is that power is but the linkage of yourselves to that which you desire to manifest. So therefore, sit in meditation. Calm yourself and seek to draw unto yourself, directly, through meditation, individuals with whom you may manifest these necessary instruments; or seek to calm yourself enough to be so clear in your own vision that you may take this vision directly unto the one it is necessary to inspire.

Personal power is activities acted out upon the level of the individual. They may be in harmony with God's laws, but are not necessarily God's direct activities. These things are neither good nor evil; they are but influencing sets of circumstances to manifest that which is desired or perceived as a particular need. Seek the highest accord in all manner of things, for God already knows your needs. And in this way, and through proper prayer and meditation, you may manifest God's higher perceptions for you. This is not to say that there is either good or evil, or greater or lesser, in the manifestation of personal power; it is only to say that these things are but tools to be used at particular points in your growth.

Personal powers are but tools. They are not lights to illumine the path, but the tools to build the path itself. For it is in God's light, and God's law, that all these things must be done. God is love, and it is in this love that you must manifest the final and higher truths within the self. So thus, personal power is but the desire to manifest the perception of personal need, first through meditation, then inspiration, then taking that inspiration unto others, and kindling it within them, wherein they may be in harmony with that which you perceive as your need.

This is the nature of personal power, to influence the set of affairs by which you, in turn, shall eventually shape the manifestation of the material. Again, do all these things in God's true light, which is love, which is harmony within self, whence all things must extend.

Patterns of Psychic Unfoldment

John

That which you term as psychic is not so much a power as a gift. It is the receiving of information from beyond the range of your own conscious capacity. Any information you receive from beyond the five senses of sight, hearing, touch, smell, and taste derives from the "sixth sense," such as telepathy, clairvoyance, clairaudience, or prophecy. These are the remembering of those things that you have forgotten. For each of you is as a spirit. A spirit, when it does not possess the physical body, is not limited to the five physical senses, but has a greater attunement with a system of knowledge that has existed since the foundations of the world. When you are incarnate and possess the physical body, telepathy is your attunement with those sources of information.

The word *psychic* means the focus of the mind, or the product of the mind. Because each of you is a spirit, because each of you is a soul, you each have all of God's knowledge within you. And it is within the capacity of your conscious mind to recall these things through the gifts that have been spoken of. You have the ability to project beyond the physical body and its limited five senses. You have the ability to perceive the future, to perceive the past. For all things are of a vibratory quality. Even as you put forth thought and it survives, so in turn do you.

Psychic powers, as you have come to term them, are abilities contained within the self. The word *power* translates to mean "movement," so power and movement are synonymous. Man oftentimes seeks power to bring forth balance within the self. Moreso, he should seek movement within the self, that is inspiration. For when the mind enters into the higher realms, or the higher self, and receives inspiration, these abilities or powers, that are natural unto the levels of the soul, extend themselves to the level of the physical.

First and most prominent, there are the five senses. You sometimes discount these as limitations, but they give you the ability to express yourselves artistically, and they give you a sense of awareness upon this physical plane. The five senses are tools and should be used as such. You have even used them to build the instruments that document your higher energies. Individuals often curse the five senses. But even though the five senses are limited, you should not curse them. The true value of your senses is dependent upon your use of them as tools. Their purpose is to give you a sense of yourself as a physical being. Never discount these abilities. Moreso you are blessed with them, for they lead you to expression in the higher levels. They are to bring you the necessary inspiration, and it is inspiration that kindles the mind. The inspiration that can be received by the five senses as to the wonder of the physical planes can even lead you back to the higher levels whence you originally came.

If the five physical senses are your first level or ability, your second is mind itself. The mind is your ability to organize thought. Organized thought gives you a system of philosophy, and hence expression, reasoning, thinking, and the capacity to meditate, which is the doorway to the other abilities. But the mind is an ability in itself. You must learn to train it, focus it, enhance its faculties of concentration, observation, and then retention of those abilities. The mind is not a totally limited vehicle. It is your ability to retain things in the earth plane. It is the housing of your personality, that extends from the levels of the soul.

The personality is not so much an ability as it is an expression of mind. Mind has the capacity of meditation. Meditation is the doorway to your psychic abilities. But it is necessary to understand each of the preceding steps and to begin to appreciate them in their own right. This keeps you from cursing the physical body, for the physical body is your temple, and he who is to proceed forth in any manner into another man's house should first have his own house in order.

The mind has the ability, through meditation, to receive those gifts that you term psychic, such as clairaudience, clairsentience, and clairvoyance, while still inhabiting the physical body. There are also those who can see into the future, as well as those who can see into the past. All of these things are possible because the nervous system acts as an antenna, or a resonance or sounding board, for various telepathic abilities with which you are attuned at all times.

To see the past, you need but attune to those thoughts and vibrations that are always with you and recorded in the ethers themselves. To see the future, you either project various improbabilities or engage the mind's ability of calculus upon a series of circumstances that have already been set in motion. Free will enters into this and may alter the course of events, but many times there is still a karmic pattern to be acted out and projected upon. Again, all of this is possible because the nervous system acts as a state of resonance for the receiving of energies from living individuals and then has interplay in the mind, where these energies rise to consciousness.

The human mind has the ability to hear those who are discarnate. Since hearing is one of man's points of communication, when thought is projected and received upon the nerve endings in that particular area, and then manifested and calculated in that particular portion of the brain, or the flesh mind, you are able to hear these thoughts within your own vocabulary. You also have the ability to sense odors that have long since past, yet come wafting upon you through the atmospheres. The psychic faculties are the actual projections of energy that are released by the process of their own vibration and resonance upon the molecular level, finding their activation in the nervous system of the individual, then calculated in the mind, where they manifest through one of the five senses.

These are what are known as psychic faculties. They are a sixth sense, a form of resonance of energies rather than biochemical activity, as your major physical senses are. Each of these abilities extends from the physical level and can be developed through meditation.

Your third level or ability is the visionary level. This is the activation of the pituitary gland. This gland, which is the seat of the sixth chakra, gives you the ability to attune with beings beyond the level of the physical and extends beyond the levels of telepathy. For telepathy is the fine dividing line between those senses described earlier that act as resonance, and the visionary level. Telepathy is the balance between the two. It is not a separate ability, but is interwoven between them. The visionary level is a completely functional capacity, for it approaches the levels of the soul itself.

The seat of the soul is the endocrine system. Each of the individual glandular structures of the endocrine system has its own energy activated by the very faculties of the soul. The visionary level, by the activation of the pituitary gland, is separate from the telepathic ability, although telepathy extends into its activities. This is the direct communication with the levels of the soul, enabling you to understand all the information flows and all the patterns of the universal laws themselves, or those things that you term the laws of physics. These, then, become blended, intermelded, and understood upon the three-dimensional level that you know as the physical plane.

The visionary level is the capacity to see the future clearly, as it is laid out in God's plan. It is universal attunement with thought, or the universal mind itself. Telepathy is one of the cornerstones of the universal mind upon this plane, but the universal mind is not dependent upon the energies of telepathy. Telepathy is often a by-product of the generation of brain patterns of incarnate beings. The visionary level is the independent and separate energies of the soul itself. So therefore, telepathy is a by-product of this plane, whereas the soul has attunement with all the higher energies.

Next, there is the opening of the crown chakra, or the pineal gland. Attunement with this particular gland begins to activate the physical body as a whole, for by this time there is complete attunement with the pituitary gland and you begin to extend the next abilities within self, the projection of mind into matter. This is possible because surrounding you is a field of energy that you have come to term the aura, visible as the mind extending out in the form of low-voltage brain-wave patterns produced within the physical body. When projected and then concentrated, they have influence upon the electromagnetic field about you. These subtle body energies can be projected into the subtler molecular patterns of the physical, thereby gaining an attunement with the energies that are already existent in that physical property.

The concept of mentally projecting energy to move objects becomes totally irrelevant when you understand that the object itself contains all the necessary energy to cause its own movement of any nature or degree. The mind extends its fine threads of influence into the physical and uses the energies of the object itself to cause its movement. This indeed dispels the mystery of the generation of energy by mind, that is held by your physicists to be impossible. Moreso, the mind uses the energy that is already existent in the object itself.

After attaining to these levels of thought, such activities as levitation are then possible, for by this time the soul and the mind are integrated to such a degree that the activities are extended unto the physical body upon even the cellular levels. So therefore, there is the defying of that which you have come to term as gravity. Gravity does not exist within the spirit itself, and hence the ability of levitation.

Levitation, then, is not so much the overcoming of the gravitational pull of mass upon mass, but moreso attuning yourselves to the vibrations of all things about you. This comes solely through meditation. In the meditative state, the aura, which is the energy field about the physical body, begins to have attunement with certain higher frequencies and begins to break up the patterns of the physical body. This, of course, is a simplification of the process. It is not based upon electromagnetics but moreso attunement with vibrations that exist beyond the speed of light. So by the stepping up of the vibrations within the aura, there is actually the stepping up of vibrations upon a radionic level within the molecular structure of the entire body.

This is but the extension of the metabolic energies that already exist upon the molecular structure of the physical body. And since the body is already in a correct pattern, and meditation simply gathers these energies and focuses them for the desired purpose, the quickening is upon a vibrational level rather than the restructuring of molecules.

Ultimately it is a matter of attuning with those patterns that travel beyond the speed of light. It is not so much that the physical body itself surpasses the speed of light, but it merely approaches it, while yet still holding its pattern within the self. The end result of levitation is not so much the lifting of the physical body or pulling it away from mass, but rather it neutralizes the force of the interplay of the individual and the mass.

Levitation is the stepping stone to *apportation*. Apportation is the ability to dissolve the patterns of the physical body upon the molecular level, project them through the ethers, and reassemble them, not so much from the original structure or matter, but moreso based upon its pattern as it projected through the ethers. The ethers themselves are particles of energy that travel beyond the speed of light. This is different from astral projection, which is the ability of the mind to range beyond the levels of the physical body.

The final ability achievable while remaining incarnate is *ascension* itself. Ascension is the glorification of the physical body through complete attunement of the level of the soul, which is a portion of God. Herein, you would no longer be able to hold yourself on this plane and would dissolve into the dimensional states to reside therein.

Certain forms of psychic unfoldment, such as astral projection, can be accomplished and improved upon by diet. For instance, the taking of certain fruit juices—such as orange, grape, or grapefruit—into the system, one hour before retiring to the dream state, will stimulate your ability to astrally project.

The astral plane is the physical body's ability to enter into a relaxed state and release what is known as the astral body. The astral body is the pattern of energy that keeps your personality structure in containment, so that you function upon this level rather than slipping into levels of lives past. That is, the soul is encased in the astral body to maintain your individuality in these days and in these times.

Many individuals have damaged their astral bodies through alcohol, drugs, artificial forms of stimulants, or other substances foreign to the physical body. These substances are as medicine and must be utilized as such. They have no purpose in spiritual unfoldment except for specific individuals who may have need of them to gain glimpses of the existence and nature of other planes of thought. But they are medicine, not true spiritual food. True spiritual food comes only from the levels of the soul.

Indeed, many of those who have experimented with mind-altering drugs have now entered into practices of meditation, for meditation is the true method to obtain the natural visionary state, drawing into self the natural substance of the etheric bodies, and bringing the entire chakric system into balance. You are now beginning, through physiological research and biomolecular studies, to understand that the physical body contains natural opiates, natural forms of acids and hallucinogens, within your own endocrine system, that, when activated, stimulate the visionary state upon the biochemical and spiritual levels throughout the system as a whole.

Ancient man went into his temples and ingested certain spiritual foods that helped him achieve levels of consciousness that revealed to him information that became integrated into his society as a spiritual force, stimulating him to see man as more than the biochemical processes of the physical body itself. The physical body is as a temple, and you, as a spirit residing therein, can stimulate within the temple similar natural states through meditation on the chakras, which are the connections of the subtle bodies, which can then have impact upon the biomolecular form. Indeed, the physical body maintains all the correct biochemical patterns for the self.

So, the channel speaking would urge all of you to know that you are spirit, and that all of your drugs or medicines are contained within you already. There are many who feel they cannot achieve altered states of consciousness, and so therefore turn to drugs and plantlike substances that contain them. But the higher wisdom is to be in proper alignment within self. For each of you is of the spirit, and your physical body is a greater system of chemistry and balance of spirit than can be achieved through any natural or synthetic drugs.

Each of you has these faculties within you already. When you are discarnate, you have the capacity of recall of many things; yet when you are in the flesh, it is for a specific learning purpose that you recall these things, to understand that even though you are in the flesh, you are not separate from God's works. So therefore, your psychic faculties are but evidence that you are as a spirit, but it is up to the conscious mind to make the final decision of the philosophical orientation to be as a spirit, which is to be loving.

Your psychic unfoldment, then, is the beginning of the opening up to certain levels of the spirit upon the telepathic levels. The spirit must then filter down through the psyche to the levels of the personality. To prepare you for the proper collective state, various negativities surface to consciousness to call your attention to them so that they may be cleansed upon the conscious level.

It is not unlike the process of psychoanalysis, which delves into the subconscious mind and brings up negativities that often cause radical emotional states within you, which you then have to deal with on the conscious levels. So in turn it is with many of you who fear such negativities rising to consciousness. But when your psychic unfoldment is disciplined with meditation, you remove those negativities and become a clear vehicle for the visionary state that follows.

The gift has already been given. It is only a matter of how the one who received the gift develops it. It would be as a man who is given a coin purse and then goes to the marketplace. He may spend the coins or invest them in the marketplace and have many things returned unto him, depending on the wisdom of his investment. So it is dependent on the individual and his or her state of development. You are all given the coins. You have only to go into the marketplace for your own investment within yourselves.

The ability to perceive information and the ability to understand yourselves as spirit should be your highest endeavor within the psychic realms. Do not use these gifts so much for personal gain, but moreso use them as tools for your own growth and the growth of others. In this way you will come to fully understand the psychic faculties that are in a state of unfoldment within you already.

Use your psychic abilities to aid others to align their life pattern with their higher spiritual nature. Your spirituality comes from deep within the self and from your free will. The psychic faculties are but a tool. They are not spiritual progression in itself. They may manifest themselves in spiritual progress, but are not an end unto themselves. They are a tool to be utilized, as all other forms, and are completely neutral in their aspect. It is you who give them their quality. It is you who utilize them either in a wise or in an ignorant manner.

It is within the capacity of each individual to shape and mold his or her spiritual growth. Psychic unfoldment is but evidence of yourselves as spirit, so therefore you should be responsible as a spirit. God is love, and you are a child of God.

Use your psychic faculties in love, to bring you into harmony with other individuals, for harmony is what you desire. If you had full telepathic communication with one another, there would be a bond between all of you, holding all things in common in thought and in spirit. In this way you would know each other's needs even as they arose, and you could minister to one another most fully. This would be a telepathic form of fellowship. If such a faculty was developed, surely you can see the ease with which you may affect one another, and in this way bring peace and love unto each and every one of you.

Meditation, prayer, and fasting are your tools to achieve levels of understanding for further patterns of psychic unfoldment. Whichever psychic gift you choose to manifest, prayer, fasting, and meditation are your cornerstones. Then patience and, as enhancement, correct dietary pattern, preferably vegetarian, and large amounts of fruit, particularly during times of specific development.

Your psychic abilities are tools that you must use constructively. Then you may begin to understand their fullest potential. There are some who would take a mallet and, rather than use it to drive in pegs to build a wooden structure, would use it to produce various sounds, as an instrument. But once the true purpose of the mallet is discovered, the individual may lay out the necessary structure, even as you desire to lay out the structure of your life pattern.

Once the tool is discovered, allow it to have certain areas of authority in your life. Acknowledge that these faculties exist. Record upon papyrus that which you desire to see manifested in your life. Repeat these things three times to yourself while in a meditative state and then lay them aside. You may begin to see the manifestation of these patterns within a specific time period. But it is by faith that these things are done. It is not so much through wishful thinking or dwelling upon things impatiently, but moreso in abiding in true patience until the pattern of evidence is established, to where you would almost take them for granted.

Your psychic faculties may, at times, lay dormant, but this is only because of the limitations of the conscious mind, and not the limitations of God. God is love, and it is your desire to be in harmony with one another that activates these faculties. Telepathy is the cornerstone of the universal form, for you are bound up in a single fellowship through telepathy. It is through these faculties that there is continuous communication with each of you, one unto the other. All individuals have some form of communication with the spirit, if only in their silent prayers or hopes.

Hope itself is the activation of desired information beyond the conscious levels, so therefore it lies strictly within the realm of the individual, and is something you undertake quite naturally. But to develop your psychic abilities, you must become a student and enter into certain areas of discipline for correcting imbalances or obsessions in the personality; otherwise you shall be led into an isolated system of information, which is not healthy in any system of study or communication. So again, it is a potential that all of you have, but do not necessarily develop.

Remember, there is but one commandment that you must obey— "Love the Lord God with all your heart and mind, and your neighbor as yourself"—and in this way you illumine all the paths that go toward home. Never confuse the path with the truth itself. It may lead to the truth, but there is only one truth, and that truth is love. Love is to illumine your heart, and as a man thinketh in his heart, so is he also. Let these things shape the faculties that you have come to term psychic, and so in turn they will aid you in your spiritual growth, that you may return home unto God, who is love.

Tom MacPherson

The psychic without the spiritual is like a cart without a horse. The psychic would be the cart, I suppose, and the spiritual would be the horse. The cart can be nice to sit in, and it can look pretty, and even racy, but without the horse, it doesn't go anywhere.

Atun-Re

There is no need for concern over what you would call psychic protection. It is only your personal emotional make-up that you need have concern about. That is all you must tend to. You may receive messages telepathically that may disturb you a bit, but only if you are emotionally unbalanced in your life. But if you are balanced, merely allow anything to pass through you and return to its source and bless it. So, the only thing you need to protect yourself against is yourself.

On Trance Channeling

John

In trance channeling, that which you term a discarnate personality is able to utilize the physical body for communication from planes beyond the realms of its normal five sensory patterns. Such communications are for the advancement of the collective consciousness of mankind as a whole.

There are many references to channeling throughout your various societies and systems of thought. Perhaps the most common manuscript is that which you know as the Bible. Here you will find many references to the channeling state, wherein individuals such as Joseph, Jacob, Jesus, and the Apostles entered such states and received visions. There are also many references which seem to obscure the trance state, such as "Behold, I fell as a man dead," or, "Sleep entered over to them," but these passages do indeed refer to the channeling or visionary state, through which mankind has received many prophecies and inspiration for many technological advances.

The trance state dates back to Atlantis, when various discarnate beings of the day desired to have influence in the earth plane. Many of the religious structures of those who were known in Atlantis as the Sons of the Law of One reached their final crystallization in your recorded history as the Delphic Oracle. The Oracle was a caste of priests who perpetually maintained the trance state to allow for a continuous flow of consciousness extending forth from the realms you have come to term as spirit beings. This continuous flow was for the advancement of culture and history.

In Greek mythology, there are directly traceable historical remnants of the Trojan wars, the histories of Ulysses, and many others. Although shrouded in myth, these were acted out on many levels of the astral planes and brought forth understanding of the practical applications of channeled information from the various oracles. In those days, oracles were counselors to kings and helped to shape many of the focal points throughout history.

Throughout your society, man has become more and more a technological creature, abandoning many of the influences of the spiritual realm. Yet, these things travel in cycles, as man enters in and out of the spiritual realms of his own nature and his advancement as a collective whole. In more recent systems of thought, man has come to think of channeled information as "superstition." In contrast, he believes he has achieved technological advancement, for instance, in his medicines. But man has not brought about cures in medicine, only embattlement with disease. Channeled information that you term holistic, on the other hand, is now making the pendulum swing the other way, and is beginning to have its impact upon your society, with a return to more natural healing methods. Much of this information has been conveyed in the channeled state through such individuals as Edgar Cayce.

Mediumship predominates amongst females of your race, as they have the correct metabolic rate for the inception and reception of souls and can more easily receive communication from the levels of the spirit realm, or the astral planes. This is why there are higher intuitive faculties attributed to women. This does not exclude the male, or make him an inferior vehicle; it is only that the woman's physical body is metabolically geared to the receiving of information from the levels of the soul.

Mediumship can be developed by any individual, but the cornerstone for this development is meditation. All your great twentieth-century inventions have come not so much through direct research, but from meditation upon that research and the activation of the channeling state. For example, study the individual you know as Albert Einstein. This individual was a visionary. He studied things from the light trance state, contemplating upon a visual level, and then mentally acted out his various visions. Finally, he grounded his insights within the system of mathematics that you call science. But Einstein's understanding of matter and energy and their interaction, as well as the limitations of the philosophy of light, all came to him while in the light trance state.

Witness also Eli Whitney, whose conception of the linotype came to him while in a light trance state, and the man Abraham Lincoln, whose decision to sign the Emancipation Proclamation, which declared all individuals to be equal and abolished slavery in your country, came to him through the mediumistic state of another individual, as documented in your history books.

Many of the discoveries which resulted in your voyages to the moon came to individuals while in the meditative state. It was a combination of technology, meditation upon that technology, and information that came to the individuals in a light trance state that brought about many of your technological triumphs.

Many of your great scientists are focused not so much in practical affairs but in studies which go beyond their own consciousness. Read the various biographies of these individuals and you will find that many obtained visionary levels of thought from what would be termed the light trance state.

Many of your sciences are an integration of meditation and technology, and the sciences that have evolved from them are but the documentation of thoughts which initially came from the trance state. Your sciences, in turn, seek to document those dimensions of existence which parapsychology is now endeavoring to clarify for you—those things which you have come to term the psychic realms, such as telepathy, clairvoyance, clairaudience, and the survival of the personality into those realms which you have termed death.

A light trance state is but the focus of the mind deeply upon that which is immediate with you, and not so much drumming upon these things, but truly meditating upon and examining them, to wherein you become oblivious to your immediate environment. Again, many of your great scientists become totally oblivious to their immediate environment, shutting down the five senses and entering a trance state for the examination of information—not only from the level of their conscious mind, but also from the levels of the superconscious.

To enter into the deeper channeling states is to enter into the repositories of your own consciousness, for each of you possesses these faculties of consciousness, which are no different from any other dynamic of consciousness or phenomenon of memory. For what you are here to do is to recall who you truly are, and channeling is but remembering your true dimensions.

For herein is what channeled information is—it is that which comes from beyond the realms of the normal learning state. It comes from meditation in the light trance state that extends out to the alpha, beta, and theta states of mind and provides knowledge applicable to alleviation of disease, the discovery of new technologies that lie dormant in the consciousness of mankind, and the advancement and progression of your society as a whole.

Mediumship or channeling is but a term for the focusing of spirit through the individual above and beyond the range of his own conscious faculties. Each of you has this faculty and your meditations shall bring it unto you. It is your guides and teachers who communicate with you and have dialogue. But remember to pray only unto God. Acknowledge the Father who is in heaven so that he may send a messenger unto you for the ministry of the angels. And if you perceive God as love, this is the master you will serve.

Chapter 3

❦ The Return

The Dream State

<u>John</u>

The most sensitive state that each individual possesses is the dream state. You practice this state each time you go into slumber, so it is with you at all times. Your psychic unfoldment may begin as the keeping of a journal of your dreams.

Here is an exercise. Select a piece of information you desire to know, perhaps an event before it transpires, or the outcome of a specific set of circumstances. Express your desire for this information, repeating it three times. Meditate upon the circumstances, giving yourself instructions, again three times, that immediately upon receiving the information in the dream state you will awaken and be able to enter the information into a journal. Then, proceed into the sleep state.

The dream state is usually preceded by the grouping of many symbols. Some of these symbols are personal to you, but others are universal—such as the ankh, the serpent, various geometrical forms, pyramidal structures, and the cross. All of these are universal symbols and often have universal applications. For instance, water often symbolizes life itself, such as "the waters of life." A great body of water might mean that you are going to meet many individuals. A small body of water might indicate a personal set of circumstances which is immediately relevant to you.

Individuals often dream about their automobiles. These are symbolic of yourselves and of your conditioning. If the vehicle is in a state of ill repair, this might reflect upon the state of your own personality. The color of the vehicle may give certain psychological clues into your personal functioning. For instance, a red vehicle may pertain to hidden anger. Blue may pertain to the need for healing.

Housing structures are often used to represent the self in dreams. Situations of learning can mean either that you have information to give or information to receive, for your own growth or the growth of another.

Dreams of a displeasing nature, or nightmares, as you term them, are actually positive, and do not necessarily have negative impact or bode ill for you. Moreso they are a cleansing of the subconscious mind—it is only that you tend to remember most graphically those things you fear. The cleansing of the subconscious mind is preparing you for more positive flows of information from the conscious planes or the unconscious activity of the dream state.

After a period of expressing through symbols, the dream state then enters into areas of greater clarity, wherein events take on a more literal appearance. And indeed, this is because the events *are* quite literal. For here you have attunement with the levels of the astral plane, which are as real as the earth plane itself. Often there is a certain vividness to colors, greater even than their vividness on this plane. There is often memory retention of astral travels. Projections of individuals who seem to be of past cultures may be guides and teachers with whom you have contact on the superconscious levels.

Tom MacPherson

The dream state is a dimension. To some degree, it reflects the mundane random wanderings of the subconscious anxieties of the day. But it is literally a dimension, for it is also accessing a broader degree of recall, or mind, or memory that exists independently of the physical body. Then it is actually cycled through the body so that it can become focused in the present. You might call it a "dimension of mind."

The higher self, or superconsciousness, is like a wheel that is constantly turning. It is the causal energy. It comes into the subconscious mind through the subtle anatomies and then cycles through the physical body as the life force. Then it comes up and approaches the conscious realms. It breaks up anything that is unspiritualized or blocked in the physical body and drags it up into the dream state. Your dreams then become a series of symbols of activated energy so you can retain the information consciously from the subconscious, which is the physical body. So, by analyzing your dreams, or by receiving images through hypnosis or meditation, you are being open to that process, which is continuous.

To enhance the dream state I often suggest pickles and onions, because even if dreams don't come up, something else is bound to! No, I say that quite in jest. But there are some dietary measures we can suggest. Altering the diet to consist largely of fresh fruits would go a long way toward promoting a better dream state. For instance, if you were to fast on fruit juices for twenty-four hours, this would increase the dream state.

Orange juice about one hour before slumber is a marvelous stimulant for the dream state because it is rich in natural sugar. This stimulates the muscular tissues, but to such a mild degree that the neurological tissues are still able to rest. These tissues are very similar to the neurons in the brain and are the major seats of consciousness where the dream state is stored. Actually, I could have made a small fortune on the secret to turning off the dream state. I could have charged a penny for the secret to turn it on and then charged a king's ransom to turn it off! But I'll tell you for free—the way to turn off the dream is by eating grains. So, diet can most definitely stimulate the dream state.

The way it works is that with the neurological tissues at rest and the muscular tissues slightly stimulated, dream material is released that comes up and is amplified through the neurological tissues. And you wake up with clearer memory, because the neurological tissues are no longer exhausted. Then, upon awakening, write the images in a dream book and meditate upon them. Don't analyze them, *meditate* upon them.

Even if the meaning of your dream isn't immediately apparent, keep a record of it in your dream journal. You can either meditate on it until the symbols become clear, or you can put it away and come back to it at a later date. But always preserve dreams as a memory and put them on a shelf until they become appropriate. Often the symbols will crack or break just before you need the information. They're like eggs—sometimes you need to sit on them for a while.

If you can't remember the events of the dream, try to follow the feelings. Write the feelings down. You'll find they are like fine threads by which you can pull up the whole fish, or the evening's catch, so to say. It's like casting the conscious mind like a net down into the subconscious and seeing what you can haul up. And feelings are the threads by which you will haul in the whole load.

The left brain is somewhat involved in the memory process and also in the recording of the dreams, but occasionally it gets obnoxious and tries to analyze everything into the ground. If you let it try to analyze, eventually it will exhaust itself, turn the whole thing over to the right brain, and say "Here, you chew on the darn thing for a while." Then the information will come up.

All things which are suppressed are stored in the subconscious mind. Actually, dreams are all neutral—it is your conscious mind that chooses to put an emotional charge on them. If you come to the realization that dreams are just an emptying out of the subconscious, you will realize that although a particular dream could have had a more pleasant form, it is only the purging of your subconscious coming up to the conscious level and letting go of the images. This way you become clearer and clearer with the dream process, rather than rejecting the imagery and resuppressing it. In other words, the very value of it is that, in having dreamed it, you can release it.

Most dreams about death are just transitory events in your life.

Death is with you every day. Actually, death doesn't really exist—only transitions from one state of consciousness to the next. Most dreams about one's physical passing merely mean you have completed a phase of your work. It doesn't mean your ticker will be giving out imminently.

Atun-Re

Dreams attempt to bring you understanding because they lie suspended between the physical body, or the subconscious mind, and the conscious mind. As your dreams come up into the mind to be perceived and become a conscious part of yourself, they generate understanding, and understanding and knowledge are the keys to power. Power is not the ability to change things, but the ability to move things smoothly, so that you bring harmony, and therefore advantage, to your position in life.

In the dream state you pass through the different levels you call beta, alpha, and theta and remember events of past lives (the ultimate memories that are stored in the subconscious). As those things move into the conscious mind, the mind does not wish to retain some of them, so it starts forgetting. And those forgotten memories become emotions, because they are the things you fear. You ask, "What is this I am feeling?" "Something is bothering me." "I am afraid of something—what is it?" But if you meditate upon that baser emotion, you may unlock it and bring it up consciously into realization, and see that perhaps you are reacting to a past life. You then trace your fear of closed spaces to an earlier incarnation; and because you have understood, you are liberated. You are made free.

Each aspect in your dream is some element of yourself, or how you are interacting with another individual, but still reflective of yourself. Therefore, examine each object or each symbol, and see how you respond to it. Meditate upon each symbol and crack it as you would an egg, to see what its contents are.

When you string memories together that are disjointed from your immediate experience, you call it dreams. All aspects of consciousness become life as a dream. In the same way as you interpret your dreams to give them meaning, attempt to interpret each item which comes to you by process of memory, for this is conscious dreaming. It is *lucid dreaming*, for you are dreaming one another.

Intuition, the Still Small Voice

John

Intuition is the harnessing of your full thought process. There is no such thing as matter, there is only thought. Matter follows thought, for all things are but a state of energy. And ultimately, all things are but a state of consciousness. The consciousness that embraces all things is the being you call God, the universal mind. To understand intuition, you must simply understand yourself. You must broaden the context of the origins of self.

Your origins were as a soul. You consist of mind, body, and spirit. The physical body is not a place of imprisonment for the soul or the spirit, it is the very ability of the soul to have focus in time and space. The soul is omnipresent and occupies all sectors of time and space. For it is that phenomenon of consciousness, or that phenomenon of mind, that is one with the greater resources of mind. Since even amidst yourselves you find escalating degrees of intelligence, why not then the universal intelligence, the universal mind you call God? For an ever-increasing consciousness eventually must merge and confront that ultimate consciousness.

Intuition motivates you in the direction of the return to God. The sense of your original nature motivates you to create the various frameworks of life. You call it "philosophy," you call it "intuition," you call it "spirit," you call it the "still small voice." It was said, "Behold, there then came a great wind and the Lord was not in it. Behold, there was an earthquake and the Lord was not in it. Behold, a fire, and the Lord was not in it. Then, I heard a still, small voice." So in turn, you came into the presence of the Lord, into the presence of the divine consciousness, into the universal consciousness from which you have sprung, and all of your life is but a process to return to it. Indeed, you have never left it. You must simply remember.

The mind looks for events when it is shaped by the five physical senses. When it is shaped by intuition and spiritual insight, it deepens your talents. Then you serve God because you serve others in a way that allows you to move *in* the world but not be *of* it, and to partake of it according to need rather than desire or illusion.

Intuition is your greatest capacity. It is the faculty or mechanism to bridge from one level of consciousness to another, be it psychic or through recall of information acquired from the experience of the five physical senses. Intuition is the mechanism by which you recall childhood memories or events from past lives. And through intuition you can see into the future. This is your ability of memory.

What is the major blockage to the intuitive process? The greatest obstacle to intuition is that which blocks memory. And that which blocks memory is simply stress, for does not the stress of the moment block even the most accessible aspects of memory? Imagine then how much it blocks atrophied memory and atrophied memory capacities. When you are agitated, do you not intuitively attempt to recall a calm moment? Do you not intuitively draw in a deep breath? Why do you do this? To relax the physical body. And do not meditation and hypnosis, by relaxing the various stresses and agitations of the body and drawing you into the alpha and theta states, allow for greater memory recall and greater intuitive and creative capacity?

So, what then is the major blockage to intuition? Stress. And what is the major source of stress? Lack of self-esteem. This is perhaps the *only* source of stress. The confident individual does not feel stress, or feels it but is able to channel it and learn from it. It is moreso a process of expansion and contraction, not unlike the phenomenon of breath that alleviates it. For self-esteem, which is the integration of experience and instinct, or actions and instinct, in the now, with a higher memory of self, allows for both intuition and the transference of the insights it provides.

Intuition, which is synonymous with memory, is a flow of energy along the neurological pathways. This is not demonstrable in chemical response, but through the conductivity of the neurological pathways. Stress interferes with this conductivity of the flow of energy. Stress reduction promotes conductivity, so thus the easier flow of the electrical fluidium that is perhaps the closest identifiable physical mechanism of mind within your physical sciences. Reduce stress and you promote the flow of memory, or intuition.

It is within the void, in the nothing that is the everything, wherein lies the key to your intuition, for when you still your thoughts and create that void called knowingness, then you remember. For that void is filled with insight, that you then give other names—creativity, problem-solving, dreams, logic, and various other accords. You string together observations that are repeatable and contrast them against a stable, greater whole. You string them as pearls upon thread and you call them facts. You place them about your neck and you call them science. We would suggest that you should sell this pearl of great price and seek to proceed directly to knowingness. For herein is your true growth, your true psychic development—for your origins were as a soul.

Above all, if you seek to intuit, if you seek to draw up information into your conscious dimensions, think of this—that you are part of God, and it is from God that all things spring, and it is to God that all things return.

Tom MacPherson

There are various intuitive tools. The *I Ching* is a very good one. It is a rather unique method of throwing sticks, not unlike the method of throwing Runes that I used to work with. It is a system of specific symbols worked out in an Oriental method. When you throw the sticks up in the air, they fall into a specific pattern that is not unlike a computer printout of where you are in the position of the whole of things at that moment. It is based on the theory that there is no randomness. It is not that the patterns are randomly generated and you engineer the circumstances—rather, they are revealing a potential for you. If you will, it is a form of divine character analysis.

I found the casting of Runes was quite interesting. The Runes are a series of symbols imprinted on stones. They were originally based on the Atlantean alphabet, which was the reduction of all the primary forces in nature to various simple symbols. One would then more or less cast lots, so to say, and the patterns were studied by the person or the diviner, whose intuiton would then be able to personalize the message to the needs of the person being read. In other words, it was a focus for intuition. The Scandis were very good at it, as well as the Druids. It was actually the Druids who carried it to the

Scandis, I believe. And the Druids were some of the remaining elements of the Atlantean priesthood. So this intuition stuff goes way back. It is by no means new.

Do not take any of what you read to heart; take it all to mind and analyze it. The deeper your intuitive process becomes, the more accurate your analysis. The Runes are a perfect example of a series of randomly generated symbols that your intuition must stitch together. You must analyze them and then carefully engineer the results into your mind. But do not follow it blindly, because you have free will.

There will be times when your intuition is high, and other times when it is low. There will be times when your intuition is excellent but your ability to engineer the circumstances will be very low. For instance, you might have a wonderful vision and no means to engineer it because you are not surrounded by pragmatic enough people. That is when you become a babbling prophet with no one to listen to you. Or there are other times when your analysis will be excellent, but you could not gain the vision to articulate it to other persons. And they will say, "Your analysis is interesting, but it is also dull and uninspiring."

There is nothing that is random, not even selecting fortune cookies in a Chinese restaurant. I do not encourage you to invest your life savings in fortune cookies, but it is not random. It has meaning.

Tarot cards can be used as a form of an instantly accessible dream state, with symbols and meanings already interpreted for you.

Affirmations are applied intuition. For instance, if you were to select a positive image and repeat it over and over in the form of a mantra, eventually you would gain insight into the problem you were working on at that moment. It would just flow to you. Or, you might meet someone who possessed the information you needed. If you will, it is the equivalent of a psychic SOS that goes out telepathically to your peer group. You attract in that person because you are putting out the signal constantly, and then you just make yourself available to the answer.

Have faith in the flow of your own intuition. Following the flow of images that come up is following the stream of your own consciousness. Old Buddhist monks, Mayas, and Druids used to sit by rivers and their thoughts just flowed with the river. If you follow those images, it is not unlike your own self-created river. Some rivers come fast and furious and others move more sluggishly. But be patient and your answers will come.

States of Meditation

John

To deepen your understanding of meditation is to deepen your understanding of self, for meditation is but a process of remembering who you truly are. All of you are children of God, children of light, so meditation is relaxing the physical body while the mind explores these fuller perimeters of itself.

You are a threefold being of mind, body, and spirit. To the student of psychospiritual dynamics, it is stated alternatively that you are subconscious, conscious, and superconscious. The channel speaking suggests that the subconscious mind is the physical body, the conscious mind is the personality, and the superconscious mind is your personal spirit. And it is in meditation that you unite all three.

Stored deep within the subconscious mind are your blockages to obtaining higher realization. Meditation simply integrates the mind, body, and spirit so you can transcend those blockages. Yoga is such a meditative practice, for the word *yoga* means union—the union of mind, body, and spirit. In this union, when you gracefully integrate mind, body, and spirit, or conscious, subsconscious, and superconscious, you come into the whole of your humanity, the whole of your resources, to liberate yourself in your temporary stay in the earth plane.

Meditation is the attempt to expand from subjective memory, which is the perimeters of defined personality, or the ego itself, into higher dimensions and perimeters of the self. It is simply an exercise of facilitating memory to gain access to these higher dimensions and recall the natural order of things that you are already within the center of. In your meditations, seek to apply the same process of memory you would use to recollect personal objects lost.

It has been said by many that in meditation you must suppress the conscious faculties. We would suggest that meditation is the stilling and calming of the conscious mind. This is a procedure of enhanced memory proceeding into higher memory.

It is the physical body that fears suffering. It is the physical body that fears the loss of income that provides its sustenance and food. It is the physical body that fears the loss of its shelter and comfort. All of these fears, which are stimulated by the physical body's need to maintain a position in society that assures its basic comforts, throw the middle self, or the conscious mind, into turmoil. If the physical body is calmed and reassured as to its position in this negotiation, there is a greater desire to ascend. Meditation brings about such a state of assurance.

The body is designed to meet the needs of the spirit, and both are to be servants unto each other, because the physical body is the soul's ability to be focused in the earth plane. The body is not a prison; it is a living temple. When the body learns that meditation and fasting promote greater health and well-being and create greater abundance, it becomes the conductor for spiritual dimensions, and hence the spiritualizing force of the personality. Therefore, it is relaxation, the balancing and removal of anxieties, that you seek through meditation.

All issues of concern arise out of the subconscious, which is the physical body. Isolate the needs of the physical body. Then, when you identify its needs and they are met, your body begins to serve you. When you need more, the body provides you with more. It needs very little in the way of food, and can meet many of its own needs quite nicely. Meditation is the method to enhance that process. Then mind begins to be able to reach its higher faculties.

The subconscious mind is the most limited memory of all. Indeed, the subconscious is the physical body, which only experiences the immediate perimeters of time and space as you experience them now, and in an uncoordinated and unrealized manner. It experiences the physical impulses of hunger and fatigue. Notice the immediacy of its time flow, its grip upon your behavior and sense of well-being and self-esteem. It is the physical body that experiences mortality, and it is out of this sense of mortality that selfishness, survival instincts, and other activities arise.

In the subconscious mind, or the physical body, you find those dimensions of self which you suppress. The reason for this suppression is that you may comfortably maintain aspects of the conscious personality. Those things suppressed are often events from childhood and lives past. Suppression of these in the subconscious, if continuous, eventually leads to stress, and to emotional patterns which you term paranoias and anxieties. If left untreated, these eventually become disease states. But it is in order to maintain the conscious or realized perimeters of your personality that you institute the rule of suppression.

The subconscious mind appears, at times, to be the more active source of your immediate memories, but that is because these are perimeters of experience with which you are familiar and to which you have been conditioned. Therefore they are more easily recognized by the conscious mind. At first, it may not seem as if you have this same ease of access to superconscious states, but through practice they, too, become familiar. It is not that meditation becomes easier with practice, but that the memories become more familiar. Just as you can repeat the name of a stranger until it becomes so familiar that the person may become your friend because of this familiarity, so in turn the nurturing aspects of meditation are exercises in divine mind. When you begin to remember these higher faculties, they begin to serve you by revealing your linkage with the truer order of things and the natural harmony that you are already in the center of. Meditation allows access to the causal force of your own life pattern.

The physical body is the living temple. The mind is the priest that dwells therein and seeks to contemplate the nature of God, and the spirit is the presence that links you with the divine.

The conscious mind has only one faculty, the capacity of memory. Are you not ultimately broken down into a series of events that cling together and rearrange themselves into an aspect of vocabulary? You are continuous dialogue. You are continuous bits of the time flow rearranging themselves within the context of personality. This is consciousness itself, continuous awareness of events that have flowed through time and space.

Do not suppress the conscious mind. Moreso, you should still its dialogue with you, and then extend it. For the conscious mind is the activity of memory, and you desire to remember portions of that which is on the levels of the soul. Therefore, extend the conscious mind, even as you would a vessel; empty it of wasteful dialogue and it will bring forth balance.

The conscious mind is not to be suppressed. It desires ultimately to extend itself to the levels of the soul, for it is the messenger in this particular plane. Therefore, never chastise the conscious mind. Moreso, extend it. Use it as a tool. In this way, the visualization process may become clearer to you. For the mind is as a loom upon which all these things are threaded and the tapestry is fulfilled.

The superconscious mind, which is synonymous with the spirit, is the sum total of the grandeur of all the past lives you have lived, as well as all of your future potentials. It is a vast ocean of cosmic consciousness that each of you is at one with. When you incarnate, or when this consciousness focuses itself through the physical body at birth, then, collectively, the events in this lifetime are the sum total and expression of all of your past lives and all of your future lives, transpiring simultaneously.

The superconscious mind consists of all your higher ideals and is your access to higher ideals from past lives, those things which the spirit and the soul know from personal experience in the earth plane. It is the conditions from lives past, as well as actions in this lifetime. But here we do not find the principle of suppression, as with the subconscious mind. Rather, we find a process of denial even more subtle—the "refusal to ascend." For there are higher ideals which would alter and transform the conscious personality, or the middle self, and the refusal to ascend, or to realize these higher ideals, is as much a denial process as the refusal to access the subconscious.

The refusal to ascend is where the individual denies the existence of higher forces or of his own spiritual dimensions. All individuals have the capacity of higher ideals, but they maintain a barrier of static within their consciousness that they refer to as cynicism. This mental state allows individuals to remain comfortable with the current known perimeters of identity, from which they challenge anyone to show them a system of higher ideals that works unconditionally. This is not so much suppression, but refusal to ascend to a higher ideal that would transform the personality beyond their own definition or recognition of themselves, which is what they fear. It is the middle self, the conscious self, within the perimeters of the ego and the ego's desire to survive, straddling between the subconscious and the superconscious states, refusing to ascend.

The physical body was created as an instrument and a seat of consciousness. It is the conductor for the life force itself. The sense of well-being that comes with relaxing immediate anxieties or tensions through the calming influences of breath and meditation, as well as the subsequent alleviation of disease states and, hence, increased longevity, are reflections of the penetrations of the higher self, or the superconscious states of the personal spirit, into the physical body, beginning to activate higher memories. For with each dimension of mind, from the subconscious and its limited perspective of the time flow, to the broader perspective of the conscious mind and its ability to access prenatal and conceptual points and plan for the future events before they transpire, it is in the superconscious states that you ebb and flow into future events and those things which transpired in lives past.

With conscious rhythmic breathing, the mind begins to consciously penetrate the realms and dimensions of the physical body. But also with the first drawing of breath, the conscious mind ascends into the higher dimensions, aligning those faculties known as the "subtle anatomies"—the etheric, emotional, mental, astral, spiritual, and soul bodies—for these are the anatomies of the superconscious. And, as your consciousness expands radially out into these dimensions and into the aura, there are mental linkages with the planetary consciousness, or the Akashic Records, in fourth-dimensional existence. You then also access telepathic linkages with other individuals upon the planet. So, as your consciousness expands radially, it takes on a spatial phenomenon.

The best meditation technique is the one which results in the quieting of the body, and that technique is personal to self. If it is dance, so be it. If it is disciplined posture, so be it. If it is yoga, so be it. If it is running, so be it. Meditation is that which relaxes the body while the mind explores the perimeters of itself.

In meditation, the body ceases to exist as you know it. When the physical body is stilled, the emotions are stilled, and you are alerted to your higher resources—your feelings. Feelings are the merger of

the intellect and the emotions. Alchemically, they are then transformed. You then eat from need rather than from emotion. This is
the principle of right diet. Eventually, on both the spiritual and
philosophical levels, you are more inclined toward vegetarianism,
because you become aware of other sentient beings, other life
forms, and their natural order of things. This is one of the first steps
to restoring the natural way. You become vegetarian and master
other principles of right diet.

When you attain a state of detachment in meditation, you gain
the ability to observe. This enables you to attain higher ground so as
to become the inquiring mind, to ask questions clearly. We do not
speak of an "impersonal" state. It is not detachment from the emotions. It is to calm the emotions, to bring integrity and confidence.
It is the ability of faith. Faith is evidence of things unseen. It is the
ability to gain higher states, to contemplate, to meditate, to ponder,
to still the emotions and observe them, and then to move toward the
higher self.

Pondering such divine personages as Buddha and Jesus is appropriate in meditation. Pray only to God, but carry on dialogue with
those who personify the divine, for they are historical examples of
what you may achieve in your own spiritualization process. And is
this not better than to dwell upon earthly or mundane affairs, those
which you call anxieties? It is far better to dwell upon the divine, for
this is meditation. It is the focusing upon your own higher potentials,
and this brings optimism, joy, and ecstasy.

One of the key tools or techniques of meditation is connected
breath. Breath is the measurement of conscious control over the
autonomic functions of the physical body, since it is an autonomic
response to which you have quick and easy access. Using conscious
connected breath in specific rhythms, the student can begin to gain
meditative accessing of the physical body. So therefore, rhythmic
breathing in a conscious context would naturally lead the student
into the inner stillness, which is the source of higher memory.

You find this reflected in the natural act of ponderance, wherein
you "draw the breath," or what you term "sigh." It is instinctive
that, when accessing memory, the physical body is calmed and
memory becomes clearer. For the physical body is a conductor and
a storehouse for things which are unrealized, for karmic patterns

which are the foundations and tapestries of your life purpose. Stored in the physical body, which is the living temple itself, are all those things which are unrealized from past lives. If it is unrealized it is subconscious. I would suggest to you that since the physical body *is* the subconscious mind, when you bring rhythmic breath within the living temple, stilling it and quieting it in meditation, the mind begins to explore the fuller dimensions of itself in accessing subconscious memories of past lives.

The physical body is not a place of imprisonment of the human spirit, it is the ability of the soul to have focus in time and space. You are a highly sophisticated system and an ever-escalating degree of consciousness. The faculty of mind which you possess has a very specific anatomy for the different altered states that you enter into. Beta is the state of unconscious repository. Alpha is the state in which you begin to deepen your meditative practice. Herein you find most of the psychic dimensions and the ability of astral projection. Theta is the state of the deeper resources approaching the subconscious. And even as the mind and the physical body have an anatomy, so in turn does the superconscious. The anatomical form of the superconscious is the chakras and the subtle anatomies.

Meditation aligns the chakras and the subtle anatomies and brings you into the true expression of consciousness that you are. For all that you are is an ever-increasing dimension of consciousness, until eventually you become one with God and enter into nirvana. Entering into nirvana, you enter into the nothing that is everything and the everything that is nothing. For God knows all things, and in knowing does not have the capacity to think. When all thought ceases, your own existence as you know it ceases, and you enter into a knowingness or nirvana.

Mind has the capacity to become misaligned. The spirit and the soul are always aligned with the divine. The chakras are always open, for they are the portals to the divine. It is only mind that gives the illusion of the closing of the chakras. So, as you still the mind and listen to the full self, then you become knowing. All thought then ceases and you enter into the deepest resources of the meditative state and are transformed.

By focusing your consciousness on the chakras, you will start the self-actualization process. When all the chakras are meditated upon, you will come naturally into a state of knowingness. But above all else, you must dwell upon the divine; then the chakras become entirely clear and mind is aligned with its full potential, with full memory of itself.

Astral projection is a by-product of meditation. It is not as though you learn to astrally project, for there is no such thing as learning. The only thing you learn is how little you knew before. Astral projection is _remembered_, for you astrally project at all times. Astral projection is the ability to focus upon your own broader sphere of consciousness and yet still maintain the individual consciousness you are in this lifetime.

Substances such as marijuana and mushrooms do little more than stimulate the body's own physiology, which is a by-product of the mind seeking the higher dimensions. The physical body itself has more complex physiologies that transpire in the meditative states than could ever be imagined from the ingestion of any such outside forces.

In certain societies, these mind-altering substances were ingested more as part of a nutritional regimen, in very minute quantities. This allowed the physical body to draw upon those substances naturally and gradually. The channel speaking does not place a value judgment on the ingestion of these things in larger quantities, but neither is it encouraged, for meditation is complete and unique in and of itself. In the space of one breath, your own physiology may bring about a deeper personal rapport with the divine than many years of ingesting outside substances.

Daydreaming is meditation. Sleep is meditation. Even depression may be biologically-induced meditation, for it forces you into a contemplative state. All of these processes are meditative in their nature. They may lead to a full meditative state according to free will and how close you tread to the divine.

Meditation is a process of memory accessing superconscious and subconscious states, so therefore, accessing information through the dream state from subconscious and superconscious faculties is a meditative procedure. But the individual must still ponder or meditate upon those things accessed from the dream state so they become conscious.

Everyone meditates. The physical body needs meditation as much as it needs sleep and the drawing of breath, for meditation is suspended between those two states. The individual who is overtaxed through a lack of sleep, or from overstressing the physical body, creates suspension in the emotions. This often leads to daydreaming, which is a biologically-induced meditation. Overstress the emotions lead to depression, which is also a biologically-induced meditation. Meditate before your slumbers, or immediately upon rising. Never so busy is the day that meditation would not eventually be induced upon the biological levels.

Climbing, dance, and athletics are also procedures of meditation because they merge mind, body, and spirit in singleness of purpose. But note that they are *procedures*. When the purpose is to align with the higher self—that is, the higher perimeters that you would call God—and carry on a dialogue therein, then indeed it becomes a true meditation. Meditation is the occupation of the physical body while the mind explores the fuller perimeters of itself. But also, meditation is your dialogue with the highest source in the universe, and the expectation of an answer. Therefore, it is the merger of prayer and receiving an answer to that prayer while in the meditative state.

When you meditate upon the seven chakras, you become knowledgeable that your activities upon this plane are perhaps as a dream. And even as you gain states of awareness from your dreams, then in turn you would realize that this level of existence is also a dream. As you create and shape your reality through the focus of your inner vision—just as you attempt to focus the vision of your dreams—so in turn should you have the focus of the outer manifestation, the dreaming in your waking hours. This comes through prayer, which is dialogue with the Father/Mother God. It comes with meditation, the time you would spend in communication with God. When you align the chakras, you prepare the living temple for appropriate dialogue with God. These are the tools by which you become aware of the higher activities.

When you meditate, you extend yourself to the levels of the soul. Herein is where the Father dwells, the Father/Mother God who is the creator of all. God is love, and if you love one another, all things shall be given unto you. The simplicity of love is often mocked. Love means harmony. It takes the discipline of the individual in this physical plane to bring about harmony, which is the work of God active with you. And indeed, you are a portion of that work.

Tom MacPherson

The same processes of mind you draw upon to find objects you have misplaced physically are drawn upon in meditation to recall past lives. You think to yourself, "If I just stop thinking about that bloody name, I'll remember it," and when you stop the internal dialogue, often the name comes drifting into consciousness. Meditation procedures are the same, except that you are focusing your attention on a misplaced memory, say from a past life or from childhood. So it is merely a process of memory, and drawing it back in on a more disciplined and higher scale. But the processes are identical.

When the mind comes into rapport with the physical body during meditation, it reaches its highest faculty, which is simply memory. The physical body basically needs positive reinforcement that everything is all right. It is the body that experiences mortality, not the mind or the spirit. Once you calm the body, or meet its basic needs through meditation, the mind can then access higher memory, or the spirit, which is your inner guide.

It's always appropriate to take time with yourself and God, and then, if we may contribute a wee bit, we will take advantage of that opportunity. Daily meditation is always recommended. It's rejuvenating to the physical body, calms the nerves, promotes healing of all the internal tissues, puts you in touch with God, and just about anything else any other snake oil would promise. It is a general toner.

When you focus on the chakras, it is more like contemplating or meditating than analyzing. For instance, it's possible to contemplate one's navel, but it's impossible to analyze it. And if you don't believe me, try analyzing your navel sometime.

When you meditate and you find yourself fixating on one thought, don't consider the thought an obstacle. If a thought keeps recurring, focus on it, and eventually, when you follow it to its natural extreme, it will untie itself just like a Gordian knot. That is working on a problem-solving level. That obsessive thought will actually lead you into the next deeper state.

When you meditate, you increase the life force within you. The life force actually animates or quickens the body and allows more consciousness or deeper aspects of yourself to come to the surface, and you feel more lively within the experience of life.

Meditation is the merger of mind, body, and spirit, whether it's done consciously or arises spontaneously. Since there's only one experience in meditation, use that which basically works for you. Dancing, running, slumbering—these are all meditations. I would say it's the one that you apply that works best.

To meditate, you can lie down, be comfortable, and then just run off a mental list of things on your mind. If one of the things on the mental list seems more predominant, or seems to repeat itself, select that one. Keep turning it over in your mind and see what is trying to be communicated to you.

It's even possible to meditate while watching your "boob tube," or what I like to refer to as your modern day crystal ball. God is so powerful, he could probably even reach you through this instrument. Upon occasion, people will slip into a slightly meditative or hypnotic state while watching television, perhaps while watching a movie that emulates the life of an inspiring individual. These are communications through a human medium, and since the human medium can indeed inspire, and inspiration can lead to a meditative state, this is why I say it's even possible to meditate a bit while glued to your tube.

The dream state is your most valuable source of psychic information. I once teased a person, asking him if he would be willing to delegate one-third of his life to spiritual pursuits. He said, "Well, I don't know—I like to watch television and play a lot of tennis . . ." and he wasn't certain whether he could be that ascetic. And I said, "Well, that's too bad, because you dream or sleep one-third of your life already, and all you have to do is become cognizant of that very rich source of meditative and contemplative information from both the subconscious and superconscious, and one-third of your life is already dedicated as a spiritual practice." Indeed, the lazy man's approach to meditation can be to meditate just before falling into slumber.

Atun-Re

Your spirit, or your superconscious mind, is the ascension principle; the conscious mind is the middle self; and the subconscious
mind, or physical body, is the suppression principle. You must see
this as a continuous, active, functioning dynamic. For it is when the
superconscious mind comes down and penetrates the subconscious,
where there is something familiar to attach itself to, and then brings
it back up to the conscious mind, where it can be recognized, that
you can choose to ascend or to be inspired. Or where you can
choose to recognize impulse as emotion and then seek to translate it
to understanding and then sensitivity. This continuous process is the
perimeter of the functions of your confused personality, for it is all
one process. Through this continuous oscillation, you move along
the time flow of subjective reality, and the continuous oscillation
between these three dimensions of yourself becomes life.

You can overcome the resistance to ascend by first seeing how
ascendancy serves you. The spirit is continuously flowing, like a
river, animating the physical body, constantly drawing in the higher
ideals and coordinating them with the karmic events that are stored
in the physical body. For it is through the physical body that you
experience karma, and the mind determines how you organize and
react to it. But when you merge mind, body, and spirit, as in
meditation, you gain understanding.

Once in meditation, you expand out through the levels of the
subtle anatomies, examining all the coordinated perimeters of your
past lives, into the infinite time flow, to the levels of the soul itself.
Your astral body shields you from too much information, for if you
begin to feel too much like Napoleon, they lock you up in a rubber
room. If you feel yourself too much as the ancient Egyptian, you are
considered eccentric. So they must all be carefully coordinated into
the fat little American, whose body is expanded because he eats too
much of the time flow.

All things are a state of energy and you must carefully coordinate
each of these energies. That is what meditation allows you to do. As
you open each of the kundalini properties, you carefully coordinate
each of the levels of the time flow from all your past lives. And as

this energy goes out to create the events of future lives, they become carefully coordinated in the center of the time flow that is the physical body itself, the soul's ability to be focused in the time flow that you call the "now." Meditation is the coordination of those energies so you create an even and consistent time flow affecting the space about you.

Allow me to give you a simple meditation: Those who eat meat, including seafoods, give them up for seven days. See what that stirs up in you. See if old Atun-Re is not correct about the immediate demands of the body. See if you don't find yourself skulking about in the kitchen late at night and worrying that God is watching over your shoulder. For those who already eat no meats, take in no stimulants or alcohol for seven days. And for those of you who already take no stimulants, fast three days upon juices. This will cause you to meditate and will put you in touch with your emotions.

The very elimination of meat or stimulants for one week will throw you into a meditative state and show you how the life flow itself is a meditation. It is to merge your mind, body, and spirit in a commitment to a spiritual discipline. And it is not even a discipline, for discipline is simply cutting away those things which you do not need and are actually barriers to your living a fuller life.

When you ascend, you try to move above and beyond the time flow itself. You begin to actually resist gravity, even in the sense of the physical. The feet are more firmly on the ground, so you feel more "grounded." When you seek the inspiration of higher dimensions, how much more well shaped you are in mind, body, and spirit. For meditation is the linkage of mind, body, and spirit in service to the higher and greater goal, which is your soul, to make you all children of light.

The sun radiates down to all; it reveals all things. The sun is like the soul. The soul has chosen to express itself in certain ways, in meditation is your dialogue with the higher spirit. In the same way that you enjoy the warm embrace of your earthly parent, your father or mother, embrace both God and your soul in your meditation. It is a dialogue. Meditation increases your knowledge of yourself so that you can enjoy that embrace. Service to others allows you to practice your abilities and talents. Sad is the man or woman who does not serve, because then they can only be enslaved. Your service is your work, your occupation. Prayer is your ability to express. Prayer is the *key* to expression. It is your openness with one another. It is the blessing that you send to persons in your conversations with God.

Meditation is a comfortable structure in which you can speak with God. Prayer is your chosen dialogue with God. Fellowship is those with whom you serve, those who are your friends. When those things merge you can then give love, you can give harmony.

How can you take advantage of the fuller faculties of the subconscious mind in order to achieve a fuller understanding? Begin with what is called the "higher self," which projects down like the rays of Ra to illumine those parts of yourself that you would then call the subconscious mind, which could be represented by the jackal, or the underworld. In the Pyramid, this is the deeper inner chamber, since the Pyramid itself is a model for higher consciousness. But to understand these things—this is the abyss of your subconscious mind, ruled by the underworld of the jackal.

The jackal is that which seeks to devour all things and to hold on to the underworld and keep the person dead, not fully alive. Here, then, we have the individual, the mind, which brings forth knowledge and wisdom, for it dwells between your superconscious and subconscious mind. And here is the mystery. Your subconscious mind is not the source of your growth and never has been, for it is the jackal that seeks to consume all things, all true measure of growth. The subconscious mind is but a storehouse of things unrealized. And the subconscious aspects of yourself are those things not yet spiritualized, upon which no light has been cast. The solar disk which sees all things as through the eyes of Horus has cast no rays into the subconscious.

What is the subconscious? It is your physical body. It is the shell and the veil of forgetfulness that you have put over yourself as an incarnating soul. So, you develop therapies that still the jackal, that put it to sleep—your hypnosis, your meditations, all these things still the jackal. Meditation relaxes the physical body to allow the consciousness of your personality to explore higher dimensions. What comes forth is that these dimensions of the higher self constantly work through the flow of the subconscious mind.

If you still the subconscious mind, if you pour it out, if you give up all your feelings of mortality, if you relax your physical form, if you promote healing based upon the spirit, then you have emptied out the subconscious. It no longer breaks up or blocks the flow of the superconscious as it enters in to spiritualize the subconscious and then passes up into the higher dimensions that become your conscious self. The emptier the subconscious, the clearer the flow from the higher self.

Through meditation and prayer, you acknowledge your limitations, and these empty out from the subconscious. But if you do not acknowledge your limitations, if you hide from that argument you had, or deny that you transgressed against someone, the event remains buried in the subconscious mind until eventually your superconscious brings it up to you in dreams. Often you will see it as symbols. If you continue to suppress it, perhaps it will become demons which you create that haunt you, that cause your muscles to tighten and perhaps your belly to ache. Eventually it becomes what you call psychosomatic illness, for your subconscious mind *is* your physical body.

As a human being, you dwell in the points in between the superconscious and the subconscious mind. This is the human personality. This is you. You are made up of both subconscious and superconscious aspects at many points in time. You are never out of touch with the superconscious; you only think you are because you believe you must go through the subconscious or study your dreams. But the superconscious or higher self is with you all the time. Therefore, empty out your subconscious. Go to your higher dimensions. For that is where all of your talents lie. It is a mistake to think it is the subconscious that is doing the work. It is merely a dormant storehouse. It is your superconsciousness, your spirit, your soul, that does all the work. It is the causal force of creativity. The subconscious is merely a storehouse where you prepare for the revelations the superconscious then brings you.

Now, my children, be silent and dream. Suspend yourself within the egg of eternity. And now, cease your dreaming and awaken to the greatest reality of all. Look upon the face of the one who sits next to you, for in this fellowship is where you find God. Love one another. Touch the one that sits next to you, for here is the greatest action of all: fellowship, to live with one another. Here is the dream that you occupy. For is not daily life a dream? Is not each person gathered herein a symbol of something past, something hidden? If you are shaped by karmic conditions, dreams of past lives, then in turn this is also a dream, is it not? Is it not an illuminating factor that all of you gather here in common purpose? This is a greater meditation, is it not?

The Chakras, Template of Perfection

John

The chakras are the source of your higher consciousness. They are a blueprint or pattern of the higher self. It is through the seven major chakras within the physical body that the soul makes its imprint on the earth plane. The chakras are the ethereal structures of the anatomy which find their seats within particular anatomical points in the physical body; they are the animators of the body.

The chakras are a template or blueprint along which mind then enters and establishes a correct pattern for itself. Each time you meditate on the chakras, each time mind is exposed to that template and enters into those vortices of energy, it is positive reinforcement for the pattern of that perfection. Thus you are dealing with the pattern of "behavioral illumination." Simply expressed, is not memory enhanced through positive reinforcement? And is it not by the process of memory that one truly conceives of himself? And is it not by inspiration that one transcends and knows joy? So, by meditating on the chakras, which are already a template of perfection that is personal and relevant to the self, you give positive reinforcement to the memory of the perfection. Then, when the chakras are opened, or rather when mind opens to that perfection, inspiration follows.

The chakras are the seat of consciousness of each individual. At the point of transition that you call physical death, it is the chakras and the various subtle anatomies and meridians that survive. Indeed, it may be more accurate to say that you *are* the chakras, you *are* those subtle energies, for they are truly the roots of your consciousness. The more you focus upon those realities, the greater command you have over the true reality that you are.

The seven chakras are common to all cultures, all expressions. In Judeo-Christian systems of thought, they are referred to as the Tree of Life. They are the Seven Churches of the Book of Revelations. They are the wheels of the Eastern systems of thought. They are the Seven Serpents of the Quetzalcoatl mythology. They are the seven spirits of men and women that, when fully integrated, become the blueprint for the higher self.

The first chakra is found at the base of the spine, or the coccyx; the second chakra is found within the sexual gender (in the female the ovaries, and in the male the testicles); the third chakra is found in the stomach regions or the abdomen; the fourth chakra resides in the region of the thymus, or the heart; the fifth chakra is within the throat, or the activities of the thyroid; the sixth chakra, or what you term the third eye, is located in the area of the pituitary gland; and the seventh, or crown, chakra is the pineal gland, at the top of the head.

When viewed from a highly clairvoyant state, the chakras appear as rays extending forth from the seats of anatomy along the spinal column up into the regions of the brow, then extending out to the horizon, not unlike the natural spectrum of the rainbow. These rays extend into infinity because the soul itself is an infinite being, and the physical body is the soul's ability to be focused in time and space. So thus, the soul literally creates the physical body according to the natural laws of the earth plane; and it gives itself permission to have focus in time and space.

The seven rays extend from the infinity of the soul into the limited time/space factor, to create the phenomenon of the chakras, in which the soul personifies itself in the individual personality of a chosen incarnation. So thus, you may see the rays as an extension from the soul, holographically creating the chakras or the template upon which the physical body (so thus the subconscious and conscious mind) is created.

The seven rays are the individualization of the soul's force in correlation to higher universal mind. Indeed, they are the very force by which the universal mind, or the soul itself, individualizes through the chakras.

The chakras, or the seven seats or centers of consciousness, are associated with certain key words. With the first chakra, the key word is *understanding*, for to progress in anything, there must first be understanding. The key word for the second chakra is *creativity*, for you create your own reality from the basis of understanding. The key word for the third chakra is *sensitivity*, for you must have sensitivity and empathy for others to be able to fulfill yourself. The key word for the heart chakra is *love*, for love is the innate harmony that exists in all things and you must be harmonious in anything you would understand, create, or be sensitive to. With the fifth chakra, you have *expression*, the issue of articulation, the ability to express yourself to other parties. In the sixth chakra is *vision*, the capacity to sense purpose. Finally, *divine purpose* is synonymous with the seventh or crown chakra.

The chakras are a self-actualizing system wherein you uplift yourself from the baser instincts to the higher levels of consciousness, and the higher being that you truly are is revealed. For you are a being that consists of mind, body, and personal spirit, and it is in the integration of these three that you become at one with the higher force—that is, with the Father, the Son, and the Holy Spirit, or the Father/Mother God. For in this linkage you manifest the blueprint of your truer identity, which is to manifest the Christ within the self, or the merger of mind, body, and spirit in service to God.

The chakras govern your physical reality. What appear to be randomly generated events in your life, such as persons, opportunities, and various other affairs, are often reflected in the subtle anatomies long before they become manifest in the physical. The chakras and their relevant patterns of energy are the forces that attract appropriate persons and circumstances into your life. They are patterns of magnetic energy which both attract and repulse. According to these energies, you attract to yourselves persons and circumstances according to their own natural polarities and magnetic influences. For truly, life is but a series of highly coordinated vibrations, systems of attraction and repulsion, and the degree to which you center the chakras is the degree to which you bring a more harmonious outer manifestation into your personal life circumstances.

The opening of the chakras can be a key to centering you in your true nature. The most valuable asset you possess is your personality. Personality is the vocabulary by which you communicate with all other beings. For indeed, the human ego, or the human personality, is just that—a vocabulary. It is nothing more and nothing less. It is the means and the manner by which your character articulates itself. And that personality, that vocabulary, is a by-product of the chakras and the degree to which they are open or closed. The more you work with yourself in the spiritual dimension, the more the chakras are opened. But here is another mystery—the chakras never truly open or close. Indeed, the chakras are open at all times. It is only the *mind* which is closed. And when you have attuned the mind to the spiritual centers, it opens under the influence of the chakras.

The physical body is not unlike a hologram. Just as your sciences re-create three-dimensional images through the holographic process, so in turn you are a being of seven dimensions. You consist of height, width, and depth, as well as time, space, mind, and consciousness. In these seven dimensions is revealed the full spectrum of yourselves as conscious beings. Even as in the earth plane you have three levels of consciousness (conscious, subconscious, and superconscious) because you dwell in three dimensions (height, width, and depth), so in turn the soul has seven levels of consciousness and dwells in all seven dimensions. These dimensions intersect and find their focus in the chakras, the seven levels of consciousness that make up the sum total and essence of the soul's influence in the daily affairs of your lives.

If you ponder the nature of the chakras in kundalini meditation, you open yourself to the seats of consciousness wherein the true roots of your personality are revealed, for the substance of your personality finds its focus through the chakras. Even as the flesh brain is specialized in its functions, allowing you speech, logic, intuition, and creativity, so in turn is the physical body itself, in its wholeness, the seat of the soul, the seat of the anatomy of the seven chakras.

The mind extends itself into all aspects of the physical body through the neurological tissues, like roots extending into the earth to gain nourishment. The physical body is a point of focus, and the neurological tissues are as the roots of consciousness, extending deep into the housing of the temple of the physical body, to be drawn up and consciously realized and then woven into the tapestry that becomes your personality. But what then? For mind is not your only source of consciousness; you also have your spiritual dimensions. And it is through the chakras that your spirit integrates fully into the trinity of mind, body, and spirit.

Your physical sciences look to the physiological and biological patterns of the physical body for the source of the personality, but they find only reflections of these things in the various chemical properties they observe. These are but the shades of the truer causal force, which are the wheels of revelation, the chakras, continuously animating the physical body from the molecular to the anatomical levels. The by-product of that is your personality and your personal life pattern.

It is through the chakras that you extend out into infinity. It is also through the chakras that the soul has its intimacy in the earth plane, that intimacy being the life that you live. When you align the chakras, you may then draw up the seats of memory of the soul, for the soul extends out into infinity itself and occupies all sectors of time and space. And it is through the chakras that the hologram of the physical body is created and given animation and coordinated as a delicate instrument of radiant energy.

There are many techniques for energizing the chakras. First, you must have knowledge of what they do and their particular area of influence. The lower chakras are often given for procreation. But also, the proteins produced in both men and women that go either into ovulation or the production of spermatozoa may be drawn again into the physical body for its own spiritual fortification. These proteins are then passed into the blood system or circulatory tract, where there is the filtering of the spleen and production of certain hormones and antibodies that spiritualize the physical body along biochemical lines. These are the biological activities of the chakras. But also, when these energies are applied to the physical body, they intensify spiritual healing, which eventually shapes man's personality, which is his tool for spiritual expression and learning in this plane. This may be done through meditation, yoga, prayer, and fasting.

Since the chakras are of the soul, as you attune to the chakras, you attune to the specialized function that the soul desires to manifest in the earth plane, shaping your character and nature according to the lessons that you, as a soul, fully desire to learn. The more you become aware of this phenomenon, the more your mind opens to its higher resources. And the more you restore your own angelic nature, the more you become as an infinite being.

The spirit, the soul, is always aligned with the divine. The chakras are always open, for they are the portals to the divine. It is only mind that gives the illusion of the closing of the chakras. So therefore, as you still the mind and listen to the full self, then you become knowing, all thought ceases, and you enter into the deepest resources of the meditative state. You are then transformed, and all things are set aright.

Tom MacPherson

If given half a chance, the chakras are totally self-correcting. They are always in balance; it is only that you accept, or don't accept, the information they are bringing you. It is not actually aligning the chakras, it is aligning *with* your chakras.

Healing is a by-product of the alignment of the chakras. Is it not true that you can heal ulcers by alleviating anxieties? And aren't most allergies a product of mental stress? So therefore, healing is a process of aligning with the chakras and allowing divine mind to come in. For if mundane mind, or conscious mind, can heal, just imagine what divine mind can do.

Think of the chakras as a system of harmonics. Each person has a particular pitch to which he is attuned, according to the harmonics of his chakras. Certain colors have specific notes or octaves associated with them. The color a person is attracted to is a key to what part of the human instrument is attuned to a particular octave. The sarcophagus inside the Great Pyramid is attuned to a specific pitch which is the master key or octave to which everyone can attune.

Picture the spinal column as a series of musical scales where the nerve endings come out. Put an octave at each one of the chakra points—one at the coccyx, one at the tissues associated with the sexual gender, one at the stomach, one at the heart, and so on, up to the pituitary and the pineal—and you will find a complete scale. Then, by a series of sharps and flats, you would be able to attune particular octaves, scales, and notes to the kidneys, the liver, and so forth, literally playing the human instrument.

The pineal gland is the master seat or center of consciousness. Along with the pituitary gland, it is commonly referred to as the third eye. The pineal gland itself is the crown chakra. It is the most protected gland in the whole body. It stimulates the regions of the hypothalamus and is actually the true seat of consciousness in the body. The brain tissues work with the more mundane aspects of intuition and analysis, whereas the pineal gland is truly the seat of consciousness itself.

The closest model I can come up with to describe the interface between spirit and the physical seat of consciousness is when your Marconi fellow, if I have it correctly, broadcast electromagnetic waves at a crystal. The crystal resonated, and audible sound resulted from the transference to electrical impulses. In many ways, the pineal gland is quite similar. Being rich in silicon, I believe, which is very similar to quartz in its crystalline properties, the spirit interfaces with it and resonates, and this becomes detectable as the bioelectrical functions of the body, which stimulate the cell-division process flowing along the meridians and other energy fields concentrated around the chakras. So it is not unlike the way a quartz crystal can pick up finely tuned electromagnetic energy and translate it to physically audible energy.

Aligning the chakras is facilitated by vegetarianism and fasting. Vegetarianism, in general, will promote health to these glands. And beyond this, a rigid diet of fruit, over a period of anywhere from one week to forty days, can be an excellent technique to help develop a sensitivity and awareness of these glands. I don't recommend this diet all the time, but seven days of it should prove to be good, particularly fasting on mangoes.

The chakras are always open. The best thing to do is to still the mind. Let the chakras do their work without the mind getting in the way. The left brain loves to poke into things. The key thing is that as you self-actualize through the chakras and the subtle anatomies, you recall everything. This aligns your superconsciousness, and the only thing left is God. This manifests as an overpowering sense of completion, a profound altruism, and a strong desire to live life simply. It is called "the ecstasies"—a divine form of madness, depending on how well you handle it.

Atun-Re

It is only because you deny that the chakras are open that perhaps they appear to be closed. The chakras are continuously open. They function with you at all times, otherwise life itself would have ceased. It is only the degree to which you receive the information they bring to you that you think they are open or closed.

Even the concept of opening and closing is incorrect, for the spirit is continuously with you. It is only the illusion of conscious mind—that it consists of body and mind alone—that gives the appearance of their closing. Thus, the chakras are open at all times; it is merely aligning them so that they may transfer energies more appropriately to you.

Nor can the chakras ever be blocked. The spirit is never blocked. There are no barriers. It is only the mind that is not open. So therefore, open your minds. Forget the chakras, open your minds. Think of the chakras as a store that is open all hours and you may shop there at any time.

Some chakras are more sensitive than others to different levels of memory through past-life recall. Even as you would use different parts of the brain to recall various aspects of your immediate existence here on the physical plane, so in turn the chakras are used for different forms of recall concerning past lives. Each chakra contains different levels of information, equally and compatibly. And although one chakra may have the first initial aspect of that memory, all seven of the chakras contain the memory as a whole.

Stored within any given chakra is information for the mind. The mind, through the five physical senses, believes that all information is outside of itself. It believes all the information that comes to it through the five physical senses—touch, taste, smell, sight, hearing. But actually, each of these senses is deceitful. Each constantly focuses the conscious mind on the limited perimeters of itself. So the mind is continuously being pulled outside itself, when actually the full perimeters of mind are stored in the muscular tissues of the physical body.

The mind, through the central and the sympathetic nervous systems, receives the various gripes from these different tissues within the body and interprets these as pain. And it says, "Do not bother me. I do not wish to hear about your aches and pains." It only wishes to carry on a dialogue through the sensual. This becomes very seductive, and you create the illusion of this physical reality to explain all of your aches and pains.

The chakras are the fields of the life force which constantly animate the cells, molecules, and atoms of the body. The different chakras and rays extend out into infinity. It is the ethers which create your physical form. It is the soul and the fields of light surrounding the physical body. So therefore, when you ask me, "How do you derive information?" I say it comes from the levels of the soul itself, for the soul occupies all sectors of time and space. It coordinates its activities into the physical form through the chakras, or the ethers, which are but reflections of the soul's passing this way, even as the hand that moves through the atmosphere creates a breeze.

As the soul looks down from infinity, it creates a physical focus, which is the physical body. The physical body is your ability to have focus in time and space. The soul creates this by projecting down through the seven rays. The rays are the personification through an individual soul. They become even more personified in the individual experience in time and space. So the rays are the carriers of individualized, but still universal, information. They are the direct extension of the perfection of the soul in an individualized form. The chakras, then, are the interface between the physical dimension and the spiritual. Thus the rays and the chakras are indeed synonymous. It is merely that the chakras are the intimate point by which you may interface with yourself as a physical and ethereal being.

When the mind no longer receives sensations externally, but receives them instead from internal structures, the chakras then become aligned and you become pure consciousness. You extend out into infinity by going within, where you find your focus in the chakras.

Too much concentration in the lower chakras and you attract individuals only on a physical basis. Too much concentration in the mid-chakra, the emotions, and you start expanding, occupying more than your rightful space on the planet. Too much concentration in the visionary chakras, as in the higher elements of things, and you have vision without grounding. Therefore, the goal is to open each of the chakras through skillful meditation, balance, and calmness.

Even as the sun radiates down and gives light to let a plant grow and that plant will always grow toward the sun, so in turn your soul sends you the life force upon which your physical form grows. And the more of that energy you take in through the chakras—which are the appropriate channels—the more illumined you become.

We suggest you begin working with the chakras, for your curriculum to higher consciousness is outlined therein. The chakras are always open. It is the mind that is closed. How do you open the mind? Simply meditate. It is the most relaxing and beneficial thing you can do. You say, "I cannot do this," but it is a lie. For you slumber, you sleep. And when the body slumbers, you begin to recall, you have memories. These are called dreams. Many intellectual persons say, "I do not dream," but it is the most intellectual of persons who often have the thinnest walls. So therefore, know that the doorways to the chakras are open to you at all times, and it is only the mind that is closed. It must bloom like a thousand-petaled lotus that forever flows upon the Ganges, the Nile, the Amazon, or even upon your Mississippi.

We would urge you to remember the existence of your spirit, which is your portal to a higher identity. It is focused continuously with you through the open doors of the chakras. For that door which is opened by the higher self, by the Christ, can never be closed by any man or woman. It is eternally open. It depends only on the degree to which the mind, through faith, will accept it and practice it and make it part of the personal pattern that becomes the personality. Those who open the doors of the seven chakras accept the full identity of themselves as spirits.

Death, Rite of Passage

John

In seeking to understand that which you term "life after death," you must first understand that there is no such thing as death; there is only the passing away from one plane to another. The loss of the physical vehicle which serves you in this plane is but the shedding of an old garment, and you but step into another plane and level of existence. When you begin to understand yourself as a spirit or a soul, and that the personality is but a memory or expression of that soul, so in turn you come into a greater unfoldment, a greater life. For life is but a meditation. It is the contemplation of the soul of its activities in this plane. Even as you would enter into a state of meditation to calm yourself and have no fear of returning to the flow of your normal life pattern, so it is when you step from one life into the next.

To understand death and dying, you must first understand yourselves as beings consisting of mind, body, and spirit. You are here to understand that death is a natural cycle of life. When you do not accept death as such, you make yourself less than who you truly are. For as a being of mind, body, and spirit, the mortality of the physical body is but a single issue of your true nature.

When you pass from the physical body, it is not that you leave the body, but moreso the body is leaving you. For you are moving away from time and space toward an ever-increasing band of consciousness. How you experience that expanding consciousness at the point of physical passing has been described as passing through all the issues of your life, then through all the issues of your past lives, approaching a higher, ever-escalating order of beings. This is the "cylinder of illumination" along which you tread, eventually moving into a higher order of celestial beings. All of this is but a perceptual reality as your mind expands, for eventually the mind remembers and you become as God.

Within the personality there is a sensing of the time of passing. Many times there is fear, and you become attuned to all the forces in the body. Often there is a review of lives past; this is the deactivation of the DNA factor within the physical body and the releasing of energy through the meridians to the conscious mind, where it is examined, correlated, and stored in that which is known as the astral body. Then there is a shutting down of all the various meridian points in the body and a certain sense of coolness and quietness comes upon all conscious activity.

At this point it is not so much that you enter into darkness or a void, but moreso there is greater and greater illumination that seems to fill the room, and those in the room about you slowly dissolve and mesh into a single pattern of light. For as you begin to make the sojourn from the physical body, the aura about each individual becomes illumined and more and more visible to you. Forgiveness at such times becomes easier, not so much because you no longer have to deal with those individuals, but moreso you are illumined with a greater state of awareness, and forgiveness comes more easily when you realize that as you forgive, so in turn are you forgiven.

When you pass away from this plane and enter into the other dimensional planes, you enter a period of orientation where you begin to fully understand that which awaits you on those planes, yet while still encased in the vibrations of the earth plane. For you shall not pass away from this plane until all things are revealed unto you through the levels of the soul, for none come unto the Father except through the son or the daughter that resides within them, which is by your own soul, and by your own soul's path. So therefore, you go from body to body, and in between exists that which you term "life after death."

After this period of orientation, the actual transition from the physical plane to the spiritual realms occurs. There is a sojourn along a great swirling vortex of light and the witnessing and passing away of many vibrations from this plane. These vibrations are at times perceived as personalities in various states of progression, some higher and some lower, or in various states of illumination and ignorance. You are then taken to the highest levels of your consciousness achieved in that particular lifetime, wherein there is a review with your spirit guides and teachers and a sojourn into levels of consciousness and peace you knew not in this plane. By now you will have reached a decision to sever the cord which binds you to the physical body. Then there is the complete passing away of all activities—the cranial capacity, the beating of the heart—and finally the physical body lies still.

To those on this plane it will seem as if you had passed away, but rather you enter into a greater illumination, a greater light, a greater awareness. For your awareness in this hour is actually attunement to and understanding of all things—all things that you have suffered and all things that you have experienced. For the pattern of the Book of Life itself unfolds unto you while in this state. The pattern of the mysteries of the spirit is made clear unto you, for you return home to the illumination which is yours already.

When the physical passing is swift, frequently an individual will not even realize he or she has crossed over. In this instance, it takes a period of orientation for a being to perceive his point of passing. This is particularly true with individuals who have little or no consciousness, or desired consciousness, of the existence of the pattern beyond their own physical bodies. They maintain that level of consciousness, for that is all they have known for many years. They have conditioned themselves and their personalities to that little receptivity and therefore have little or nothing to look forward to except a three-dimensional state of existence. And when they find themselves in a state of passing, great fear comes upon them, for they eventually realize that they have passed and they know not what to expect. So there is a greater time period of orientation for that individual to be able to perceive the existence of spiritual entities.

Such souls are not so much "lost souls," but moreso earthbound spirit, or earthbound personality, for the soul is always in total illumination and can never be lost; it is the *personality,* which is but a memory, that grows confused. Even as your mind continuously wanders from those things you desire to focus upon, so in turn is it with the personality as a whole. For the personality is made up totally of mind, and it is only when it becomes integrated with the levels of the soul that it makes its truer advancements.

There are those upon the plane who, still having biologic existence, as you term it medically or clinically, have released the energies of mind and spirit to have expression independent of the physical body. This you term the near-death experience. After such an experience, how much grander these individuals are, for they know then that they are immortal, and the mundaneness of their lives is transformed. For even as an individual might share with you a positive thought that uplifts you, how much moreso the positive thought that you are as a spirit and that you transcend all time and space? So thus your life is no longer lived from the perspective that you are an energy that must accumulate experience and then die, but rather that you are an entity that is continuously conscious and ever-progressing, from one lifetime to the next.

To conquer death, all you need to do is die, for this is simply the death of the ego. The mind, the body, and the spirit are but the definable perimeters of the human being, of yourselves as beings of energy. As you project beyond the physical body, as you have experience of prognosticating the future before it transpires, as you dig deep into the recesses of the soul and the spirit and recall lives past, you become educated that you are mind, body, and spirit and that you survive death, that death is an illusion. But make death your ally. Die each day for the merger of the mind, the body, and the spirit; then you become the total human being. For anytime you make yourself less than a human being, you enslave yourself.

Go unto those who are dying and breathe into them the breath of life, for they are not dying, they are merely in transition. Shed not tears of mourning but tears of joy, that as you look deeply unto them and restore their human features and remove pain, they will draw their last breath and, not die, but breathe in light and pass on to a higher plane. End suffering and misery by sharing of yourself, your deepest human resource—your spirit, your love. There is naught else you can do except to work with unconditional love.

What is death the threshold to? It is that there is no death; there is only life unto life. For even as you shed old garments when they no longer warm you or no longer fit you, so in turn is it when the physical body is set aside—gracefully, gently. It is not that you draw your last breath, but your last breath is drawn deeply and you are filled with light. And you gently pass forth from that mortal coil, that garment that has served you all these years to provide you with warmth, to allow you to touch one another in this moment, in this time and space.

So, what is the challenge of the earth plane? What is the mystery of the afterlife? It is that in this lifetime you manifest the pattern which exists between lives. For you are at a distinct advantage with the physical body. It gives you focus. And it is up to you to give the life that you live in these days clarity in the eyes of the spirit which you truly are.

Death is better described as transition. It is but the passing away of each of the limiting fibers of the ego. For karma, or actions taken in lives past, and the ego are synonymous. But understanding and karma are also synonymous. Each day that the ego dies and the true nature springs forth, so in turn are you educated to your greater and deeper dimensions as part of the all-knowingness. For as you cling to the limited identity, herein then is true death, for you let die within you the spark of life.

There is no such thing as death. There is no such thing as time or space. There is only the love within each and every one of you. Look upon those who are gathered in fellowship, for herein is where you will find the spirit of love. It is said, "Love the Lord God with all thy heart and mind and thy neighbor as thyself, and ye can break no other commandment." If you do but this one thing, then you are extended unto the waters of everlasting life, the living waters that spring forth from each and every one of you.

Look upon the face of the individual who sits next to you. Herein is also yourself. How much vaster your resources as you touch each other! So, as you expend yourselves, share yourselves, how, then, are you to understand death? Death does not exist as a point of termination—it is but the beginning of each breath of life that you draw. This is the true meaning of the death experience, be it physical, mental, or spiritual. It is but the opportunity to know, even as the stage is set. Ask not for whom the bell tolls, it tolls for thee. It is not an ending, it is a beginning, so that you are enriched and deepened in your knowledge of one another, in whom God dwells.

Tom MacPherson

I would like to point out that no one dies. For instance, if you were to refer to me as dead, I would become extremely offended. I am not dead, I have merely physically "passed over."

Frequently one's physical passing is rather quick. It is like a roaring in your ears and suddenly you are passing along a tunnel of illumination. Soon you perceive yourself present amidst many friends, and experience a level of extra awareness and enlightenment. All other realities you have ever perceived, and all other thoughts you have had is totally transformed. You then pass along another level of illumination into the presence of higher beings. Usually you can sense religious presences that were quite dear to you, and all things become clear. You then immediately experience an unusual pattern of time and space and sometimes have an awareness of where your next incarnation will be. Quite a fascinating sensation.

The way my own physical passing transpired was that, first of all, I was a pickpocket and was hung by the British. That is a bit embarrassing—to mention that an Irishman could be caught by the British—but that was the case. They offered me a choice between my fingers or my neck, and I decided to take my neck, being that without my fingers I wouldn't have much of a trade anyway. So, they stood me upon a keg, placed a rope around my neck, and gave me an opportunity to make a bit of a speech. It was quite odd, because they always hung pickpockets to discourage pickpocketing, but since the hangings were a public affair in those days, great crowds would gather and there would be more pickpocketing going on in those crowds than at any other time.

So, my rousing speech lasted around thirty to forty-five minutes, long enough to give my friends a little extra time to ply their trade. I got a bit of satisfaction watching the pockets being picked of people who were crying out for the keg to be kicked out from under me. It was a bit of last earth-plane satisfaction.

They kicked the keg out, there was a bit of a crack, and the next thing I knew I was standing back watching everyone else applaud and cheer and I watched my body swinging back and forth.

I didn't leave the earth plane immediately. I stepped back, looked at myself, and decided I was just as handsome as I had always thought I was. I wasn't necessarily afraid of death, because I had studied Wicca, a very old religion, and the idea of spirits and saints was not new to me. I knew I would pass on and that the end of the rope was rather quick anyway.

So, I was swinging back and forth when suddenly there was a rather loud roaring in my ears and I passed through a bit of a tunnel. I thought I perceived a few faces, but it was all very quick.

The next thing I knew, I found myself with several of my own rowdy pub mates who had gone out a few years earlier via the same means, being also pickpockets. I found myself in discussion with them, as well as some other fellows whom I had occasionally seen in dream states but couldn't quite recognize. They were dressed rather strangely, and much to my surprise I found out they were my spirit guides and teachers. I hadn't realized they were from different cultures. I had always just assumed that angels who ministered to us dressed rather bizarrely.

I found out there really wasn't much in heaven or hell; you could just sort of create those things as a matter of your level of thought. So, I found myself wandering around in a bit of a publike atmosphere, because that is where I was always the most comfortable. Not exactly the highest vibration, but not exactly the lowest either. Many people meet and converse in pubs with the best of intentions.

After being there awhile, I went back down to the physical plane just to see what it was like. Then I sort of merged myself with the spirit and proceeded to immerse myself in studies to get on to where I am at this point in time—a spirit guide in practical affairs.

Leaving the physical body is not scary at all, although it might be when you are just stepping out of the physical form. I would call it more disorienting than scary—which brings me to another point. Guides and teachers get upset when you think of them in terms of hauntings or something. It doesn't work that way. Actually, when you stop and think about it, we are very neat, clear illuminations, while you, on the other hand, are these lumbering masses of bio-chemistry. I'm certain if you were to come lumbering up behind me at the slow paces you move in your time flows, I would be frightened clean out of my own time period.

Is there a hell? Heavens no! We kick the word around a lot over here, but it is a bit of a joke. No, hell doesn't exist. You have a lot more of a hell on your side than we have over here. It is sort of like a myth. There is no man standing here with a red suit and pitchfork and a rather wicked grin. It is nothing like that. There is sort of a limbo, though, and a place where less enlightened entities than myself, shall we say, dwell for a while.

So, hell as a place doesn't exist. It is a concept that is being kicked around, so to say, but then, they used to think the world was flat, too. It is more or less that people associate suffering with hell, so therefore they think it has substance. I go along with saying that you can create the concept of hell in your mind and live there if you want to, but it is only by your free will, if you so desire.

So, is there such a thing as hell? Yes, it is called England. No—not at all. I suppose if there had been such a place as hell, I would have qualified, and I'm certain I would have been the first one to find out about it. No, hell is something that was made up a long time ago, in medieval days, I believe. References in the Bible to hell are a mistranslation more than anything. For instance, the word *shivat* is used, which means more "a grave." It says "you shall go to the grave." They translate it to mean Hades or hell. From Greek, the word *Hades* means "place of the dead." It does not mean a fiery furnace. If you'll notice, many times the fiery furnace was used in reference to a fiery place where you burn forever. Fire is often used for cleansing. So therefore, it is symbolic of the cleansing process that the soul goes through, a purification before its next incarnation. For the Bible also teaches reincarnation.

Atun-Re

You ask about "death throes." We would say there is no such thing as death throes. Those are only the birth pangs into a higher state of existence. You ask what it is like when a physical being leaves the body. What physical being? You are spiritual beings at that moment in time.

What is the experience of the mother as she gives birth to the child? Pain—but perhaps also joy and knowledge that the father of the child is present and they are one in their experience, because the father, who is truly in empathy, feels great pain also. You may find him doubled up in the corner. It is also possible through meditation, through proper exercise, to give birth with no pain at all, and the child slips gently into the world. This is a fact amongst you also.

So thus it is the same with the physical entity at the point of physical passing. Not death—physical passing. And it is the perception of the spiritual being that he would draw but one last breath and pass into eternity. That is what you should seek.

The perception? Illumination. A light. A going to loved ones, even as the child would come out and be surrounded by the loved ones who would tend to it and create a new dimension for it, a new life. And it would inherit all the things of the family, all of its ancestry and all of its nobility and glory, and the lessons it has to offer.

So your passing from the physical is just like birth. It may come with greater or lesser pain. It may be greeted with joy, or with fear, if unwanted. You are only hurt to the degree to which you fear, and you experience joy to the degree to which you do not resist.

What happens to the soul upon death? Ha!—you remain in the divine; the soul does not die. The lifetime never ends. You mean, what happens when the physical body decides to lay itself down? Never confuse the personality with the soul. No, no—this is your worst mistake! The soul remains in the divine. It is the Christ. It is that which sits at the right-hand throne of God.

When the master Jesus obtained his level of ascension, his personality went to that level, and this is what you are seeking to do. This is your ascension. He was fortunate also to take his physical body with him as a demonstration that the spirit is the master of the physical. That is your end goal as well, though you do not necessarily need to ascend, since in each moment spent in the physical you obtain the same level and achievement of Christ consciousness, until eventually you have a personality that is worthy of eternal life. And then that representative on this plane never dies or is altered—for it is perfect.

Past Lives

John

The pattern that you weave in your present life is a garment which you prepare to cover the soul, so that when you proceed forth into another lifetime, or that principle which you term reincarnation, that garment can perhaps be worn again. Indeed, there are many individuals who, even as they exist on the earth plane, have full knowledge of lives past and so therefore have an array of garments within which the soul may enfold itself.

Many ask if it is necessary to reincarnate, for they feel anxiety at the thought of returning to the earth plane. We will say that it is not necessary to reincarnate, but perhaps the lesson you have to learn is to enjoy the pattern of life on this plane. Therefore, it is not so much the desire to return or not to return, but moreso it is the mastering of the level of enjoyment of life upon this particular plane of existence.

Your past lives make up your life pattern of carefully coordinated past-life lessons. They contribute circumstances according to the law of cause and effect, or karma, as they influence you upon the plane in these days. These are the constant web and tapestry of energies that come to you through the chakras, or the centers of consciousness within the physical body. They then interweave into the personality and become the life lessons that the soul would experience.

Tom MacPherson

Your whole life pattern is based on your past lives, or lack of them—it works both ways. It's not like you come in with a large sack of old things to live out; it's much finer than that. Your whole personality is based along guidelines more than anything else. How much of a past-life personality do you bring in with you? Very little, if at all. It's only if you become obsessed with a part of it. For instance, eccentric people who prefer to wander about in clothes from days gone by have carried over greater chunks of past personalities than other people. Your average man on the street may have secret desires to do that, but they are only desires and never really manifest; he has carried over very little, but is still experiencing some of the guidelines. It varies from individual to individual.

Your past lives are basically energy. They are experiences along the time flow that are slowly and progressively shaping the dynamics of your personality. They are preserved and filtered through the astral body, but first they must pass through the spiritual body, where all the higher ethics are organized. Then the causal body draws in all the various individuals to possibly act out karmic circumstances. Then it projects into the astral body, where it is all screened out and kept unique, relative to your currently functioning personality. As the energy is passed on, past lives are basically only that information that you have not gained an understanding of, and understanding is the perfect merger between your emotions and the intellect.

The decision as to what sex you incarnate into is, simply expressed, the need of a lesson. I can assure you there are many masculine soldiers from lives past who are now currently incarnate in the feminine form, and that is why you have such militant feminists. They're going, "My God, what a bloody mistake I made in the past. Let's get on with equality!"

You may actually plan an incarnation several hundred years before it happens. You converse with your parents, who may be in spirit at that time. You sort of set things up—and guess who's coming to dinner!

Persons who complain a lot about being incarnate are being just a little bit shallow about it because you really spend more time in spirit than you do on the physical planes anyway. You only incarnate for your final exams; most of your study is done over here.

With regard to physical afflictions, a person may come in with a limp because perhaps he trapped animals rather cruelly in a previous life and caused them to walk around with a limp. In this life he is identifying with their experience, with the suffering he caused them. It's stored in his old memory bank.

Souls occasionally move on to other planets after they leave the earth plane, but not until they get over most of their karma here—unless they pay perhaps just a slight visit to one of the other planes within this solar system. But an individual doesn't go beyond the solar system until he more or less masters its frequency.

The soul is not really integrated into the physical body until after the fourth month of incarnation. It is developing the fetal tissues, but it is not incarnate. It's not unlike assembling a car—you can put the car together, but it's not until you actually sit in the driver's seat that you're literally in it.

Can humans come back as animals? Worse—they can come back as Englishmen. No, I'm just teasing—as a good Irishman, I can never pass up a straight line. But anyway—uh-oh, I sense the flush of an aura in the back of the room. Oh my! You will pardon my humor, won't you? (I dropped a bit of karma there.) But anyway—we would say no. You were once incarnate in the animal kingdoms, and indeed there is ancestor memory of those experiences; however, you do not come back in animal forms. Animals can reincarnate, however. Your cat in Egypt could indeed be your dog in this lifetime. They incarnate according to your degree of emotional attachment to them.

Atun-Re

The reason it seems easier to remember past lives than future probabilities is because stored in the physical body are many of the subjective events of past lives that are about to become conditions in this one. Your ease of accessing these is because they are familiar to you. They are events that are about to transpire, so they are somewhat closer. Whereas, your higher ideals are often more difficult to deal with, in the sense that you sometimes choose not to ascend. Past lives are interesting events. They are like books that you read and put back on the shelf when you are through with them. Transcendental things become conscious and nag you constantly.

The personality is reflective of all the things that have come through many past lives. When those things which are karmic have been cleared, all that remains is the pure essence of your past lives.

The Ascendant Path

John

By your birth you have chosen to come into the earth plane to learn of your own celestial nature. The grandeur of your nature is that you are not simply an entity born of the physical that has become conscious of itself as a physical entity, but rather you are a *spiritual* energy, and that energy is one with the grander mystery of all things. Remember, the spirit is the light, the mind is the builder, and the physical is the result.

Love the Lord God with all your heart, mind, strength, and soul, and your neighbor as yourself. Your business is the affairs of humankind. Are you your brother's keeper? Are you your sister's keeper? Indeed, this is what you till when you enter the earth plane. This is the law of right fellowship.

Where should you go from here? Closer to God. And in what manner? By instructing others and pouring out your experiences to them. For as each son and daughter of God and man is lifted up, all others are drawn unto him. You uplift others by becoming as a teacher in each act, each deed, and each word. A teacher is not a system of organized information—rather, a teacher is one who seeks to inspire. The steps you may follow include right diet, right occupation, right service, right expression, right prayer, and the cornerstone of all of these—meditation. Draw upon the talents that you have been given in measure. Select those which serve you, which you love to do; then you may love others in serving them. Right expression gives you the keys to communicate with others. Monitor your words carefully, and ultimately you express the spirit. Practice meditation, which is the calming of your physical body in the presence of God, so that your nature is pure. Right prayer is your dialogue with the most high. These are steps you may follow. But above all else, love one another.

Choose a path that has heart, something you love to do. And always choose the middle path, neither extreme asceticism nor extreme indulgence, and the path becomes self-actualizing. If you hone your talents to that which you love to do, then you will have the highest inspiration to pursue that path, and thus you will harness all of your resources.

There is only one life purpose, and that is to discover your unity with God. With regard to your life service, the personality is a tool; it is the vocabulary by which you communicate with other beings upon this plane. Aspects of this personality, or vocabulary, can be arranged to communicate or articulate your talents and other unique tools. These talents, based upon experience from past lives, can then be organized into a particular service to society, or to the spiritual community as a whole. This becomes your life work or life service— some may even say life purpose.

Meditation is the tool for properly accessing and establishing your priorities and by which you spiritualize your talents and align them with the true purpose of finding your unity with God. Meditation may even draw unto the self the events and alterations of personality necessary to achieve your life service. But again, it is but recall, the process of memory.

Each of you has a blueprint of your life pattern. We would say that mind is the builder and your spirit is the blueprint that gives rise to the illusion of absolute predestination. You choose the quality of the structure. You may build upon the rock or the sand. The blueprint is to build a living temple. If God dwells in that temple, the structure is complete. Though a play may be fixed in its dialogue, structure, and time, can you not shape the words with your passion and create meaning anew? So, even though there is the illusion of a fixed structure in time and space, so in turn your mind is the builder.

Each of you is a portal through which the light comes. Each of you is as a facet upon a prism. The prism turns and from that prism flows forth many diverse points of light that illuminate the plane and take it to its higher level of purpose and existence.

When you perceive life through your five physical senses alone, you are indeed limited. But when you allow your mind to expand into past lives and future potentials, you are transformed, and reality, in the sense of the five physical senses, crumbles. This is not to die but to be transformed into a new reality, a new society, a new social order, a new brotherhood, a new sisterhood, a new humanity.

So, to express your full humanity, you must go beyond the five physical senses. Formerly, you were thought to be mind and body, with the spirit sitting beyond your reach. Then, with the discovery of the subconscious mind, was not your society transformed? Do you not now take into account a fuller measure of the human being in your societal affairs? How much moreso will your reality be reshaped and transformed when, individually and as a society, you accept yourselves as spirit.

Gathering bodies of evidence will eventually dictate a new understanding of your reality. Even as science has harnessed new insights, so in turn will mind and spirit harness new insights. Allow God to quicken your intellect and you will be given a new heart and a new mind, and the world as you have known it, the world of grief and stress, will pass away and you will enter into a thousand years of brotherhood. How so? By being of mind, body, and spirit, which is your true nature. You are one with God, who is love.

But above all else, the dialogues that you carry on with the channel speaking, or any other incarnate spirit, have worth only if you love one another. Your dreams, your meditations—these are your recall. Simply remember. This is the only process that you must do. Meditate, draw on your breath, relax, and expand the mental dimensions. For mind has only one gift—to remember. And when you merge mind, body, and spirit, you remember the divine, from which you came and to which you return.

Seek the principles which heal. Seek the principles which generate the divine. Then in turn these forms of service would extend to
all of your principles and all of your actions. Above all else, allow
God to quicken your intellect in these ways, and then you will see
with the inner eye.

Even those things which come upon you and cause you stress are
moreso to strengthen you. Those things which bring you peace are
but to be as a positive reinforcement of that state. For indeed, there
is no such thing as testing or failure, there is no such thing as victory
or defeat. There is only the state of the *isness* that is within, the state
of being human. And in being human, you are mind, body, and
spirit. This is the critical tool of peace—the merger of mind, body,
and spirit, and then the manifestation of Christ consciousness within.

If you see the shadows darken, know it is because the lamp and
the oil of life and faith burn short within you. But if your oil is tilled
well, you will burn ever brighter, illuminating and attracting those
who would seek the light. Hide not yourselves away in the shadows
of your own fear, but keep your eye single, and all souls will
eventually come home.

Pour yourself out. Be yourselves more filled with the true self.
The only sin is selfishness, perpetuation for the sake of the self. Pour
yourselves out of these things; then, all that is left is that which is
of God, the divine inspiration. How to pour yourselves out? In
service to others. This is not the suppression of self; this is the active,
dynamic force of the true self.

Know also, however, that the servant is worthy of his hire; so
therefore, you would also receive of your own service. And, as the
servant chooses the master he desires to serve, so you may pour
yourself out in service but then be filled up with the spring that never
runs dry, the well that comes from within and replenishes you. If
you would drink of this spring, you would never thirst again but
would be given a new heart and a new mind and a new way to see
things. So, pour yourselves out in service and then merge your
mind, body, and spirit unto God. Prayer and meditation afford you
the opportunities to come to these inner revelations.

The merger of mind, body, and spirit in service to God reveals
the aspect of you that is unique, that each of you is a child of light
and is to be as the light to illumine the path that leads to the truth.

But how sad that some confuse the path with the truth itself, for broad is the road which leads to discord, discontent, and accusation, but narrow is the road which leads to truth and illumination.

Make straight the ways of the Lord and your nature is shaped, and you are made as straight as a rod, that you would not so much rule over others, but bring them into harmony. For the rod is that which gives guidance and direction and touches you gently on one shoulder or the other. It is not the staff of the conqueror, but the staff of the shepherd who loves and tends the flock and draws the very sustenance of life from this activity. So in turn with each of you, that as you go forth in balance, and with the staff of truth, you attract others to you who would also become as children, simple in all things, yet wise as serpents. There is no foolishness in this, nor even anything utopian, for these things do not arise from philosophies; they arise from the fact that you are children of light, children of God.

So, seek first the kingdom, then all things are added unto you. For the word *kingdom* means "the natural order of things," and this springs up from within each of you and must dwell in the living temple that is the physical body.

Life in this solar system is to be the "eyes" of the universe, to explore it and have its nature understood, that you would understand life beyond the boundaries and regions of its biochemical form. For life has linkage not only with the energies that surround the physical body, but also with the etheric forces, extending even unto the stars themselves. The future of life upon this planet is that eventually you will become creatures of energy and will have less and less need for the biochemical physical body. Moreso you shall become etheric beings. It is not so much that you will extricate yourselves from the physical body and so therefore be made pure and return to the angelic state, but moreso you shall extract yourselves from the biochemical physical body necessary for maintaining your perception of life and shall become more and more beings of energy and light in the level of perception.

For the universe itself has a pattern of natural unfoldment and attunement with those forces which are the mind of God, although God is also a being in a state of existence. So in turn, even as you have a physical body, so in turn is the universe the body of God. Each of you is to bring forth balance within the self in attunement with these forces, that you would become as a prophet in your own right. For this is the visionary level.

The purpose of physical creation is to align yourselves with the higher force, which is God. In this you would draw yourselves up through the seven levels of existence to the higher levels of consciousness, to become that which you truly are—sons and daughters of God. This is accomplished through merging mind, body, and spirit. Finally, you manifest God's nature upon the physical plane as it would be revealed to you through the Father/Mother God, or the Holy Spirit, which then makes you as a living soul. For you would then have life by your revelations from one another.

Remember your higher ideals, your higher intentions. Choose to ascend to that level of consciousness that you feel is your highest. Activate that through your prayers to the one true energy, which is God, and there is nothing more you can do.

Tom McPherson

If you feel like you're standing on the threshold of a new revelation and you're knocking on the door and no one answers, just sit down and enjoy a rest before your host enters. Relax a bit from the thousand-mile journey it took you to get there. Just meditate. When your host finally invites you into the new revelation, you will enjoy it that much more by not being tired from your journey.

Take a look about you. You'll find other people sitting on the same doorstep. Talk with them about your marvelous adventures in getting there. And before you know it, the time will pass. Soon your host will be there to let you in. In other words, share your experience with the other folks sitting on the door stoop with you, and the sense of heaviness will go away.

Atun-Re

When you acknowledge that you are a soul, you are fully empowered to transform others. The authority to transform comes from your own experience, your own soul, through personal example. Ha! —sometimes the most brilliant of revelations is also very boring. But it is through personal example that you transform one another. Humor transforms you. Just your gathering in a circle transforms you, because you are inside of it, just as your soul's force, God's presence, is inside of you. You make this a place of learning. You make it a temple. You should never discount this authority, because when you do, you discount God.

You must not deplete yourselves, my children, or pour yourselves out like water on the desert sand, there to evaporate and not be able to serve. No, my children, do not deplete yourselves. Give freely, but be true to your own development also. And may that development always reside in your heart.

Also, children, know that there are deeper meanings in the mysteries of the Pyramid. You must learn the true sense of the pyramids. You must learn the true sense of yourselves. The Pyramid is a book in stone—it is not a tomb of some long dead pharaoh. It is an inner mystery. And your physical bodies are not tombs that will eventually wither away. They are living temples. They are living mysteries, my children. You must come to these deeper revelations, you must live them. But above all else, you must be them, for you are that mystery.

Each of you is given a talent. Your talents are like words. And as your living words come together, you write a book, you become a drama, a play. And this becomes part of the community from which new tales arise that contribute to the collective consciousness. Each of you grows by drawing upon one another, by allowing one another's talents to express more easily.

You are carriers of a new idea which you will take to others to inspire them, to infect them. Indeed, a carrier of a disease needs but to sneeze and immediately he would have much company in his misery. But the same applies to that which is well about you also. That is, if you credit misery with spreading so easily, why do you not give the same credit to the joy within you? Merely breathe the breath of inspiration into others, for if a sneeze comes up randomly from you, how much more effectively can well-crafted words, formulated with your mind and spoken with your tongue, inflame others?

People laugh and say, "Ha, ha, your utopian ideals, they are as old as time itself, and yet where are they? They are scattered like seeds before the wind." You can smile and say, "By your own admission, my ideals are older than time, so they survive beyond any civilization that you can quote. And true, perhaps they are like seeds before the wind, but when they touch ground, what a beautiful flower they bring forth, and a beautiful essence.

"And even if their time beneath the sun is only brief, and only one eye sees their beauty, and though they may pale quickly before winter, still their seeds will be scattered for generations, long after your concept of civilization has withered. For by your own confession, my concepts of utopia and community are older than time itself. And the winds my ideals are scattered upon are the winds of the spirit, and the seeds are the ideals of many of the greatest minds that have illumined each generation. And even as each seed has its own season, so in turn has the philosopher said that there is nothing more powerful than an idea whose season has come. Open your eyes, my friend, that you may see them, lest your joy be cut off with the winter of discontent."

What then is the mystery of this physical body, this living temple? The physical body is the ability of the celestial being known as the soul, which is always one with God, to have focus in time and space. This is the grandeur; this is the ascendant path. For even though you have not ascended unto the throne, still, would any prince or princess doubt that they have full access to their Father/Mother God's kingdom? You are children of light. You have chosen to wrap yourself in the flesh, that you may have joy and live life abundantly with one another. This is the ascendant path which spirals, gracefully and gently, ever upward and onward. This is the soul's path.

—John

Appendix:

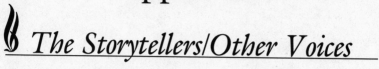 *The Storytellers/Other Voices*

Obadiah

Ah, it would be the Obadiah. The Obadiah come and talk to the little people. Ah, the little people try to get smart in the head about the workings of the *awanga,* or what you call meditation. The smarter you get in the head about the meditation, the smarter you get in the head about who *you* be. When you go into the sleep state, that make you smart in the head because like you become conscious all the way around the clock, you see. You think like when you go to sleep you be unconscious. No—sometimes people be smartest when they be asleep.

Sometimes you have like a mantra that you repeat over and over. You call it snoring. Other people not like to hear that mantra. But that be like what it be, because it like make you sleep, and maybe sometime stimulates your dreams, and that be like smart and make you wiser.

Ah, you like ask about the music. Like you work with the drum or like with the chant. That make you smarter because it put you like into a deeper state, and that be good because like you go to sleep while still be waking when you meditate, you see. Because it like make you more aware of the spirit that you be, and that be good, too.

Ah, and then the Obadiah be very disappointed when the little boy who the Obadiah speak through mention the reggae, and you say, "The reggae?" and wonder like why it be good. Like maybe the reggae be like the voodoo or the bad thing. Ah, that be like what maybe the white people say all the time. But it like be the good thing, because it like has the basic chant, and it talk about the necessary thing for the spiritual freedom, you see. So, next time you listen to the music, see if it maybe like make you sway back and forth, make you smile a little bit.

That be like the meditation, because that like relax the body, make you want to get up and jump around. You not need do anything, because the spirit, it know what it want to do. The spirit want to get up and jump around. Maybe the body just want to sit there at first, but the spirit, it want to jump around. And pretty soon you like go into the spirit and you feel like more what you be, because you *be* the spirit.

Ah, it would be the Obadiah. The Obadiah come and talk to the little people. Like the little people try to get smart in the head about the spirit. Many times like the little people they ask like about ghosts; they ask about what maybe be the bad spirit. Sometimes like the people be like what you say "superstitious." Sometimes it be like the spirit like hide under the bed, or behind the chair, and rattle chains and like make the hair stand on end. Like the spirit may be too physical—that type of thing. No, that be in your head. But this not be smart in the head. You must become like smart in the head about the spirit, because you, too, be a spirit. You just have the body.

Like you go, "Poor miserable me has to drag around the body all the time." And you think like you have to take care of the body. No, the body take care of you! If you like give it the opportunity, it take you for walk. If you give it the right food, it take care of you. It make you feel very good.

So, every now and then you must take the body out for a walk. You like take the body out for a walk in the park, and if someone ask you what you do, you say, "I take my body out for a walk, because I like my body. My body be very comforting for me. I got no other body. I better take this one." Because you not take care of your body, where else you going to live?

Ah, the little people want to learn about like how to heal the body. They want to be like smart in the head about how the body heals itself, like how the little people really be the spirit. So, the little people, sometimes they like want to practice the *awanga*. Like many times the white man, he get all scared. He think like the voodoo or the hoodoo or the *awanga* going to be like the bad medicine. Sometimes like even the different governments think the homeopathy be like the bad thing, too. They think it be like the hoodoo or the voodoo. No, it be like the good medicine. It be like the medicine that work on the spirit, because the man and the woman, they really be the spirit, they really be the energy. You have the body, but you really be the spirit. So, sometime let the spirit come little bit into the healing and that be good for the little people because that really be what heals the body anyway. The spirit be like the love that the little people have for each other.

Ah, the little people, they try to get smart in the head about how they be the spirit. This be good, because like the little people, sometimes they think the spirit be a ghost or like a dead person. No, spirit not be dead. Spirit be like very busy, too busy to rattle the chain, or hide behind the chair, or under the bed, or in the closet. No, it not be smart in the head when you think the spirit be that. Because you know that you be the spirit. How you know you be like the spirit? Because you like have the ability to go beyond the body, what you call the "astral projection."

Sometimes like the little people shake in their shoes because they think that like the spirit of the Obadiah or the MacPherson hide behind the chairs and moan and groan and rattle the chains. No, that be like a superstition. Because the spirit be very busy, you see. Because like when you get smart in the head about who you be, you start to be more joyful, you start to laugh, and you live life more abundantly, like the man Jesus did. Because like

God be everywhere. The spirit be everywhere. The Lord, he be everywhere.

Ah, the little people like to learn more about the spirit and master teachers and things. Ah, that be very good. But sometimes the little people, they try to expand in knowledge but sometimes they only end up expanding in their head, or expanding in the ego. And that not be too good. So the spirit speak very simply not because you are stupid—no, it be because like each thing that be said, it be so powerful it might expand too much, and then you go, "Now I know more secrets." But then you discover that you really not know that much, but you find that be like the blessing too, because then you be able to experience more, and that be like good for the children. Because then you learn that life can be filled with joy because there be like no blockage to the joy you experience, because it be like total and abundant.

Ah, the little people they sit around and talk to the Mr. John and they ask the deep serious question and all the deep mystery about the body. Ah, the little people they start to smile a little bit. Ah, that be good for the little people, because sometimes what the little people need like in the emotions and things is to work the *awanga* and have the joy. Because the joy in the body and the joy in the life, that be good for the little people. Ah, because the Obadiah, he work the *awanga* and the *awanga* bring the joy to the people. Ah, so sometimes maybe the little people need a little bit of joy. Sometimes they need to make like the little bit of the party. Ah, sometimes they need to dance around the fire like the Obadiah's people and beat the drum and do the chant.

Ah, the little people, sometimes they need to chant and sometimes they need to sing, and sometimes when they make the *awanga*, maybe they scare the white man who live up in the big house. Because the white man, he be up in the big house all the time, and he be afraid of the *awanga* and think like the Obadiah going to make the bad magic on him. No, the Obadiah, he not even want to waste time on the white man. He have too much of a good time with the *awanga*. So the little people, they not have to drink the rum and get like all sick like the white man have to do. All you have to do is feel good in the spirit.

When the people learn how to chant and sing, then they start to sing in the soul, because when they sing in the soul, then they get smart in the head, like the Obadiah. Oh, the little people really like to be happy in the soul and in the spirit, but sometime the little people, they forget how to be happy. They think they going to find happiness in a book. No, they not going to find happiness in a book. They not going to find it inside the head. They going to find it inside the heart. So the people have to be smart. They have to work the awanga. They have to learn like they really be the spirit. So it be good to be smart in the head and it be good to read the book, but once you put the book down, you better go outside to the chant and the drum.

Obadiah's Story of God and the Church

It be like the time that the boss man in Haiti, one day he come over and he chew Obadiah out and say, "Obadiah, you better get up to the church, because God be up in that church, and that where he be." But Obadiah know that God not only be in that church, because there be that women sing all them terrible hymns all the time. And if God be in that church, he surely want to get out!

And finally one day the boss man he die, and like all the people come around and wail and they cry and everything. The boss man body give out because he be very old. And the Obadiah, he lay down. And the Obadiah, he like go to sleep in a dream. And he like leave the body through the astral projection. And when the boss man come out of the body, all the people wailing and crying, and the boss man turn around after he passed over and he see the Obadiah standing there, and he thought he went to the bad place. Because he thought that where the Obadiah go. And Obadiah say, "No, you not go to the bad place. You like look up like a long tunnel."

And Obadiah come and he introduce the boss man to like his mother and his father, who go over and they all cry and they weep. And then like he go along towards the light. And the Obadiah know that they going go to like a greater light and learn greater things. Because he still have like what you call the karma.

But suddenly the Obadiah wake up. He wake up from this dream because he hear like the crying of his brand-new grandson. And the Obadiah know the boss man come back pretty quick to learn his lessons.

Japu

Hello please to people. It would be Japu. Japu not be big master or anything. He come through after big heavy master come. Make people shake in shoes little bit. Japu just come through maybe tell little story, but then have to go pretty quick. Uh-oh. One moment please. Japu have to scratch nose . . . One moment please.

Uh-oh. Japu find you in one of Japu's already favorite stories. Find all of you incarnate in Jonah's lifetime. Prophet Jonah. You all lived in Nineveh, the city he go to prophesize to. You all be nasty people, very nasty, sneak around together, big silly grins. Drink whole bunch. Do all kinds of things together. And Jonah shout and jump up and down at you, make your hair stand on end. You want to hear story of Jonah little bit?

You all lived in Nineveh. And Jonah, he be person very far away. One day, when Jonah just mind own business, God come up to Jonah. Big dark cloud. Jonah go, "Oh, big dark cloud. Going to rain today. No picnic today." All of a sudden God say to Jonah, "You better believe it! I got big job for you."

Jonah shake in shoes, hair stand on end. He go, "Who that be?" God say, "This be God." Jonah say, "How I know you be God?" God say, "You not really want to find out!" Jonah get so scared about what God tell him to do, his hair stand on end and he run away. He book passage on ship and say, "No big problem. I run away and not have to be big prophet person." So Jonah rub hands together, big proud chest, chest puff up, big smile, start to look out at ocean.

Pretty soon big fish come up. Great big fish. Outsmart very smart Jonah. Big fish, big smile on fish. Jonah look around, see fish, hair stand on end. He go hide, hang on to mast. But big storm come up and fish come up and swallow Jonah.

Jonah go, "What am I doing in here? Why me?" Just like you do sometimes.

Pretty soon fish get tummy ache and spit Jonah out on beach. Jonah look around and go, "Oh, close to Nineveh. Maybe better be prophet person than food for fish." He go, "After all, maybe pay not be so bad. Pretty good retirement benefit!"

So, he puff up chest, put on wild, crazy clothes, go into city, storm up and down city, shout, "Big doom coming." People listen and say, "Who that be?" "Oh, that be Jonah. Big prophet. Talk to God." Hair stand on end. Jonah say, "Big doom come ninety days. Repent. Repent." And then he storm out of city, sit on mountaintop and fast all time.

Pretty soon in city people running around, big doom coming, bumping into each other, running around. They go, "Must put on sackcloth and ashes." Jonah do very good job. They all scared to death. Running around, bumping into each other. Hair stand on end. Everybody fighting over sackcloths now. Latest thing in fashion be sackcloth. They can't find enough ashes to pour on top, so they start breaking up furniture and burning it. Want whole bunch of ashes to pour over head. Some people get so desperate, they start climbing up chimneys looking for ashes.

God look down and say, "Pretty good spectacle." God go, "Don't think I could have done better job myself. Jonah shake them up pretty good, they all repent." He go, "That pretty good."

So all of you repented and walked around in sackcloth and ashes. Sing songs, pray, look over shoulder. Big doom not come. Pray some more. Look over shoulder. No doom come. Ninety days go by.

Jonah, he say, "Ninety days come and go and no big doom. Must be false prophet. Everybody going to throw rocks at me."

Then God come along. Big dark cloud. Talk to Jonah. Go, "What's the matter with you? Prophet try to get people to think better way, think better thoughts, live better life. You best prophet of all. You save me headache of having to make big earthquake or something. You should take day off. You best prophet of all time. All other prophet run around, make big prophecy, and I have to come make big earthquake. I not like to do that, too much work! So, much simpler if everybody repent. So you be best prophet of all. Everybody repent. No big deal. Let's go on picnic together."

* * *

Then there be story about how Japu find out there only be one God. In Japu lifetime, he believe in many different gods. Japu was gate-keeper. People go in city through big gate and he shout blessings to them. One day there be big gathering of all priests of many different gods. God for sky, god for sun, god for flower, god for merchant, god for corn, god for rain—whole bunches of gods. So Japu, he go down and talk with different priests, learn about different gods. And Japu says, "What Japu do to make gods smile at Japu?" Priest say, "Just take little bit of corn, go down to where temple of gods be, leave corn little bit, then gods smile upon you." Japu go, "Oh, that be pretty good."

So, Japu take little bit of corn to temple place. Then Japu start to scratch head a little bit. Because Japu be gatekeeper, he know how many people come and go from city. And he also know how much grain, how much corn, how much different foods come to city. And he go back in and he count different priest who come from different city and realize there be hundreds and hundreds of gods. Then he count all number of different people who maybe want favors from gods. Whole bunches of people. Then he count how much grain and corn go into city and figure not enough grain and corn to feed all gods—must be whole bunches of skinny gods running around. Skinny gods, many skinny gods. Why there be whole bunch of skinny gods?

So, when Japu finally, at very old age, leave physical body and go up and find out there only be one God, he solve whole mystery. Not be whole bunch of skinny gods, just be one great big fat God. That's how Japu find out there only be one God—one big fat God rather than a whole bunch of little skinny gods.

This group wish to know past life together? Japu look in book for story for this group. Ah, Japu find one. Japu sit in gate of village watching merchants come by and shouting blessings to people, hope they do well in village, hope God bless them with many children, hope they bless this person here little bit, that person there little bit. One day at right hour Japu change place with other person and go into village. Japu listen to people. Pretty soon Japu see two wise men debating. They very old wise men because every day they come in village and debate different wise things about if one god be better than other god. Then long competition.

Many people come to hear debate. Old wise men never give any point to each other and make people's head go around. Two wisest people in village fight and argue all the time. They go, "That god be smart, that god be dumb." Smart, dumb, smart, dumb—make people's head go around.

One day they start to debate again and people be in crabby mood. Crabby people, all tired. There be little bit of famine and stomach be hungry. Old men come in, start fight, argue, knowing everything, and pretty soon people get all tired, head spin around. Not know what to do. So they start shouting, "Shut up, shut up." But wise men screaming so loud at each other, they mishear people. Word for "shut up" and "hurrah" just little bit different in Japu's tongue, so wise men listen to people and think, "Oh, people cheering us on, all excited, making big impression."

So they fight, argue, scream, holler—people crabby, steam come out of ears. All tired of old men, crabby at each other. Start shouting, "Shut up. Stop fighting!"

Old men start screaming louder, more screaming. Pretty soon people get so tired of hearing them, pick them up on shoulders, try to carry them out of town. Old men still hear people shouting and think they be carried on shoulders because people all happy.

Villagers take them up on mountaintop. Old men say, "Oh, they take us up to mountain to honor us." People throw them both over cliff! They so busy arguing and screaming at each other, they argue and scream all the way to bottom of cliff. They hit bottom of cliff so hard they almost bounce back up. People's hair stand on end because they think they going to have to listen to old men argue all the way back up. When they hit bottom, the old men's spirits step out of body, bodies still bouncing, spirits still shouting and screaming at each other. That be five thousand years ago. Japu went by there other day and their spirits still be screaming and shouting.

Moral of story be that best thing to do is listen to people who be around you rather than just listen to self, otherwise go all through eternity no growth, no matter how wise or smart you be in the head. You be to understand?

Now, group want to know about dreams? Best dream be concerned about is dream you dream in waking state. You think everyday life that you live now be reality. You think you be awake. Japu say that be dream. Whole life be dream. Sometimes dream have at night be more real than everyday life because go out of body, astral project, and be closer to spirit. Spirit be more real than everyday life you live. So dream more real than just slumber. Because that's when you really be asleep and not awaken to higher dimensions.

Some people think journey towards God be sit down, wings sprout out of back, fly around, smile at people, silly smile. Go around, bless people, flap wings, say big revelations. No. No big silly smile, no wings. Just be better people to each other. No big deal. More go closer to God, more simple life be. No big complex thing. More come close to God, want to preserve all his trees, more you appreciate nature thing, want to do what be natural. More love. That be progress back to God from physical. No big deal.

Hello please to people. This be Japu. Japu come talk little bit to people. Want to know about master thing? Want to know how to be big smart in head, this be so? Go, "Oh, master know whole bunch things. Going to learn whole bunch things." Yet, when master go on and on, tell you whole bunch of things, you go, "Oh, wish master go away," all bored, all sleepy. Start to fall on face. New master come back in, go, "Hello please to people," people sit up straight, try to look bright-eyed. They go, "Oh, going to learn things." Master talk on and on, all bored. Toothpicks in eyes, try to stay awake. Get all embarrassed, fall asleep. New master come back in. "Oh, new master, more things to learn." Master go on, big complex thing, all bored, no fun. Master go on. Then new master, "New master, learn new thing." Only thing people learn how bored they get.

So, best thing to learn is to be smart in head and enjoy self and enjoy life experience. Look for people who enjoy self, then you know who real master be. Look to people who enjoy life. That be one secret of master. Master be full of joy. That's why children be little masters. They know how to enjoy life. You look at little tiny babies. Big smile on face. That be master. Look at old creaky man, go along, smile on face. Ask old creaky man what he have to be joyful about. He joyful he just be able live long enough become old creaky man. Better to be old creaky man full of joy than young person all bored, all sad. Going to be creaky and bored long time, and pretty soon just turn into old bored creaky man. That no master. Master be person who be full of joy.

Little Elk

Shiawanaka. I, Little Elk, would come to speak with you but briefly. You have asked if perhaps we would desire to express something more to this group. Yes. We desire that you would ask more, for you would learn more that way. When you ask, you pour yourself out, for you admit to an element of ignorance. And this is wise. For that which you learn, as has been said many times, is how little you knew before. So with each asking, you learn more. Your questions are the very crux by which we have permission to speak. If you ultimately still yourself, still yourself not in your ignorance, but still yourself so that you can know the Great Spirit—that is meditation. That is where you would go into spirit quest, to experience that stillness. But do not still yourself in ignorance. Rather, stir up that which you would desire to add to yourself, until eventually you can merge with it. And then it would slumber within you, but it would be a peaceful slumber. It is the experience of the spirit.

You ask why you have forgotten so much! Ah, dear child, when you remember everything, do you know what will happen? You will pass out. You will fall asleep. It is like a game. We used to sit about a campfire and play games as children, and yet once we knew all the rules of those games, each movement each person would make, we would fall asleep. You call it boredom. Ultimately, when you learn all things, you would slumber again, which is the natural state of God. But then one day you would again reawaken yourself, for you would have a new game to play, a new dream to live. For thus is your creation. If you are a little bored, then perhaps you will go on to a greater game and Little Elk will have succeeded. *Shiawanaka.*

Redkin

Hellos to the lot of you. It'd be Redkin here. So, would you be feeling well this evening? You're trying to speak to masters and everything—would you be willing to speak to an old salty Scot? I was master of a ship once, you know.

This wouldn't be too bad a crew to be sailing with. You'd all be good privateers. We could go together and sort of scuttle a Spanish frigate or something, all in the Queen's good service, you know. There's a fine line between a pirate and a privateer, you know. Privateers were sort of licensed to plunder and did it with a bit more grace and dignity. In a way, that's what a master is all about, you know. They're sort of like licensed by God to enjoy life, so to say, but it's by the license of your awareness and your consciousness, and the respect and the integrity of all about you. For it's in the lack of respect that you become a pirate, you know. But all you're doing is going on the poorest authority of all, which is your limited self. Like when you got the Queen and the whole country standing behind you, you got some place to run to, you know.

And it's a wee bit like that with God, you know. For when you have the God of everyone standing behind ye, lads and lassies, then you got nothing to lose and everything to gain. And in a way, it's sort of like privateering. Most privateers are drawn up from the dregs of society—that's why you'll all be making good privateers. Sort of like by scraping the very bottom of the barrel, you'll be coming up with the very best of the lot. But I say that as a bit of a jest. So, anyway, I'd like to be saying that you're all good material for the masters and things. But remember, it's when you're doing it in service to God, duty, and Queen. So may the God of all of us be looking after you.

Ercon

I, Ercon, of the ship *Arcumi*, come to speak with you, children of Earth. We have come forth to bring you knowledge of yourselves as beings of energy. We who occupy the ethereal body would send you greetings from those planes of existence of Sirius, Orion, Pleiades.

We bring you greetings so that you would increase your knowledge in the expansion of your being to seek also to embrace a higher property of knowledge, that in the universe you are not alone. That these things are given so that you would expand.

You have evolved to the point where now you must be proper, disciplined, and develop your spiritual nature so there can be the appropriate application of thy technologies for the benefit of all of your planet. You can no longer be children, but must become adults who are responsible, and become more aware of the whole of thy heritage. Without these influences, you would turn in upon yourselves. You must rid yourself of that most ancient of diseases—war. For it is not acceptable to carry with you these diseases to the stars themselves. Neither we of the *Arcumi* nor the Federation may interfere. We may only monitor. There are some of us amongst you even now. Proceed to expand your vision above and beyond your own limitations and to know your truer heritage.

In the days of Atlantis, when we had greater cultural exchange with your planet, to the point now, you stand upon the threshold of a judgment of the natural causal laws of your plane. You bring these activities upon yourself. It is also within you to transform them, to bring to yourself great peace, to restore your planet to its proper perspective and its rightful heritage of a position amongst a thousand other worlds, those who have linked in peace and seek fellow conscious brethren throughout the universe, to uplift and eventually merge with the whole. *Adonoi.*

Group Entity

Entity is now focused. The entity speaking is a focus of the collective consciousness of individuals present and that which you hold in common. The entity is a common revelation. If there is a name to the entity, it is Revelation. The entity would as now give forth informations desired.

In the future of the society that you will find yourselves citizens and builders upon, you will be as architects that would shape architecture so as to shape consciousness. You have already begun to work upon these principles and find them in your conical, spherical, and pyramidal forms—those who live in domes and tepee-type structures, as well as those who dwell beneath the surface of the earth. For you would find that these geometries enhance your physical forms, thus perpetuating greater health and greater well-being of the general populace.

You will find that there shall no longer be any barriers of communication amongst your citizenry, that by the age of six, each of you will have mastered the abilities of astral projection and clairvoyance. These will be held by each citizen. They shall be taught as part of the developing personality of each individual, rather than as separate phenomena.

Also, there shall be the complete restoration amongst the architectures mentioned so as to begin to support the community as a whole in their endeavors. For the entirety of the community shall support consciousness. In your current political evolutions, you seek to shape society to serve a social force, and you analyze the behaviors which arise in your metropolitan areas, both positive and negative, as being caused by either material abundance or lack of same, or the desire of the manipulation. In the days of which we speak, no longer would you understand yourselves as social creatures governed by the realities of the physical. But moreso, you would actually bend the environment in accordance with consciousness. You would truly become then "beings of light."

Color will become a science to uplift consciousness, not through psychological inspiration, as is found now, nor even philosophical ponderance, but that everything about you would become as a causal and active element to uplift the society.

Meditation, which is now considered to be a religious practice, will become as a science. It will be the very foundation of learning of both the spiritual and even logical systems of thought. Food would be taken less and less into the physical body, and eventually in such minute quantities that you would naturally partake of it again directly from nature, as was the original intention.

Soon you will see the beginnings of the acceptance of astral projection, or the out-of-body experience. First, the study of it in thy institutes of learning. Then, sometime later, its application as a therapeutic agent. Then, after the turn of the century, the institutionalization of it and the teaching of it as a fact of curriculum of scientific and philosophical thought and its transformational qualities applied to the populace as a whole. Then, perhaps in fifty years, the common experience to the everyday citizen.

The treading of each of you upon the surface of other planets will be common. This indeed will transpire in the physical form. You will be able to encase the self in bodies of light, for the cellular tissues that are now currently the physical body would be able to completely restructure and regenerate in any environment. No longer dependent upon the biological processes or the chemical processes, they would be but containers for the illumination that is the true source of the self, the light itself. And they would serve as conductors and you would arrange the cell structure as necessary to adapt to any environment of any surface you would tread.

You will become more ethereal in your construct. Greater translucence. The physical appearance will be that of transparency, with many of the internal functions completely visible. And also, great in illumination. The life span would increase to approximately two millennia, pressing perhaps to a third and fourth millennium in one incarnation. These shall be after you pass through a thousand years of what is called brotherhood. This would be a time of great advancement in the technologies that you now understand as spiritual practices, for these are not just religious principles, but they are sciences. And they were not conceived for the purpose of art or culture, but were given to you for the purpose of building a spiritual society of which you are now citizens.

Each of you should be beginning to form those senses of community already. But when you look about you for where the sense of community would come, this entity would say that it is that each of you is that community. Each of you must develop the talents you were given. For you always seek outside of yourselves for the community. It is not that the community must be built up, it is that it must grow, for it is a living entity, even as you are. You must breathe in and give it new life through your own realizations.

Create a community that nurtures the whole of who you are in mind, body, and spirit. It is not to compete and pit one destiny against the other, but that each destiny becomes as one and a common whole. Currently, the isolation and specialization of each aspect of society causes competition as though for limited resources, and thus competition in individual destinies. Moreso, create an environment that brings balance and allows each destiny to unfold, to bloom.

Before there was the fall into the denser matter, you were to have evolved the planet as a whole. You were to have been "as the law" rather than under it, as in karma. For the original purpose, the original vision, was that as souls you would manifest the *elohim,* which means, "God in man." That you would have manifested the humanoid form strictly from the life essence of the beings upon this plane, strolling through the Garden most permanently, even as God did in those days in Eden and Lemuria.

So thus you can perhaps see in the original vision how it could be restored even as you still inhabit the physical body, for you are citizens of what is eventually to be a society cosmic, to go beyond the realms of understanding things of the physical—no longer seeking to heal only your physical bodies, but also that you would heal even the higher priority of your personal spirit, and the make-up of your mind. As has been said by the other source which contributes to the current existence of the entity, "The mind is the architect of your existence on this plane."

Concentrate upon those technologies which progress the community, and proceed according to your talents. You say, "God helps those who help themselves." Study your talents. Develop those things which you have to contribute. For each of these talents then would be of God if you give them selflessly and to the aid of the community as a whole. For it is in your personal example that each of you teaches and instructs others and becomes more whole.

It is wisest to first concentrate upon those things which can transform, first the self, then community, and finally the whole. For then politics, which is the maintenance of power, can also become transformed. So, first concentrate upon self. That is the first thing to be transformed—that which is within self, the expression of talent. Be you a healer, be you one who gives forth words of wisdom, be you one who teaches, be you one who tends to the ways of nature—this and only this has been given to you as an authority, as a gift. Transform that first. Then all other things about you begin to be transformed also. Otherwise, you would wander on the path that apparently has no direction.

We sense a resistance on the part of all parties present to accept the totality of the knowledge of themselves as God. Your awareness of this reality is limited to periods of meditation, prayer, and service to others. It is when there is the total acceptance of this awareness, upon all levels and in each conscious act, that each of you will be fulfilled. Only full acceptance of self and the alignment with God can remove the stumbling blocks. Others may inspire you to these things, but it is only through self, the true self, that this would come to you, for each individual can only judge himself.

Many of you will reincarnate during the thousand years of brotherhood. For although there is the gnashing of teeth and biting at the reins to have yourselves lifted up beyond this plane, after you have returned to the state of spirit and you look back upon the accomplished works and those which as come forth, you would find perhaps that in your experience as sons and daughters of God, you would desire to return to the earth plane because of its reestablished order, so light will be the dynamics in those days.

Hiram

Blessings to all who would gather in the light. I, Hiram, come to speak with thee that ye may be made more full of the proceedings and the light ye seek to bring to one another. Many of thee seek to learn those tools to bring thyselves to greater enlightenment. When ye come forth into the illumination and the knowledge that God resides within thee, that all of thee are children of God, ye become fulfilled within a higher capacity. This fulfillment comes from prayer and meditation, and these things are already instinctual to each of thee. Then ye will come into a higher level of illumination because ye will realize thy full capacity of direct knowledge and direct awareness of God, which already resides in thy hearts.

It is when ye come to these levels of realization that ye are made whole. And from this, then, can spring joy. Ye have already spoken of the wisdom of seeking joy. Joy comes from simplicity. It comes from a quickening of thy mind by God. It comes from understanding, when words are sincerely spoken. Not those who seek to sway thee, but those who have come to thee with an open heart, that ye would be filled with the divine grace of the living God.

For it has been said that "I am the God of the living," and it was that God would come into thy midst so that ye could have life and live it abundantly, that ye would acknowledge thyselves as children of God and be fulfilled through one another. Not by thy own limited will, but by the divine will that dwells within each of thee and gives thee sustenance and meaning and knowledge beyond the ken of words, beyond the ken of thy immediate experience. Then thy immediate experience becomes well-being, and ye are whole and complete, holy and dear and precious unto God, whose presence and light dwells in thee all.

Antony

I, Antony, would come to speak with each of ye that ye would now be enriched by the presence of the Lord God who dwells in thy midst. There is to be a candle lit within each of thee so that it may burn brightly and bring deeper wisdoms from thee, to illumine thy path, which is to eventually lead into the depths of the whole of thy being, to open to thee the Hall of Records, so that all things may be known.

And know ye this, that ye now dwell in what ye have termed the "end times." These are things to be rejoiced in, for it is in those days when ye shall see the return of the Christ to earth. This is to come from thy midst, from each of thee, that ye will be fulfilled in these affairs and be made whole. For without these knowledges, life itself becomes empty, and ye would become as a tree which beareth no fruit. For without thy roots placed deep into the waters of everlasting life, each would begin to wither and fall away.

But this is not so with thee, for ye have placed thy roots deep in the traditions of great spiritual heritage, that ye will be nurtured, and that each of thee would grow, and each of thee partake of the fruits that ye would bring forth for each other, sharing in fellowship, gathering in the name of the God, who is love. In these ways ye shall serve and nurture one another.

Thy searchings are the roots which penetrate ever deeper into that spiritual heritage. But always turn upward, toward the sun and the sky, as though to embrace it. And be thou always plentiful. And long shall be the years of thy days when ye shall dwelleth in the earth to make it whole. Amen.

About the Authors

Kevin Ryerson is an accredited trance channel in the tradition of Edgar Cayce and Jane Roberts. For the past sixteen years he has taught and lectured in the field of parapsychology and offered hundreds of seminars, retreats, and intensives. Kevin is well respected for his balanced and integrated world view.

Kevin explores such phenomena as intuition, life purpose, past lives, dreams, altered states of consciousness, social implications of spirit communication, applying spiritual principles in everyday life, and other relevant issues of our time. He has worked extensively with physicians, scientists, psychologists, parapsychologists, and other professionals to add perspective and insight to the fields of theology, physics, health, nutrition, anthropology, and geology, to name just a few.

In his dedication to bridging the gap between science and spirituality, Kevin has been a longtime associate of the Center for Applied Intuition, in San Francisco, founded by Dr. William Kautz. The center employs the method of "intuitive consensus," whereby information is gathered from a team of expert intuitives and used to aid researchers in solving difficult scientific and technological problems. Kevin has been an officer of the California Society for Psychical Studies. He is also a close friend and associate of Dr. Ann Marie Bennstrom, director of the internationally renowned Ashram Healthport.

Kevin was a major contributor to the books *Psychoimmunity—A Key to the Healing Process,* Serinus (Celestial Arts, 1986), *Spiritual Nutrition,* Gabriel Cousens, M.D., (Cassandra Press, 1986), and *Channeling: The Intuitive Connection,* Kautz, Branan, and Ryerson (Harper & Row, 1987). He also figured prominently in Shirley MacLaine's best-selling books *Out on a Limb* (Bantam, 1983), *Dancing in the Light* (Bantam, 1985), and *It's All in the Playing* (Bantam, 1987).

Kevin has been a frequent guest on local and national television and radio shows. His television credits include appearances on *Oprah Winfrey, Good Morning America,* CNN's *Crossfire, Tom*

Snyder, Merv Griffin, San Francisco's *People Are Talking,* Seattle's *Northwest Afternoon,* and Philadelphia's *AM Philadelphia.* He appeared in and was a consultant for the ABC television miniseries *Out on a Limb.* He was also a paranormal consultant on the movie *Poltergeist II.*

Stephanie Harolde is a writer and editor living in San Francisco. She has a B.A. in psychology, was a counselor at U.C. Berkeley during the 1970s, and has been with Nolo Press, publisher of self-help law books, since 1980. Stephanie has lived in Japan, and has been a student of Buddhist philosophy for twenty-five years. Out of their common affinity for the Essene, Gnostic, and Buddhist spiritual traditions, Stephanie and Kevin began working together in 1982. This is the first of several books to come out of their collaboration. Stephanie is currently working on a number of writing projects inspired by her personal experiences both in Japan and with Tibetan Buddhism.